Social Studies Plus!
A Hands-On Approach

Editorial Offices: Glenview, Illinois • Parsippany, New Jersey • New York, New York
Sales Offices: Parsippany, New Jersey • Duluth, Georgia • Glenview, Illinois • Coppell, Texas • Ontario, California

www.sfsocialstudies.com

Program Authors

Dr. Candy Dawson Boyd
Professor, School of Education
Director of Reading Programs
St. Mary's College
Moraga, California

Dr. Geneva Gay
Professor of Education
University of Washington
Seattle, Washington

Rita Geiger
Director of Social Studies and
  Foreign Languages
Norman Public Schools
Norman, Oklahoma

Dr. James B. Kracht
Associate Dean for
  Undergraduate Programs
  and Teacher Education
College of Education
Texas A&M University
College Station, Texas

Dr. Valerie Ooka Pang
Professor of Teacher Education
San Diego State University
San Diego, California

Dr. C. Frederick Risinger
Director, Professional
  Development and Social
  Studies Education
Indiana University
Bloomington, Indiana

Sara Miranda Sanchez
Elementary and Early
  Childhood Curriculum
  Coordinator
Albuquerque Public Schools
Albuquerque, New Mexico

Contributing Authors

Dr. Carol Berkin
Professor of History
Baruch College and the
  Graduate Center
The City University of New York
New York, New York

Lee A. Chase
Staff Development Specialist
Chesterfield County
  Public Schools
Chesterfield County, Virginia

Dr. Jim Cummins
Professor of Curriculum
Ontario Institute for Studies
  in Education
University of Toronto
Toronto, Canada

Dr. Allen D. Glenn
Professor and Dean Emeritus
Curriculum and Instruction
College of Education
University of Washington
Seattle, Washington

Dr. Carole L. Hahn
Professor, Educational Studies
Emory University
Atlanta, Georgia

Dr. M. Gail Hickey
Professor of Education
Indiana University-Purdue
  University
Fort Wayne, Indiana

Dr. Bonnie Meszaros
Associate Director
Center for Economic Education
  and Entrepreneurship
University of Delaware
Newark, Delaware

ISBN: 0-328-03597-1

Copyright © Pearson Education, Inc.
All Rights Reserved. Printed in the United States of America. The blackline masters in this publication are designed for use with appropriate equipment to reproduce copies for classroom use only. Scott Foresman grants permission to classroom teachers to reproduce from these masters.

Contents

Welcome to *Social Studies Plus!* v
Assessment ix
Glossary of Theater Terms 1

Unit 1
Teacher Planner 2
Long-Term Project 4
Unit Drama 6

Chapter 1
Short-Term Projects 12
Writing Projects 14
Citizenship Project 16

Chapter 2
Short-Term Projects 18
Writing Projects 20
Citizenship Project 22

Unit 2
Teacher Planner 24
Long-Term Project 26
Unit Drama 28

Chapter 3
Short-Term Projects 34
Writing Projects 36
Citizenship Project 38

Chapter 4
Short-Term Projects 40
Writing Projects 42
Citizenship Project 44

Chapter 5
Short-Term Projects 46
Writing Projects 48
Citizenship Project 50

Unit 3
Teacher Planner 52
Long-Term Project 54
Unit Drama 56

Chapter 6
Short-Term Projects 62
Writing Projects 64
Citizenship Project 66

Chapter 7
Short-Term Projects 68
Writing Projects 70
Citizenship Project 72

Chapter 8
Short-Term Projects 74
Writing Projects 76
Citizenship Project 78

Unit 4
Teacher Planner 80
Long-Term Project 82
Unit Drama 84

Chapter 9
Short-Term Projects 90
Writing Projects 92
Citizenship Project 94

Chapter 10
Short-Term Projects 96
Writing Projects 98
Citizenship Project 100

Contents

Unit 5
Teacher Planner.................... 102
Long-Term Project 104
Unit Drama....................... 106

Chapter 11
Short-Term Projects............... 112
Writing Projects 114
Citizenship Project 116

Chapter 12
Short-Term Projects............... 118
Writing Projects 120
Citizenship Project 122

Chapter 13
Short-Term Projects............... 124
Writing Projects 126
Citizenship Project 128

Chapter 14
Short-Term Projects............... 130
Writing Projects 132
Citizenship Project 134

Unit 6
Teacher Planner.................... 136
Long-Term Project 138
Unit Drama....................... 140

Chapter 15
Short-Term Projects............... 146
Writing Projects 148
Citizenship Project 150

Chapter 16
Short-Term Projects............... 152
Writing Projects 154
Citizenship Project 156

Chapter 17
Short-Term Projects............... 158
Writing Projects 160
Citizenship Project 162

Unit 7
Teacher Planner.................... 164
Long-Term Project 166
Unit Drama....................... 168

Chapter 18
Short-Term Projects............... 174
Writing Projects 176
Citizenship Project 178

Chapter 19
Short-Term Projects............... 180
Writing Projects 182
Citizenship Project 184

Chapter 20
Short-Term Projects............... 186
Writing Projects 188
Citizenship Project 190

Unit 8
Teacher Planner.................... 192
Long-Term Project 194
Unit Drama....................... 196

Chapter 21
Short-Term Projects............... 202
Writing Projects 204
Citizenship Project 206

Chapter 22
Short-Term Projects............... 208
Writing Projects 210
Citizenship Project 212

Chapter 23
Short-Term Projects............... 214
Writing Projects 216
Citizenship Project 218

Additional Prop Suggestions
for Unit Drama 220

12 Month Calendar: History and Holidays 221

Welcome to Social Studies Plus!

Using Activities to Launch Social Studies Classes

Most educators are all too familiar with the "banking" metaphor of learning, where students sit passively as receivers of information. Educators also know the need to switch that construct to a vital one where students *participate* in the wide world that social studies class can reveal. To jump-start this new metaphor, it helps to have a variety of dynamic and broad-range activities that draw life and direction from the content and skills of basic social studies curriculum. In this way, students begin to realize that the issues of social studies concern things they care about.

Social studies, of course, is about both the forest and the trees. It covers the whole world—big and little events, heroes and ordinary people, issues of justice, morality, and ethics. Social studies is also about the *specific*—the content and skills connected with historical fact and assessing controversial issues that students learn to work with at their own levels of understanding.

When we teach social studies, it is important to join all the important historical, political, and economic aspects of the curriculum with the concrete ways students learn and express themselves. It makes sense, then, to engage students in many different kinds of activities so as to appeal to the varied ways students tackle any curriculum but especially the broad curriculum of social studies. A variety of approaches helps students internalize what citizenship means and how important participation is for a democracy to thrive.

Social Studies Plus! Overview and Purpose

Social Studies Plus! begins with Scott Foresman's social studies basal scope and sequence and then sets up engaging activities that invite students to think independently about events and issues in both the past and present. Some activities create a storytelling atmosphere, where students can move from the concrete to the abstract. Some *Social Studies Plus!* activities place the student in the middle of an historical event and ask the student to take a position and justify it. Other activities promote discussion, questioning, and analysis about the consequences resulting from events, ideas, and persons' actions. Not only should the ideas presented open students' thinking and get them interested in social studies curriculum, the activities should also help students see that they have something at stake in the issues of being a citizen.

Social Studies Plus! offers several approaches in which students may participate:

- Students may create simulations by playing various roles; for instance, they may become members of an immigrant family arriving at Ellis Island, or they may act out the parts of weary soldiers at Valley Forge under General George Washington.

- Students may dig into hands-on activities by drawing themselves on "living" time lines as characters in the early colonies or on the Underground Railroad.

- Students may use their math and graphic organizer skills to map out or graph the fast clip of progress during the Industrial Revolution.

- Students may design labor union broadsides or cartoons about the 1920s, which then may trigger critical discussions of moral and ethical issues.

- Some students may use biographical sketches of famous people in history to stimulate their own writing of persuasive speeches, poems, or news articles that show a variety of perspectives.

Each unit follows a basic progression. First, a Long-Term Project presents a unit theme for students to work on throughout the study of the unit. Second, other unit themes are presented in creative and dramatic form in a six-page Drama section. Third, a number of Short-Term Projects, Writing Projects, and Citizenship activities further develop the topics covered in each chapter.

Read ahead to see how each unit is mapped out and how to make the most of all the projects and activities presented in *Social Studies Plus!*

Unit Development

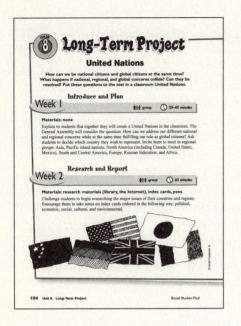

Long-Term Project

Students are offered a Long-Term Project that may last several days or weeks. The goal of the project is to extend the main ideas of an entire unit and allow students enough time to perform one or several tasks. For instance, students may draw, make graphs, do an interview, or complete some research on one topic. With the Long-Term Project, students have time to enter into the discussion of an issue, or they launch into making something concrete, such as a model, diorama, puppets, and so on. The unit project, then, allows students to integrate key social studies concepts and skills in an organized, and often artistic, way.

These unit-sized projects may suggest that the teacher set the context or recall topics at hand, or the teacher may choose how much background to give students. Students do not always need prior experience with the topics presented. Procedures for handling the project are laid out in easy-to-follow steps where teachers may choose the grouping and specific tasks so that, by unit's end, everyone contributes to an overall display or project. Students usually end up choosing what goes into a report or display, allowing them the chance to *own* a part of the display. One of the most enlightening parts of the unit project happens when students present their endeavors to one another or to other classes. A close second to that experience occurs when their audiences ask the students questions and the students become experts for the moment.

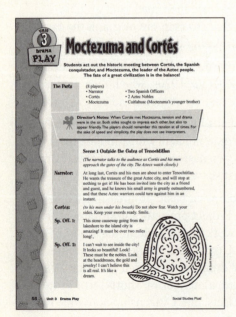

Drama: Plays

Every activity in the Drama section of *Social Studies Plus!* is aimed at creating a dramatic and physical reaction in students to some social studies issues. All the activities give students opportunities for improvising.

The plays are presented either as fully written scripts or as plays with some written lines and suggested ways for improvising additional lines and scenes. In addition, most plays are based on the following parameters:

- The plays take no longer than 30–40 minutes at a time, although play practice and presentation may extend over several class periods.
- The plays are appropriate for each age group in both dialogue and plot complexity.
- The plays are accompanied by a director's guide that will help the student-leader or teacher by providing plot summary, prop and theater term suggestions, or character descriptions.

Drama: Scenarios

Scenarios give students the opportunity to act out brief scenes that draw on their spur-of-the-moment reactions as well as promote their abilities to think on their feet. These scenarios relate to the topics and skills at hand and do not require outside research. Each scenario will:

- provide students with a purpose and focus for the scenario,
- often suggest a conflict relevant to the students' life experiences,
- be easily done in the classroom with a few optional props,
- take only about 10–15 minutes to present,
- and often allow students opportunities to think beyond their usual perspective about facts and people.

There are several common theater terms used throughout the Drama section. See the glossary on page 1 for a full set of theater terms. You may want to copy the page and make it available to the students.

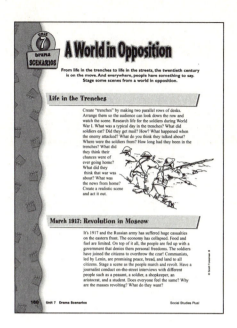

Chapter Development

Short-Term Projects

The goal of the many Short-Term Projects is to extend the chapter content. No projects are repeated from the Teacher's Edition. Rather they proceed from the themes and topics of interest in the Student's Edition and so allow students a myriad of hands-on activities. These projects are oriented toward engaging students in the following ways:

- Short-Term Projects engage small groups, partners, individuals or the whole class in relevant activities.
- They encompass a wide variety of activities: map making, debates, theme mobiles, banners and collages, speeches, time lines from Ancient Egypt to the town of Egypt, Maine, and many more.
- They suggest ways for the students to have fun with social studies topics and skills.
- They cover skills to help students think "out of the box."
- They offer directions that students may follow without much adult assistance.
- They integrate various subject areas into a social studies project.
- They can be completed in about 20–30 minutes.

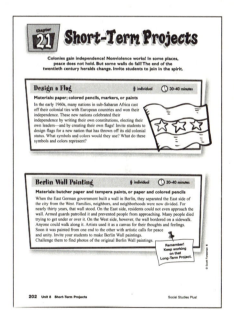

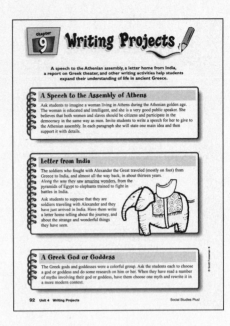

Writing Projects

In a grab bag approach, some Writing Projects allow a wide swath of creativity and some take students through brief, but rigorous, expository writing. The Writing Projects should also include the following goals.

- The Writing Projects engage students in a variety of dynamic writing applications of social studies content and skills and can be completed in about 20–30 minutes.
- They serve as a bridge between students' (a) prior knowledge and life experiences and (b) content of the core text.
- They provide a connection between concrete/operational understanding and the application of social studies concepts/skills to a student's life.
- They should help students experience social studies in ways other than rehashing dates and events.
- They should be intriguing enough to make teachers and students *both* want to try the activities.

Citizenship

Social studies always deals with citizens of the past and present. To show students how important participation is in a democratic society, these activities focus on the traits of a good citizen.

- Each Citizenship page may require some research, creative writing, interviews, or artistic endeavors.
- The goal of this page is to make students more aware of how to spot citizenship traits in their own actions and in the larger neighborhood or community around them.

Blackline Masters

Each chapter has at least one blackline master for students to use to further extend one or more of the activities in the unit or chapter. Some of these pages engage students in crossword puzzles, cartoon strips and storyboards, graphic organizers, map and graph making, and various kinds of artwork.

Assessment for *Social Studies Plus!*

The rubrics suggested for use with *Social Studies Plus!* materials are intended to aid teachers in recording a range of the students' linguistic and cultural experiences.

The emphasis of these rubrics is placed on thinking rather than rote learning, performance and successes rather than failings, and on each individual's development within grade-level expectations. Obviously no rubrics are a substitute for the teacher's classroom observations. A teacher's notes on students' abilities to gain knowledge based on experience is key in helping teachers make students understand what they need to learn.

The rubrics presented in *Social Studies Plus!* pertain to assessing students' achievements while they are engaged in exploring the social studies content and learning new skills. Applying these rubrics to the students' work gives them concrete feedback and helps them monitor their own progress toward meeting performance standards. These rubrics are oriented toward assessing the variety of ways students may approach the content and skills of this program.

Writing Rubrics

Writing, because it is specific and tangible, may be easier to evaluate than most other subjects. Both analytic and holistic rubrics are used to evaluate writing. Many teachers use holistic scoring because it evaluates a writer's overall ability to express meaning in written form.

Analytic rubrics tend to incorporate spelling, punctuation, and grammar accuracy, yet they also address some complex aspects of writing assessment. This rubric is based on the assumption that teachers will be looking at students' abilities to begin handling some stages of the writing process in relation to social studies content. Once students have some specific ideas of how to improve their writing, they can begin to be their own editors.

4-point rubric

4 Excellent   **3** Very Good   **2** Satisfactory   **1** Needs Improvement

Six Traits for the Analytic Writing Rubric

Content Quality and Idea Development
genre well controlled, interesting, clear, complex, organized, details in place

Voice
specific, honest, appealing, clear point of view, appropriate use of action verbs, easy to follow

Organization
complete text, details in place, smooth transitions, fluency of thought, builds anticipation, creates interest, contains beginning, middle, and end

Word Precision
interesting, precise, and vivid word choice, strong verbs, understands appropriate phrasing, handles repairs well

Sentence Fluency
variation in sentence structure and length, uses sentence patterns when appropriate

Mechanics
correct grammar and spelling, sensible paragraphing, formal and informal punctuation used appropriately, easy to read

Rubric for Narrative Writing

	4 Excellent	3 Very Good	2 Satisfactory	1 Needs Improvement
Content Quality and Idea Development	• well-developed story • well-focused on the topic • clear ideas are well-supported with interesting and vivid details	• fairly well-developed story • focused on the topic • ideas are well-supported with details	• sometimes strays from topic • ideas are not well-developed • more details are needed	• poorly focused on the topic • ideas are unclear • few details are given
Voice	• voice is fitting for the topic and engaging • well-suited for audience and purpose	• voice is fairly clear and seems to fit the topic • suited for audience and purpose	• voice rarely comes through • not always suited for audience and purpose	• voice is weak or inappropriate • no sense of audience or purpose
Organization	• well-focused on the topic • logical organization • sequence is very clear • excellent transitions • easy to follow	• generally focused on the topic • some lapses in organization • has a beginning, middle, and end • some transitions • usually easy to follow	• somewhat focused on the topic • poor organization and some difficulty with sequence • few transitions • difficult to follow	• not focused on the topic • no clear organization • no clear sequence • difficult to impossible to follow
Word Precision	• precise, vivid, and interesting word choices • wide variety of word choices	• fairly precise, interesting, and somewhat varied word choices • wording could be more specific	• vague, mundane word choices • wording is sometimes repetitive • more descriptive words are needed	• very limited word choices • wording is bland and not descriptive
Sentence Fluency	• uses complete sentences • varying sentence structures and lengths	• uses complete sentences • generally simple sentence structures	• occasional sentence fragment or run-on sentence • simple sentence structure is used repeatedly	• frequent use of sentence fragments or run-on sentences • sentences are difficult to understand
Mechanics	• proper grammar and usage • correct spelling • correct punctuation • correct capitalization	• few errors of grammar and usage • mostly correct spelling, punctuation, and capitalization	• errors in grammar, usage, and spelling sometimes make understanding difficult • some errors in punctuation and capitalization	• frequent errors in grammar, usage, spelling, capitalization, and punctuation make understanding difficult or impossible

Social Studies Plus!

Rubric for Persuasive Writing

	4 Excellent	3 Very Good	2 Satisfactory	1 Needs Improvement
Content Quality and Idea Development	• clear position is well-supported and insightful • complete control of topic • many facts and opinions to support position • presents a convincing argument	• clear position is somewhat supported • good control of topic • some facts and opinions to support position • presents a fairly convincing argument	• position is taken, but not supported • some control of topic • few facts and opinions to support position • presents a weak argument	• no clear position taken • little control of topic • no facts and opinions given • no argument presented
Voice	• voice is strong and engaging • specific, honest, engaging point of view • well-suited for audience and purpose	• voice is fairly strong • generally clear, honest, engaging point of view • suited for audience and purpose	• voice rarely comes through • general, vague discussion of topic • not always suited for audience and purpose	• voice is weak or inappropriate • no particular point of view presented • no sense of audience or purpose
Organization	• well-focused on the topic • logical organization with reasons presented in a clear order • contains beginning, middle, and end • easy to follow argument	• generally focused on the topic • organization is mostly clear but reasons not always presented in a clear order • contains beginning, middle, and end • usually easy to follow argument	• somewhat focused on the topic • poor organization with only a few reasons presented • no clear beginning, middle, and end • difficult to follow argument	• not focused on the topic • no clear organization • no reasons presented • no clear beginning, middle, and end • no argument presented
Word Precision	• precise, persuasive word choices • interesting word choice • fluency of thought • appropriate use of action verbs	• fairly precise, persuasive word choices • wording could be more specific • generally appropriate use of action verbs	• vague, unpersuasive word choices • wording is general and not convincing • wording is sometimes repetitive	• very limited word choices • fails to persuade • wording is redundant and bland
Sentence Fluency	• uses complete sentences • varying sentence structures and lengths	• uses complete sentences • generally simple sentence structures	• occasional sentence fragment or run-on sentence • simple sentence structure is used repeatedly	• frequent use of sentence fragments or run-on sentences • sentences are difficult to understand
Mechanics	• proper grammar and usage • correct spelling • correct punctuation • correct capitalization	• few errors of grammar and usage • mostly correct spelling, punctuation, and capitalization	• errors in grammar, usage, and spelling sometimes make understanding difficult • some errors in punctuation and capitalization	• frequent errors in grammar, usage, spelling, capitalization, and punctuation make understanding difficult or impossible

Rubric for Expressive/Descriptive Writing

	4 Excellent	3 Very Good	2 Satisfactory	1 Needs Improvement
Content Quality and Idea Development	• "paints a picture" for the reader • well-focused on the topic • clear ideas are well-supported with interesting and vivid details	• creates some clear images for the reader • focused on the topic • ideas are well-supported with details	• sometimes strays from topic • ideas are not well-developed • more details are needed	• poorly focused on the topic • ideas are unclear • few details are given
Voice	• voice is fitting for the topic and engaging • well-suited for audience and purpose	• voice is fairly clear and seems to fit the topic • suited for audience and purpose	• voice rarely comes through • not always suited for audience and purpose	• voice is weak or inappropriate • no sense of audience or purpose
Organization	• well focused on the topic • logical organization • excellent transitions • easy to follow	• generally focused on the topic • some lapses in organization • some transitions • usually easy to follow	• somewhat focused on the topic • poor organization • few transitions • difficult to follow	• not focused on the topic • no clear organization • no transitions • difficult to impossible to follow
Word Precision	• precise, vivid, and interesting word choices • wide variety of word choices	• fairly precise, interesting, and somewhat varied word choices • wording could be more specific	• vague, mundane word choices • wording is sometimes repetitive • more descriptive words are needed	• very limited word choices • wording is bland and not descriptive
Sentence Fluency	• uses complete sentences • varying sentence structures and lengths	• uses complete sentences • generally simple sentence structures	• occasional sentence fragment or run-on sentence • simple sentence structure is used repeatedly	• frequent use of sentence fragments or run-on sentences • sentences are difficult to understand
Mechanics	• proper grammar and usage • correct spelling • correct punctuation • correct capitalization	• few errors of grammar and usage • mostly correct spelling, punctuation, and capitalization	• errors in grammar, usage, and spelling sometimes make understanding difficult • some errors in punctuation and capitalization	• frequent errors in grammar, usage, spelling, capitalization, and punctuation make understanding difficult or impossible

Rubric for Expository Writing

	4 Excellent	3 Very Good	2 Satisfactory	1 Needs Improvement
Content Quality and Idea Development	• well-focused on the topic • clear ideas are well-supported with interesting details	• focused on the topic • ideas are well-supported with details	• sometimes strays from topic • ideas are not well-developed • more details are needed	• poorly focused on the topic • ideas are unclear • few details are given
Voice	• voice is strong and engaging • well-suited for audience and purpose	• voice is fairly strong • suited for audience and purpose	• voice rarely comes through • not always suited for audience and purpose	• voice is weak or inappropriate • no sense of audience or purpose
Organization	• well-focused on the topic • logical organization • excellent transitions • easy to follow	• generally focused on the topic • organization is mostly clear • some transitions • usually easy to follow	• somewhat focused on the topic • poor organization • few transitions • difficult to follow	• not focused on the topic • no clear organization • no transitions • difficult to impossible to follow
Word Precision	• precise, interesting word choices • wide variety of word choices	• fairly precise, interesting word choices • wording could be more specific	• vague, mundane word choices • wording is sometimes repetitive	• very limited word choices • wording is bland
Sentence Fluency	• strong topic sentence • varying sentence structures and lengths • uses complete sentences	• good topic sentence • generally simple sentence structures • uses complete sentences	• weak topic sentence • simple sentence structure is used repeatedly • occasional sentence fragment or run-on sentence	• no topic sentence • sentences are difficult to understand • frequent use of sentence fragments or run-on sentences
Mechanics	• proper grammar and usage • correct spelling • correct punctuation • correct capitalization	• few errors of grammar and usage • mostly correct spelling, punctuation, and capitalization	• errors in grammar, usage, and spelling sometimes make understanding difficult • some errors in punctuation and capitalization	• frequent errors in grammar, usage, spelling, capitalization, and punctuation make understanding difficult or impossible

Class Projects Rubric

Social Studies Plus! presents numerous projects, for both individual and group work, making the rubric for the elements of content and skill more general. Many of the students' products resulting from these projects may be assessed as well by placing some in student portfolios or displaying them in the classroom. The rubric below is a general guide for assessing the projects.

Individual/Collaborative Projects

Directions: Copy the rubric for either groups or individuals. Circle the appropriate number for individual and collaborative participation in the projects.

Skill/Performance	Excellent	Very Good	Satisfactory	Needs Improvement
1. Collaborative reading/ understand task	4	3	2	1
2. Group listens to group leader	4	3	2	1
3. Group members listen to one another	4	3	2	1
4. Group understands cross-curricular skills needed	4	3	2	1
5. Group designs and constructs project in organized way	4	3	2	1
6. Individual uses right skills for environmental and historical research	4	3	2	1
7. Individual plans and executes art/craft project	4	3	2	1
8. Individual uses prior knowledge to complete task	4	3	2	1
9. Individual uses skill strategies, such as comparison, analysis, outlining, and map reading to complete task	4	3	2	1
10. Individual shows ability to reflect on what is the topic and what is important	4	3	2	1

Drama Rubric

Directions: Make a form for each student. Circle the appropriate number for each individual's participation in the play or scenario.

Student Name: _____

Skill/Performance	Excellent	Very Good	Satisfactory	Needs Improvement
1. Understands task	4	3	2	1
2. Plans own part	4	3	2	1
3. Understands the movement in front of group; maintains eye contact	4	3	2	1
4. Researched and practiced part	4	3	2	1
5. Willing to improvise in context	4	3	2	1
6. Projection and diction	4	3	2	1
7. Concentration and poise in acting	4	3	2	1
8. Language clear and delivered with enthusiasm	4	3	2	1
9. Understood content correctly	4	3	2	1
10. Delivered in believable way	4	3	2	1

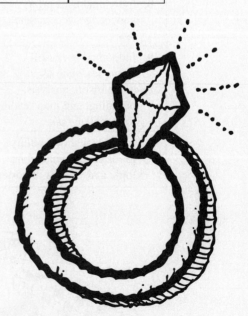

Glossary of Theater Terms

backdrop: a painting that shows the setting for a play; it hangs at the back of the stage, and scenes are played in front of it

blocking: setting the actors' positions and moves during rehearsal

center stage: in the middle of the stage

cue: a signal (a word, phrase, sound, or other action) to an actor or actors to enter, exit, or to begin a speech or action

downstage: the part of the stage that is nearest the audience

enter: to come onto the stage from the wings

exit: to leave the stage

Improv Directions: instructions for actors about moments when they must make up lines or actions

improvise: when actors make up material on the spot or in rehearsal

mime: a form of acting in which actions are used without words

monologue: a speech by one person

pantomime: the silent telling of a story through gestures, body movements, and facial expressions

pre-set: the set-up of the stage that is in place as the play begins

prologue: a short scene that comes before the main body of a play and introduces the theme

prop: any item needed by actors that they can carry on and off stage

ritual: a set of actions with special significance for the community, performed in a formal, stylized way

role-play: to improvise a character in a given situation

scene titles: signs written in large letters for the audience to read, announcing the titles of scenes

script: the written text of a play

scripted: written down, when all the lines are on the page

setting: when and where the action of a play occurs

stage directions: directions to the actors, usually in parentheses

stage right: the right-hand side from the actor's point of view, onstage, facing the audience

stage left: the left-hand side from the actor's point of view, onstage, facing the audience

tableau vivant or tableau: literally, a living picture; a scene where actors freeze to form a picture

unscripted: parts of a play that are not written down, where the actor(s) must improvise

upstage: relating to the rear of the stage

Teacher Planner

Long-Term Project pages 4–5	Materials	⏱	Lesson Link
A "Living Time Line" of Early Civilizations and Cultures Students make a time line on the advances made by early civilizations.			Lessons 1–3
Week 1 whole class/group Students select one of the many early civilizations to create a time line about.	long roll of paper, tape, colored pencils or markers	1 session 2 hrs.	
Week 2 group Students research their chosen culture, and decide how they will present their living time lines.	pencils, paper	1 session 2 hrs.	
Week 3 group Students construct artifacts appropriate to their civilization.	as needed to make "artifacts"	1 session 2 hrs.	
Week 4 group Students present their living time lines, beginning with the earliest civilization and ending with the most recent.	props and artifacts from Week 3	1 session 1 hr.	
Unit Drama pages 6–11			
Scenarios: Life and Times in Early Cultures group Students role-play skits about hunter-gatherers, King Solomon, and the Great Basin Paiute people.	props (optional)	5 sessions 25 min. each	Lessons 1–3
Play: Gilgamesh and the Secret of Eternal Life group Students perform a play about the mighty King Gilgamesh searching for eternal life.	props, costumes (optional)	1 session 2 hrs.	
Chapter 1 Short-Term Projects pages 12–13			
The Skills of a Hunter-Gatherer group Students brainstorm a lists of skills needed by people living in hunter-gatherer societies.	paper and pencil	1 session 30 min.	Lesson 1
An Exhibition of Early Tools group Students draw picture of important tools from early history.	pencils, paper, markers or colored pencils	1 session 20–30 min.	Lesson 1
The Three Sisters individual/partners Students make up short stories about corn, beans, and squash.	paper, pencils, markers or colored pencils	1 session 20 min.	Lesson 2
Early Technological Advancement Award individual/partners Students create medallions to honor an invention or technological advance.	BLM p. 17, construction paper, pens, markers	1 session 20–30 min.	Lesson 2
The Clock of Humanity group Students draw a "clock" and figure out a way to divide it up into thirty-five sections representing 100,000 years each.	paper, markers	1 session 20 min.	Lesson 3
Handprint Wall whole class Students make a modern-day "cave painting" with handprints and pictures of important activities.	paper, paint, paint brushes	1 session 20 min.	Lesson 3

Chapter 1 Writing Projects pages 14–15	Materials	🕐	Lesson Link
Legend for a Distant Past individual Students make up stories about how the early people learned to perform different survival tasks.	paper, pencils	1 session 30 min.	Lessons 1–3
Future Archaeologist individual Students write archaeologist's reports on the uses and significance of different artifacts.	paper, pencils	1 session 25 min.	Lessons 1–3
A Skara Brae Life individual Students write journal entries for a boy or girl living in the Skara Brae village before it was abandoned.	paper, pencils	1 session 20 min.	Lesson 2
The Development of Culture individual Students write and discuss some achievements, and put them in the correct sequence.	paper, pencils	1 session 20 min.	Lesson 2
A Rare Find individual Students suppose they are archaeologists writing in a diary on the eve of an amazing discovery.	paper, pencils	1 session 25 min.	Lesson 3
Chapter 1 Citizenship Project page 16			
Responsibility whole class Students discuss what is so important about a doctor's responsibility to his or her patients.	paper, pencils	1 session 35 min.	Lesson 2
Chapter 2 Short-Term Projects pages 18–19			
Sargon's Story individual Students invent pictograms to tell the story of the Mesopotamian King Sargon.	paper, pencils, colored pencils or markers	1 session 15 min.	Lesson 1
Surplus! group Students create a board game about the development of civilization.	BLM p. 23, poster board, markers, dice, objects for game pieces	1 session 30 min.	Lesson 1
War-Peace Plaque partners Students paint a place for our times, based on the Standard of Ur.	paper, colored pencils, markers or paint and brushes	1 session 20 min.	Lesson 1
Model Ziggurat individual Students construct a model ziggurat, based on the Ziggurat of Ur.	markers, construction paper, glue, cardboard, art supplies	1 session 20 min.	Lesson 2
The City of Babylon individual/partners Students paint a picture of Babylon.	paper, paint, paintbrushes	1 session 30 min.	Lesson 3
Scrolled Document individual/partners Students write stories from the Old Testament or Torah onto scrolled paper.	roll of drawing paper, pencils, two long sticks	1 session 30 min.	Lesson 3

Teacher Planner

Chapter 2 Writing Project pages 20–21	Materials	🕐	Lesson Link
Traveling On! individual Students write journal entries about a single day of travel.	paper, pencils	1 session 20 min.	Lesson 1
Polytheism vs. Monotheism individual Students write about the difference between polytheism and monotheism.	paper, pencils	1 session 20 min.	Lessons 1–4
Life Before and After the Invention of the Wheel individual Students write essays about life before and after the invention of the wheel.	paper, pencils	1 session 20 min.	Lessons 1–4
The Gods of the Sumerians individual Students write stories about one of the Sumerian gods.	paper, pencils	1 session 20 min.	Lesson 2
Hammurabi Reflects on His Place in History individual Students write stories about Hammurabi as he reflects on his life and accomplishments.	paper, pencils	1 session 20 min.	Lesson 3
Abraham and Isaac: A Play individual Students write a play telling how God tested Abraham and the covenant God and Abraham made.	paper, pencils	1 session 30 min.	Lesson 4

Chapter 2 Citizenship Project page 22			
Fairness whole class Students create a document called "The Ten Rules of Classroom Fairness."	paper, pencils	1 session 45 min.	Lesson 3

NOTES

Long-Term Project

A "Living Time Line" of Early Civilizations and Cultures

Skara Brae, the Sumerians, the Phoenicians—which came first? Agriculture, writing, coins—when were these advances made? Put it all together in one time line, and then make the time line come to life!

Which Came First?

Week 1 whole class/group 2 hours

Materials: long roll of paper, tape, colored pencils or markers

- Briefly list the events and civilizations of the time period from 3.5 million years ago to 2,500 years ago to help students learn the sequence in which cultures rose. Jot down on the board the dates of eras, cultures, and important technological or other advances.

- Tape the paper on the wall, draw a time line on the paper, and enter the information from the board at the correct points along the line. Mark the entries for the first humans and for 3.5 million years ago.

- Divide the class into five or six groups, and have each one pick one culture on the time line to learn about and present.

What's So Special About That?

Week 2 group 2 hours

Materials: pencils, paper

- Each group researches its culture, focusing on cultural or technological advances such as in agriculture, transportation, writing, and art.

- Discuss: What methods or materials did this culture use that had not been used by earlier cultures? Which people or events associated with the culture should we know about?

- Each group may present its research through a short skit, mock interview, verbal presentation, or other means. Groups may choose to make their own artifacts and will need time to assemble their materials.

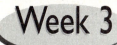 ## A Presentation and an Early Artifact!

👥 group 🕐 2 hours

Materials: as needed to make "artifacts"

Groups continue to work on their presentations. If a group is going to present a skit or short play, have it make simple props using construction paper. When groups are ready, they can practice their skits, interviews, or other kinds of presentations. Make sure they are ready to answer questions from the rest of the class about their respective cultures.

- Have the groups construct their artifacts from the materials brought in from home. They should be able to say why they chose the artifact, how it relates to their culture, what it is made of, and how the people of the time made and used it. Each artifact should be labeled showing what it is, the time it came from, where it came from, the materials it was made from, when it was discovered, or who invented it.

Ask the Experts!

 👥 group 🕐 1 hour

Materials: props and artifacts from Week 3

The "Living Time Line" comes to life! Each group makes its presentation, beginning with the earliest civilization and ending with the most recent. As each group presents, the members stand by their place on the time line. When the presentation is over, the rest of the class may ask members of each group questions about anything that was not covered in the presentation. At the end of the presentations, the labeled artifacts can be displayed in a "museum case" on a table or shelf in the classroom.

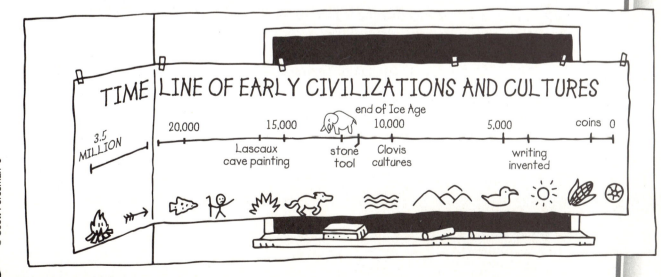

Life and Times in Early Cultures

Early cultures and civilizations come alive as hunter-gatherers go about their daily life, King Solomon dispenses justice, the Great Basin Paiute people travel south with the help of the animals—and more!

King Solomon the Wise

King Solomon is the wisest king ever to have ruled the Hebrews. One day, two women come to Solomon, one of them holding a baby in her arms. Each claims to be the mother of the child. They ask the king to solve the dispute. What does he tell the women he will do? How do the two women react? What do their actions reveal about the women? How then does he reach a fair and just solution? Act out the scene!

The Legend of the Great Basin Paiute People

Remember the legend of the Great Basin Paiute people? Ice blocked the pathway of the people. Two ravens flew up and struck the ice and cracked it, one after the other. Coyote urged them to try again. The ravens struck the ice again, and finally it broke. The people were able to continue their journey.

Make this legend into part of a short play about the migration of the Great Basin Paiute people southward across America. Include two or three human characters, with names, and four animal characters—the two Ravens, Coyote, plus one other.

The Story of Deborah

Deborah foretold that a woman would win a war for the Israelites against their enemies, the Canaanites. She chose General Barak to find soldiers and lead them into battle. Barak was worried since his troops were far outnumbered, but he followed Deborah's clever battle plan, and it worked! The Canaanite army was crushed. Their leader, Sisera, escaped on foot. Deborah's prophecy of a woman winning the war was therefore true.

Create a play about this story. Think about what Deborah and Barak discuss when they plan for the battle. What does Sisera say to his troops at the beginning of the battle?

Enheduanna Reflects on War

Enheduanna, high priestess of Ur, was the daughter of Akkadian King Sargon. He conquered one city-state after another in Sumer, creating a huge empire. During Enheduanna's life, battles raged across the land for years on end, bringing the glory of victory, but also all the sorrows and miseries of war. Enheduanna was a poet. One of the poems she wrote describes the horrors of war. Have students compose a poem which states the suffering involved in war. Then have them read it aloud.

Simulation: The Hikers and the Iceman

Some hikers are taking a walk high up in the Alps. Suddenly, they come across the body of a strange-looking man, just at the edge of a melting glacier. He is dressed in skins and carries a small knife, an ax, and a leather bag filled with food. He begins to stir. He has been sleeping for five thousand three hundred years! What questions do the hikers and the iceman ask each other? What can the hikers find out about how the iceman lived, what he ate, how he spent his days, and the tools he used and how he got them? What does the iceman learn about the hikers? What does he think when he finds out they are traveling in the mountains just for fun?!

Gilgamesh and the Secret of Eternal Life

Mighty King Gilgamesh goes in search of the secret of eternal life. Along the way he encounters strange creatures, gods, and men. What will he bring back when he returns from this fearsome journey?

The Parts: (6–8 players)
- Narrator
- Gilgamesh, king of Uruk
- Scorpion-man, guard
- Scorpion-woman, guard
- Shamash, the god of the Sun
- Siduri, goddess of Wine
- Ziusudra
- Ziusudra's Wife

Director's Notes: There are many lines in this play! They can be memorized, or players can substitute their own words. Encourage them to sound dramatic, poetic, and old-fashioned, as the Epic of Gilgamesh was first told over four thousand years ago!

Shamash, the sun god, can be the same player as Scorpion-man. Siduri, the goddess of wine, can be the same player as Scorpion-woman.

Scene 1

(Narrator stands downstage, to one side, throughout the play. Scorpion-man and Scorpion-woman stand guard on one side of the stage, and Gilgamesh begins to walk toward them slowly from the other side.)

Narrator: Look at the mighty warrior, King Gilgamesh of Uruk! He is on a journey no man has ever before attempted. He seeks to find the secret of eternal life!

Gilgamesh: Who are these fearful creatures? They make me shiver!

Scorpion-man: Stop! Where are you going? Why do you come here? What is the purpose of your journey?

Gilgamesh: I am traveling to find Ziusudra, the man who was given eternal life by the gods. I, Gilgamesh, will learn from him the secret of *immortality!*

Scorpion-woman: No mortal has ever entered here. On this path, you will walk in total darkness for twelve leagues.

Gilgamesh: I will go! I am not afraid! Open the gate!

Scorpion-man: The gate is open for you, mighty Gilgamesh. You may go through. *(Guards mime opening the gate. Gilgamesh walks through. Guards exit.)*

> **Theater Talk**
>
> **downstage:** the front of the stage, close to the audience
>
> **stage left:** the far left of the stage as the actor faces the audience

Scene 2

(As the Narrator speaks, Gilgamesh and Shamash meet at center stage, then Shamash exits.)

Narrator: So Gilgamesh walked through twelve leagues of darkness, and came out into the garden of the gods, where the flowers were made of precious jewels. There he met Shamash, god of the sun.

Shamash: Gilgamesh! Where are you going?

Gilgamesh: I am on a journey to discover the secret of eternal life! I want to be forever young, forever powerful! No one can stop me. I am afraid of nothing in this world!

Shamash: I see you will not turn back. Go on, then, brave king. But you will not find what you are looking for! *(He exits. Gilgamesh continues his journey to stage left, where he meets Siduri.)*

Narrator: Even so, Gilgamesh travels onward. See, he has come to the house of Siduri, goddess of wine, refresher of men on the journey to the underworld.

Gilgamesh: *(knocking)* Let me in! Open the door!

Siduri: Who are you? You look like a thief and a murderer to me. This door is staying locked!

Gilgamesh: But I am Gilgamesh, great king of Uruk!

Siduri: *(opening the door)* If you are Gilgamesh, why are you here? Where are you going, and what do you seek?

Gilgamesh: I have traveled long and far. I am seeking Ziusudra. I will ask him the secret of eternal life, and then I will never fear death!

Gilgamesh and the Secret of Eternal Life *continued*

Siduri: But, Gilgamesh! All men must die! Enjoy your life while you have it... make every day a day of feasting and rejoicing... but immortal life is not for mankind.

Gilgamesh: I have traveled too far to turn back now. Where will I find Ziusudra? Show me the way.

Siduri: You will do what no man has done before. You must cross the ocean, the waters of death. Go to the shore. You will find Ziusudra's boatman there. He can take you across. *(Siduri pours Gilgamesh a drink from her jug which he drinks. Siduri exits.)*

Scene 3

(As the Narrator speaks, Gilgamesh mimes walking to the shore, meeting a boatman, and setting off with him. They are pushing the boat forward with long poles, and Gilgamesh is steering.)

Narrator: Gilgamesh goes down to the shore, to find the boatman, and they begin the journey across the ocean.

Ziusudra: *(peering)* I don't recognize the man who is steering that boat. Who is he? Why is he here? I can't see who it is...

Gilgamesh: Ziusudra, it is I, Gilgamesh, great warrior and king of Uruk. I have traveled where no man has before and crossed the waters of death. I have come to get the secret of eternal life!

Ziusudra: But, Gilgamesh, nothing lasts forever! I was given eternal life by the gods, but which god will give *you* eternal life?

Ziusudra's Wife: Husband, let us give Gilgamesh a test. If he can stay awake for six days and seven nights, you will give him the secret of eternal life.

Ziusudra: Very good. So it shall be.

(As the Narrator speaks, they lead Gilgamesh to a room where he sits down and immediately falls asleep. Ziusudra's Wife brings in the plates of bread.)

Narrator: But look! How quickly our hero falls asleep! He sleeps soundly, for *seven days*! Each day, Ziusudra's Wife bakes him a little loaf of bread and leaves it by the bed. At the end of seven days, there are seven plates of bread sitting by the bed.

Gilgamesh: *(waking)* Ziusudra, I just was nodding my head for a second when you touched me and woke me.

Ziusudra: No, Gilgamesh, that is not so. Look at the loaves of bread by your bed: seven days you have slept, and each day my wife brought you a fresh loaf of bread. Look at them now!

Ziusudra's Wife: The first loaf is dried out, the second has gone bad, the third is soggy, the fourth has turned white, the fifth is moldy, the sixth is still pretty fresh... and here is the seventh when you woke up!

Gilgamesh: Oh no! I have failed! What am I going to do? I have come all this way! Shall I return with nothing to show for all my efforts?

Ziusudra: Wait. I will tell you a secret, a secret of the gods. There is a plant that grows at the bottom of the sea. It has a prickle, like a rose. This plant gives new life. It will make you young again, and strong. Find the plant and return home with your precious prize.

(As the Narrator speaks, Ziudsudra and his wife exit, and Gilgamesh mimes swimming and searching for the plant.)

Narrator: Gilgamesh did not even wait to say good-bye. He was already making his way to the bottom of the ocean where he found the prickly plant. He started his journey home again, across the wide ocean.

(Gilgamesh comes downstage and addresses the audience.)

Gilgamesh: But do you know what happened? Even that small victory was taken from me. Along the way home, I stopped to bathe in a well of fresh water and a serpent took my plant! Now, a snake in the wilderness will be young forever, while I grow old and die!

Narrator: Gilgamesh entered the walls of his city empty-handed. But he gave orders for the story of his journey to be written on a stone tablet and the tablet to be displayed on the walls of the city.

(Ziusudra and his wife come downstage.)

Ziusudra: He did not learn the secret of eternal life... *(pausing)* and he lost that powerful plant that would have kept him young. But he gained knowledge! Yes! He returned home a wise man.

Ziusudra's Wife: And who is to say that he did not gain immortality of a sort?

Chapter 1 Short-Term Projects

Through a diverse group of questions, projects, and activities, students explore early humans, their cultures, and the continuing effort to learn more about these distant ancestors.

The Skills of a Hunter-Gatherer   group   30 minutes

Materials: paper and pencil

Prehistoric humans may not have had any formal education, but they did have skills. These skills, such as knowing how to hunt or how to find edible roots and berries, helped them in their constant battle for survival.

Invite groups of students to make a list of skills needed by people living in hunter-gatherer societies. They should include skills like making tools such as stone arrows and spearheads and making fire. Once they have the list, ask them to write down if anyone they know has similar skills. What skills are they lacking? Ask students to speculate about their ability to survive in a primitive environment.

The Clock of Humanity   partners   20 minutes

Materials: paper, markers

How slowly, or quickly, have human cultures and civilizations developed? Have students draw a blank "clock" on a piece of paper and figure out a way to divide it up into thirty-five sections representing 100,000 years each. The clock will start at 3.5 million years ago and go around to the present. Have students mark in important developments in human culture and civilization.

The Three Sisters   individual/partners   20 minutes

Materials: paper, pencils, markers or colored pencils

Corn, beans, and squash are sometimes referred to as the "three sisters." They were the staple of the diets of many early cultures and civilizations. Have students make up short stories, legends, cartoons, or lessons about the three sisters, using only pictures (no words).

12   Unit 1   Short-Term Projects   Social Studies Plus!

An Exhibition of Early Tools

group — **20–30 minutes**

Materials: pencils, paper, markers or colored pencils

Have students make a list of a dozen tools from early history and then choose five or six of the ones they think are most important. Have them draw detailed pictures of the tools for an exhibit on early man. They should label each tool and tell about its origin, what it was made out of, and what it was used for.

Remember! Keep working on that Long-Term Project.

Handprint Wall

whole class — **20 minutes**

Materials: paper, paint, paint brushes

When prehistoric men and women made cave paintings, they showed the things that were most important to them: wild animals, hunters, and their own handprints. Ask the students what pictures of their world would they leave behind.

Have students make a modern-day "cave painting" with handprints and pictures of important activities. It's OK for students to overlap the pictures, or draw things in mismatched sizes. Ask: What will the paintings tell people thousands of years from now about us?

Early Technological Advancement Award

individual/partners — **20–30 minutes**

Materials: blackline master (page 17), construction paper, pens, markers

Have students choose one skill or innovation that they think was the most important.

- the use of fire
- the discovery of paint
- basket making
- the bow and arrow
- growing plants
- pottery making
- domesticating animals

Have students complete the blackline master. They may also want to create a medallion to honor the invention or technological advance.

Chapter 1: Writing Projects

The story of how humans harnessed fire, a journal entry from Skara Brae...here are opportunities for students to get involved in the life and study of early mankind.

Legend for a Distant Past

Invite students to make up a story about one of the following:
- how people found their way across the Bering Strait
- how people learned to use fire for cooking
- how people learned to domesticate wild animals
- how people learned to make and use boats
- how people learned to make clay pots stronger by cooking them in a fire

Remind them that legends do not have to be realistic.

A Skara Brae Life

Have students find out more about Skara Brae through research on the Internet or in books. Invite students to write a journal entry for a boy or girl living in the village before it was abandoned. What kinds of chores and daily tasks would he or she have to do? What kinds of tools or other equipment might he or she use during the day? What would the food and clothing be like? Remind the students not to mention anything that was not yet in use about forty-four hundred years ago.

A Rare Find

Invite students to suppose they are archaeologists writing in a diary on the evening of an amazing discovery. While they were exploring a cave in a remote area, they stumbled upon a spectacular wall painting filled with figures of humans and animals. Encourage the students to describe their thoughts and feelings as they looked at figures that had not been seen by humans for perhaps twenty thousand years!

The Development of Culture

Invite students to think of some of the most important technological or cultural advances from the beginning of human culture and civilization until sometime around five thousand years ago. In what sequence were these advances made? Is the sequence important? Why? Have the students write about and discuss some of these achievements, putting them in the correct sequence. They should explain why it was necessary for each development to come before the next, and how each advance was linked to future technological advances and cultural developments.

Future Archaeologist

Archaeologists find objects from long-extinct cultures and make educated guesses about how these objects were used.

If an archaeologist from the 24th century were searching through the trash and ruins of our civilization, what objects might he or she find? What educated guesses might he or she make as to their uses? Write the list of objects below on the board. Invite students to choose six or eight of them (or substitute others of their own choice) and write an archaeologist's report on the uses and significance of each in the "ancient culture" from North America in 2002. Tell them that some of the archaeologist's guesses should be correct (or nearly correct), while others should be wrong. The "wrong" guesses can be very funny while still sounding serious!

List of objects: football helmet, fork, steering wheel, hair clip, credit card, fashion model doll, can of soup, flute, key ring, pliers, hand-held computer game, coins, sunglasses, dental retainer, in-line roller skates, computer keyboard.

Chapter 1: Citizenship

Responsibility

In the Stone Age, healers were trusted with the responsibility of helping the sick and wounded. Find out about Hippocrates, and how his ancient oath continues to embody this trust and responsibility even today.

Have you ever thought about the trust that patients put in their doctors, and the responsibility that doctors have to do their best and be honest and caring? When new doctors are graduating from medical school, they actually *take an oath* and *swear* to uphold their responsibilities to patients, their profession, and society. The oath they swear is based on one written more than twenty-four hundred years ago by a doctor in ancient Greece!

Hippocrates was born in 460 B.C. He was the first doctor to believe that illnesses were caused by something physical, not by the curses of an angry god. He traveled widely, founded a medical school, wrote books, and taught for many years. He is most famous for writing the Hippocratic Oath. Today, updated versions of the oath are used in medical schools around the world. Look at the excerpts from the ancient and modern versions:

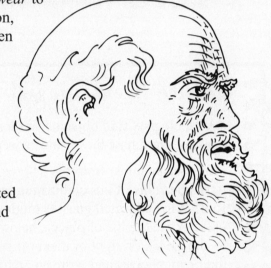

Oath of Hippocrates

I will give no deadly medicine to any one if asked, nor suggest any such counsel. . . . Whatever, in connection with my professional service, or not in connection with it, I see or hear, in the life of men, which ought not to be spoken of abroad I will not divulge, as reckoning that all such should be kept secret. . . .

Modern Medical Oath

I will not provide treatments which are pointless or harmful, or which an informed and competent patient refuses. . . . I will do my best to maintain confidentiality about all patients.

Have students research Hippocrates, his oath, and his medical theories and discoveries.

Have them discuss what could happen if a doctor were not responsible. What is something that a patient must be responsible for? Why?

16 Unit 1 Citizenship Project

Social Studies Plus!

Name _____   Date _____

Early Technological Advancement Award Nomination Form

Name of person making the nomination: _____

Affiliation (circle one):
American Association of Wheel Makers, U.S. Agriculture Group, Historic Association of Animal Breeders, National Tool-Makers Club, Northern League of Potters and Basket Makers

Other (please specify) _____

Technological
Advance Being Nominated: _____

Reason for nomination: *(Why is your advance the most important? How would human development and culture have been held back if the technological advance you are nominating had never been made?)*

_____

_____

_____

_____

_____

_____

_____

Date submitted: _____   Signed: _____

Chapter 2: Short-Term Projects

Invent a board game, make a model, and paint a picture of Babylon. These short-term projects will get students involved and thinking about the peoples of the Fertile Crescent.

Sargon's Story

👤 individual   20–30 minutes

Materials: paper, pencils, colored pencils or markers

Students invent pictograms (simplified pictures representing words or things) to tell the story of the Mesopotamian King Sargon—how he was abandoned as a baby, placed in a basket of reeds, floated on a river, rescued by a gardener, and eventually rose to be a king and empire builder. Students should make a code to accompany their pictograms.

War-Peace Plaque

👥 partners   20 minutes

Materials: paper; colored pencils, markers, or paint and paintbrushes

Students draw or paint a "war-peace" plaque for our times, based on the Standard of Ur. Students should draw their figures in relief—in profile, without a three-dimensional perspective—as the Mesopotamian artists did.

Model Ziggurat

👥 partners   30–45 minutes

Materials: markers, construction paper, glue, cardboard, craft sticks, cardboard boxes, cartons, tubes, egg cartons, etc.

Students construct a model ziggurat, based on the Ziggurat of Ur (see textbook, page 41). Have them draw on the paper before they fold it, and make the walls of the model look as if they are made of bricks. Details such as entrances, staircases, decorative patterns, and pathways should be included.

Remember! Keep working on that Long-Term Project.

Surplus!

👥 group 🕐 30–40 minutes

Materials: blackline master (page 23), poster board, markers, dice, small objects for game pieces

Each new technological or cultural advance brought early human cultures closer to achieving the agricultural surplus needed for civilization to develop.

- Have students create a board game about the development of civilization. The goal of the game is to accumulate the most agricultural surplus. Pass out copies of the blackline master for students to use to write down the rules of their game.

- Challenge the students with these questions: How did agricultural surplus allow people in early cultures to specialize? How did this lead in turn to further advances? What natural or man-made obstacles were setbacks for early cultures? How can students incorporate these advances and obstacles into their game?

The City of Babylon

👤 individual/partners 👥 🕐 20–30 minutes

Materials: paper, paint, paintbrushes

Have students paint a picture of the legendary city of Babylon with its hanging gardens, the giant ziggurat, the Ishtar gate, and temple walls with relief sculptures of animals. Before they begin, it might be useful for them to research Babylon in books or on the Internet to get ideas for their painting.

Scrolled Document

👤 individual 🕐 20–30 minutes

Materials: long roll of drawing or other paper, pencils, pens, colored pencils, two long sticks (these can be dowels, chopsticks, drumsticks, real sticks from a tree, or just pencils)

Have students choose a story from the Old Testament. If the students don't know any, have them research Bible stories and pick one they like. Students will write their stories on the roll of paper and attach the two ends to the sticks. They are creating a scrolled document, like the Hebrew Torah. They can also use a roll of construction paper to fit around the outside of the scroll to make the cover. They can illustrate the cover with pictures or "illuminate" it by putting in decorative borders.

Chapter 2: Writing Projects

Through a legend, journal entries, a play, and two essays that compare and contrast different cultures and time periods, students continue to deepen their knowledge of the people of the Fertile Crescent.

Traveling On!

Invite students to suppose that they are traders traveling by donkey and boat between the various city-states of the Fertile Crescent. Before writing, they should think about the following questions. What goods do they carry to trade? What goods will they take back to their homeland? What difficulties and dangers might they encounter? What sights might they see? Then have them write a journal entry about a single day of travel.

The Gods of the Sumerians

Have students write a story about one of the Sumerian gods: Anu, god of the heavens; Enlil, god of wind; Enki, god of water; or Ninhursag, the mother of the gods. Remind the students that stories about gods are often filled with tales of their anger, jealousy, revenge, spite, and favoritism! Sometimes stories about the gods seek to explain a natural phenomenon, such as why the mountain peaks are white, why blood is red, or how man came to tame animals. They may want to research details on these gods in books or on the Internet. Encourage them to make their stories colorful, lively, and filled with drama.

Hammurabi Reflects on His Place in History

Hammurabi is now an old man with many accomplishments behind him: military successes and empire building. How does he wish to be remembered by history? Invite students to write a story about Hammurabi as he reflects on his life and accomplishments. What is he most proud of? What does he regret? What about him does he think will be remembered by future generations?

Polytheism vs. Monotheism

Most of the people of the Fertile Crescent—the Sumerians, Akkadians, Babylonians, and others—were polytheists. Ask the students to explain what that means. The Jews (also called Hebrews or Israelites) were monotheists. What does that mean? Invite students to write about the difference between polytheism and monotheism. In addition to differences in religious beliefs and practices, what might be the differences in art, architecture, law, literature, or other aspects of culture they can think of?

Abraham and Isaac: A Play

Abraham is considered to be the first Jew because he was the first to make a covenant with God. Ask the students to recall the story of Abraham and his wife, Sarah, their son, Isaac, and God's test. (See the Old Testament, Genesis 17–22, or a book of Bible stories). Invite the students to write a play with these characters (Abraham, Sarah, Isaac, God, and also the ram with its horns caught in the bushes), telling about how God tested Abraham.

Life Before and After the Invention of the Wheel

Ask students to imagine what life was like before the invention of the wheel. How did life change after the wheel was invented? How was the wheel used, and how did this make life easier? Students should research early uses of the wheel in books or on the Internet. Invite them to write an essay about life before and after the invention of the wheel.

Chapter 2 Citizenship

Fairness

Throughout history, people have struggled to create laws and societies that were fair. Using the example of the Code of Hammurabi, students create their own rules for fairness.

The Code of Hammurabi was an early attempt to create laws to establish fairness in business dealings, to create a just society, and to prevent the strong from oppressing the weak.

- What other important documents have students read or heard about from other time periods, in America or other countries, which tried to set out a framework for creating a more just and fair society? Who are some of the people students have heard about who fought for fairness and justice in their societies?

- Figuring out what is fair and just is something that we still deal with today, on many levels. On the national level, our Congress, courts, and the executive branch of the government argue about the best ways to improve our society and make it fairer; these arguments and decisions also happen at the state, county, and local levels of government. Even in our schools, and at home, we try to make rules and procedures to solve disputes in a fair way.

- Ask the students to discuss the current ways the class deals with solving disputes and figuring out what is fair. What rules already exist? Does everyone follow those rules? Do the rules have the intended effect of creating fairness? What new rules or procedures could be added that would help?

- Invite students to create a document called "The Ten Rules of Classroom Fairness." They can work together as a class, in groups, or individually. The rules can be written up as a poster and hung in the classroom.

Name _____ Date _____

Surplus!

Rules of the Game

Some terms to consider when designing your game: irrigation, domestication of animals, agriculture, early farming, empire, climate, disease, warfare, city building, social divisions, trade between citystates, bricks, coins, writing, religion.

_____

_____

_____

_____

_____

_____

_____

_____

_____

_____

_____

_____

Unit 2 Teacher Planner

Long-Term Project pages 26–27	Materials	⏱	Lesson Link
Creating a New "Ancient" Civilization Students create the outlines of a newly discovered twenty-five-hundred-year-old civilization in Africa or Asia.			Lessons 1–3
Week 1 group Students decide where their chosen civilization was from, and what the physical environment was like.	none	1 session 1 hr.	
Week 2 group Students develop information about their chosen civilizations.	pencils, paper	1 session 2 hrs.	
Week 3 group Students work on their presentations, including drawings and charts.	paper, pencils, colored pencils	1 session 2 hrs.	
Week 4 group Students present their civilizations at a "Gathering of Experts."	drawings, diagrams, materials from Weeks 2 & 3	1 session 1 hr.	

Unit Drama pages 28–33			
Scenarios: Ancient Worlds Live Again group Students role-play skits about interpreting oracle bones, planning a pyramid, and conducting a sacred ritual.	props (optional)	5 sessions 30 min. each	Lessons 1–3
Play: The Flight of the Animals group Students perform a play about Buddha as a lion living in the forest.	props, costumes (optional)	1 session 45 min.	Lessons 1–3
Play: Prince Rama and Sita group Students perform a play about Prince Rama, based on a poem written more than two thousand years ago.	props, costumes (optional)	1 session 1 hr.	Lessons 1–4

Chapter 3 Short-Term Projects pages 34–35			
A Wall Painting in a Tomb individual Students paint a wall mural showing a wide variety of activities from Egyptian life.	piece from roll of paper, pencils, watercolors and brushes	1 session 20–30 min.	Lesson 1
A New Alphabet group/partners Students make their own sound pictures for every letter in the alphabet.	pens, paper	1 session 20–30 min.	Lesson 1
The Death Mask of a Pharaoh individual Students construct a death mask for the mummy of an Egyptian pharaoh.	construction paper, scissors, markers, colored pencils, string	1 session 20 min.	Lesson 2
An Ancient Egyptian Building group Students make drawings for a proposed Egyptian palace, temple, or other building.	poster board, pencils, colored pencils	1 session 30 min.	Lesson 2
A List for the Afterlife partners Students make a list of the kinds of things that have been found in Egyptian tombs.	paper, pencils	1 session 20 min.	Lesson 2
A Map of an Ancient Land individual Students draw a large map of ancient Egypt and Nubia.	poster board, pencils, colored pencils	1 session 30 min.	Lesson 2

Chapter 3 Writing Projects pages 36–37	Materials	🕐	Lesson Link
O Mighty Nile 👤 individual Students write poems to praise the Nile River.	paper, pencils	1 session 25 min.	Lesson 1
See the Wonders of Egypt and the Sudan! 👤 individual Students write a modern-day travel brochure for tours to Egypt and the Sudan.	paper, pencils	1 session 20 min.	Lesson 1
A Summary of Research on the Rosetta Stone 👤 individual Students research the Rosetta Stone and write a summary about their findings.	paper, pencils	1 session 20 min.	Lesson 2
Once Lived a Noble Ruler 👤 individual Students write biographies of an Egyptian or Nubian ruler.	paper, pencils	1 session 20 min.	Lesson 2
Another Day on the Job 👤 individual Students write journal entries about their day of work on a construction site.	paper, pencils	1 session 25 min.	Lesson 2
Two Letters Home 👤 individual Students write letters from Howard Carter, the man who discovered Tutankhamen's tomb, to his home.	paper, pencils	1 session 20 min.	Lesson 3

Chapter 3 Citizenship Project page 38			
Courage 👥 whole class Students discuss different occupations that require a measure of courage.	paper, pencils	1 session 45 min.	Lesson 2

Chapter 4 Short-Term Projects pages 40–41			
A Watercolor Painting 👤 individual Students make a watercolor painting after the Chinese style.	paper, black ink or watercolors and brushes	1 session 30 min.	Lesson 1
Make and Compare Climographs 👥 partners Students make climographs for different cities, plotting levels of precipitation and average temperatures.	pencils, paper, colored pencils or markers	1 session 20–30 min.	Lesson 1
Equivalency Charts 👤 individual/partners 👥 Students make conversion charts and change measurements into the metric equivalents.	paper, pencils	1 session 20–30 min.	Lesson 1
The Story of Silk 👤 individual Students find out how silk cloth is made.	poster board, pencils, colored pencils or markers	1 session 30–40 min.	Lesson 2
Words of Wisdom 👤 individual Students come up with a wise saying that will be helpful to people in a thousand years.	paper, black pens, thin dowels, string or yarn	1 session 30–45 min.	Lesson 3

Chapter 4 Writing Projects pages 42–43			
A Decree from the Emperor 👤 individual Students write a decree from the emperor commanding all the provinces to begin work on the Great Wall.	paper, pencils	1 session 20 min.	Lesson 2
Short Biography of a Famous Man 👤 individual Students research and write reports on some of the important people in Asian history.	paper, pencils	1 session 25 min.	Lesson 2

Teacher Planner

Unit 2

Chapter 4 Writing Projects *continued*	Materials	🕐	Lesson Link
A Journal of the Day individual Students write journal entries for a long hard day of factory work.	paper, pencils	1 session 20 min.	Lesson 2
A Letter Home individual Students write letters home explaining the wish to take the entrance exam for civil service.	paper, pencils	1 session 20 min.	Lesson 3
When Heroes Made Inventions individual Students write a legend explaining how a useful tool was invented.	paper, pencils	1 session 20 min.	Lesson 3
Bronze: Research and Summarize individual Students practice making their presentations.	paper, pencils	1 session 25 min.	Lesson 3
Chapter 4 Citizenship Project page 44			
Respect whole class Students think about how their lives would change for the better if there was more respect in the world.	BLM p. 45, paper, pencils	1 session 45 min.	Lessons 1–3
Chapter 5 Short-Term Projects pages 46–47			
A Map of the City of Mohenjo-Daro individual Students create a city map of Mohenjo-Daro.	paper, pencils, colored pencils	1 session 30 min.	Lesson 2
Ashoka's Columns partners Students make "rock markers" with inscriptions about tolerance and nonviolence.	construction paper, pens, markers, rubber bands, paper clips	1 session 20 min.	Lesson 2
Numbering Systems partners Students practice writing numeric information in three different numbering systems.	paper, pencils	1 session 20 min.	Lesson 3
Empire group Students invent a board game called Empire!	large piece of heavy paper, pens, markers, dice, small game pieces	1 session 30–45 min.	Lesson 3
A Time Line of History partners Students draw a time line of the history of the Indian subcontinent.	paper, pencils	1 session 30 min.	Lesson 3
Chapter 5 Writing Projects pages 48–49			
The Death of a Civilization individual Students write about several possible explanations for the demise of the Indus River Valley civilization.	paper, pencils	1 session 20 min.	Lessons 1–2
Research and a Report individual Students write reports on important people in ancient India.	paper, pencils	1 session 30 min.	Lesson 3
A New God or Goddess individual Students write about a new god, one with several special attributes and holding symbolic objects.	paper, pencils	1 session 20 min.	Lesson 3

Chapter 5 Writing Projects continued	Materials	⏰	Lesson Link
Buddhism and Hinduism individual Students write reports comparing and contrasting Hinduism and Buddhism.	paper, pencils	1 session 20 min.	Lessons 3–4
A Hindu Festival individual Students research a Hindu festival and write reports on their findings.	paper, pencils	1 session 25 min.	Lesson 3
An Animal Story individual Students write animal stories in which they are the main characters.	paper, pencils	1 session 20 min.	Lesson 4
Chapter 5 Citizenship Project page 50			
Caring whole class Students discuss how caring for others affects their own lives.	paper, pencils, crayons, markers	1 session 40 min.	Lessons 1–4

Unit 2 Long-Term Project

Creating a New "Ancient" Civilization

Students create the outlines of a newly discovered twenty-five-hundred-year-old civilization in Africa or Asia and present their findings. They include details of its culture, agriculture, architecture, and scientific development.

"Finding" a Lost Civilization

Week 1

 group   1 hour

Materials: none

Explain that the class will invent a civilization that existed twenty-five hundred years ago. Its development should be roughly similar to the cultures of ancient Africa or Asia.

Have the class decide whether the civilization was in Africa or Asia and what the physical environment was like. Discuss how this environment affected the culture.

Divide the class into five groups with each group assigned to one topic: (1) religion, (2) names and myths, (3) way of life, (4) social structure, (5) arts and crafts.

A Framework of a Society Emerges

Week 2

 group   2 hours

Materials: pencils, paper

Groups develop information about the civilization by answering the questions below.

Group 1: Were the people monotheists or polytheists? What were their gods' names?

Group 2: Name this civilization. Choose names for the people, their language, and their country.

Group 3: What was the way of life for most people? Did they hunt, farm, fish, or trade?

Group 4: What was the social structure? Was everyone equal, or was there a kind of ruling power?

Group 5: What arts and crafts did the people create?

Week 3: Filling in the Gaps

 group · 2 hours

Materials: paper, pencils, colored pencils

Groups continue to invent details about the culture. They should also be working on what they will present, including drawings and charts.

Group 1: Give details of some of the culture's religious rituals and/or festivals. These could relate to seasons, agriculture, gods or rulers, or other things.

Group 2: Invent the creation myth of the civilization. Include references to the physical environment and the main gods or goddesses (ask Group 1).

Group 3: What tools did this culture use? Draw and describe one special tool. What did the people know about math, astronomy, and medicine? What about weights and measures? Did they have coins? Give details.

Group 4: What was the role of women in the society? Did they do the same things as men? How were children taught? How were people punished?

Group 5: What were the houses like? What were they made of, and how were they built? Did people live in a city, in villages, or separately? Did they have temples, palaces, or other important buildings?

Week 4: A Gathering of Experts

 group · 1 hour

Materials: drawings, diagrams, and other presentation materials from Weeks 2 & 3.

At the "Gathering of Experts" a number of important archaeologists have come to discuss this newly discovered civilization. One person from each group takes a turn presenting information on its area of expertise. Perhaps you can introduce the "expert" and welcome that person. All the members of the group should be prepared to answer questions from the rest of the class.

Ancient Worlds Live Again

Interpreting the oracle bones, planning a pyramid, conducting a sacred ritual in a temple sanctuary...these and other scenes bring the ancient worlds of Africa, China, and India to life.

Interpreting the Oracle Bones

A family living in China during the Shang dynasty is troubled because their fields are very dry and their animals are not healthy. They go to see the man who interprets oracle bones and ask him about the future of their crops and animals and what the weather will be like for the rest of the season. The man writes the questions on the oracle bones, heats them up until they crack, then interprets the meaning of the cracks. What other questions might they ask? How easy is it to interpret the answers? Act it out!

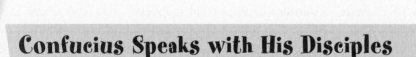

Confucius Speaks with His Disciples

A group of disciples speaks with Confucius, asking questions about life and seeking clarifications on his moral teachings. The disciples sit around their teacher and speak to him with great respect. Confucius answers thoughtfully, with dignity and authority. He speaks of the middle way; of the important virtues of respect, humility, and humanity; and of the importance of leading by example. The disciples ask questions about their own lives, about the role of the ruler in a society, and about the meaning of his teachings.

Simulation: The Pharaoh Makes a Plan

A pharaoh sends for the top royal advisors, and some of the most prestigious royal architects and builders in the kingdom. He (or she) wants to begin work on a new pyramid, a spectacular tomb to confirm the pharaoh's position as the mightiest ruler ever. The pharaoh and his or her people discuss the location of the pyramid, and what special considerations will be made to honor particular gods. Be creative.

Traders Along the Ancient Silk Road

A group of traders has stopped in a town somewhere along the Silk Road, in western China, during the Han dynasty. They are carrying goods from China, such as silk and jade. Other merchants have arrived from distant lands such as India, Afghanistan, and Persia. They are carrying spices and carpets. Some middlemen have also arrived to buy goods to sell later at a profit. Not everyone speaks the same language. Re-create this lively scene!

Offerings to the Gods

A group of singers, dancers, and musicians (with instruments such as rattles and tambourines) accompanies the temple priests as they walk to the temple sanctuary. Only the priests are allowed to enter. As they go in, carrying burning incense, they sprinkle purified water from the temple's sacred lake. The high priest says, "I am the pure one," and breaks the clay seal on the door of the shrine where the golden statue of the god is kept. The high priest decorates the statue and then makes an offering of food to the god. The shrine is closed up again, and the priests leave.

Social Studies Plus!

Unit 2 Drama PLAY

The Flight of the Animals

When Buddha is a lion living in the forest, he learns firsthand why it is important not to believe everything you hear.

The Parts: (8 players)
- Lion (Buddha)
- Deer
- Ox
- Tiger
- Hare
- Wild Boar
- Rhinoceros
- Elephant

Director's Notes: In this play, Buddha tells what happened when he was a lion. For the part marked "Lion (Buddha)" in the script, the lion is being Buddha telling the story, and the player should talk directly to the audience. When the part is just "Lion," the player should talk to the other animals. For fewer than eight players, remove some animals from the play. For more than eight, have the extras join in as more hares, more deer, and so on. As they are running away, the animals should feel free to improvise additional lines. Stage directions are in parentheses.

stage right: the area of stage at actor's right hand as he or she faces audience

(Lion stands stage right, at the front, talking to the audience. Hare is sitting stage left, at the front.)

Lion (Buddha): Once I was a lion, living in a forest near an ocean. One day, Hare was sitting in the forest, thinking about how frightening it would be if the earth caved in. Suddenly, a huge ripe mango fell off the tree near him and crashed to the ground. *(Another player drops a mango right near Hare's head.)*

Hare: *(jumping up and screaming)* The earth is caving in! The earth is caving in! *(Hare runs slowly in a circle; Deer enters and stands stage left.)*

Lion (Buddha): Deer saw Hare running away in terror.

Deer: What is the matter? Why are you running? What has happened?

Hare: The earth is caving in! The earth is caving in! *(Deer and Hare run around the stage, both shouting. Wild Boar enters and, when Deer and Hare complete their circle, Wild Boar speaks to them. Repeat this sequence for all animals.)*

Wild Boar: What is it? Help! Help!

Hare & Deer: The earth is caving in! *(All three circle the stage in slow motion, shouting, and flinging their arms in the air. Lion looks on with an expression of amusement and disbelief.)*

Ox: Save me! Save me! What is it? Where? Help!

Hare, Deer & Wild Boar: The earth is caving in! *(The four circle the stage.)*

Rhinoceros: Where? What? Help! Mommy! Mommy!

Hare, Deer, Wild Boar, Ox: The earth is caving in! *(They all circle the stage.)*

Tiger & Elephant: What is the matter? What is it? Help! Tell me!

Hare, Deer, Wild Boar, Ox, Rhinoceros: The earth is caving in! *(All circle the stage.)*

Lion (Buddha): The animals were all racing toward the ocean, and I knew they would drown if I didn't stop them.

Lion: Stop! You say the earth is caving in, but did any of you see it? Did you, Elephant? Tiger? Or you, Rhinoceros, or Ox or Hare?

Hare: I didn't see it, Lion, but I heard it.

Lion: Come with me. We will go see what made that sound, then we will return and tell everyone. *(Lion and Hare go offstage. The other animals wait. Lion and Hare return with a mango.)*

Lion: My friends. It was not the earth caving in. It was just this juicy mango falling off its tree. Go home. But before you go, tell me what you learned today. *(Ox raises his hand.)*

Ox: I learned that I shouldn't always believe everything I hear!

Prince Rama and Sita

Prince Rama, his wife, Sita, and his stepbrother, Lakshman, are in exile in a terrible forest ruled by the demon Ravana. See what happens when Rama insults Ravana's sister!

The Parts: (8 players)
- Narrator
- Sita
- Ravana
- Ravana's Uncle
- Prince Rama
- Lakshman
- Ravana's Sister
- Hanuman, king of the monkeys

Director's Notes: This play is a part of a long poem about Prince Rama called the *Ramayana*, written more than two thousand years ago! The story in the poem is acted out all over India during a whole month, at the time of the festival Divali. The message of the poem is that good conquers evil. Encourage the players to add in additional lines.

(All actors are onstage. Narrator is at stage right.)

Narrator: Prince Rama, his wife, Sita, and Rama's stepbrother, Lakshman, are in exile in a forest ruled by the demon Ravana. This story begins when Ravana's sister is trying to convince Rama to marry her.

Ravana's Sister: My dear Rama, wouldn't you like to marry me?

Prince Rama: I'm sorry, but I am already married to Sita.

Ravana's Sister: Fine! Then I'll just send her away!
(She pushes Sita, but Lakshman intervenes.)

Lakshman: Hey! You can't do that! Stop! *(Comforts Sita and sends Ravana's Sister away. All exit. Ravana's Sister walks until she comes to Ravana and Ravana's Uncle.)*

Narrator: Ravana's Sister was insulted by how she was treated by Rama and Lakshman. She told her brother, and he asked his uncle, a crafty magician, to help punish Rama.

Ravana: Uncle, you are very clever and evil. Help me show these people who is boss around here!

32 Unit 2 Drama Play Social Studies Plus!

Ravana's Uncle: I will change myself into a golden deer, and then we shall see! *(All exit. Sita, Rama, and Lakshman enter on the other side of the stage. Later the uncle comes in, disguised as a golden deer.)*

Sita: Oh, Rama! Look! Look at that beautiful deer! I think it is made of gold! Please get it for me? *(Deer runs off.)*

Rama: Sita, I would do anything for you! Lakshman, stay here and guard my wife while I catch that deer for her.

Lakshman: Have no fear. She shall be safe with me. *(Rama exits.)*

Narrator: Rama went off to catch the deer, and the uncle led him deep into the forest. Sita becomes worried about her husband.

Sita: Lakshman, where can Rama be? Why is he taking so long? I'm scared. Won't you go find him for me?

Lakshman: I will go, Sita, but first I will draw this magic circle of protection around you. Remember, don't go out of the circle for any reason. *(Draws circle around Sita then runs off.)*

Narrator: When both Rama and Lakshman were gone, the horrible Ravana saw his chance. He disguised himself as a hermit begging for food.

Ravana: *(walking slowly and unsteadily)* Oh, I am so hungry, my lady. Do you have a crumb to spare for a poor man like me?

Sita: *(stepping out of the circle without thinking)* Of course, I do. Here, take this. *(Just then, Ravana throws off his disguise, grabs her, and drags her away.)*

Narrator: *(Sita, Ravana, Rama, and Lakshman mime what the Narrator says.)* Ravana took Sita to his island kingdom of Lanka and asked her to marry him. When she refused, he locked her up! Eventually, Rama and Lakshman realized they had been tricked. A bird helped them to find Sita. Rama and Lakshman called on the Hanuman, the king of the monkeys to help rescue Sita. *(Hanuman enters.)* Hanuman built a stone bridge to the island and they all fought the demon and rescued Sita.

Sita: Oh, Rama! You saved me!

Rama: Don't worry, that demon will never bother you again!

Social Studies Plus! — Unit 2 Drama Play — 33

Chapter 3: Short-Term Projects

Students create a wall painting in a tomb, invent a new hieroglyphic version of the alphabet, construct a death mask for a pharaoh, draw a regional map, and make architectural drawings.

A Wall Painting in a Tomb

individual 20–30 minutes

Materials: a big piece from a roll of paper (or regular paper), pencils, watercolors, paintbrushes

The walls of Egyptian tombs were painted with scenes that showed the journey of the pharaoh's body to the afterworld, the daily life of the royal family and of common Egyptians, and scenes from the lives of the gods and goddesses. Have students paint a wall mural showing activities from Egyptian life, including hieroglyphic symbols. Remind them to draw the people in profile, as the Egyptians did.

A New Alphabet

group/partners 20–30 minutes

Materials: pens and paper

Hieroglyphics were, in part, pictures that reminded the Egyptians of sounds. If an Egyptian was making a set of hieroglyphics to represent the word *barn*, he might draw a *b*at (to remind him of the sound /b/), an *a*rm, *r*ain, and a *n*ewt. The collection of sound pictures, would be read as "b-a-r-n," barn. Have students make their own sound pictures for every letter in the alphabet, and then use it to write their names or sayings.

The Death Mask of a Pharaoh

individual 20 minutes

Materials: construction paper or card stock, scissors, markers or colored pencils, string or yarn

Have students construct a death mask for the mummy of an Egyptian pharaoh. Students can draw the outline of the mask and color in the design they want, or they can cut out shapes in other colors of construction paper and glue those on to look like inlays of stone.

34 Unit 2 Short-Term Projects   Social Studies Plus!

A Map of an Ancient Land

♦ individual   🕒 30 minutes

Materials: poster board or paper, pencils, colored pencils

Students draw a large map of ancient Egypt and Nubia. They include the Nile, its six cataracts, and both ancient and modern cities. Ancient cities (Memphis, Thebes, and Meroe) should be shown with black dots on the map, modern cities (Cairo and Khartoum) with black squares, and the sites of archaeological interest with black triangles. Remind students to include a key and scale and the names of bodies of water.

Remember! Keep working on that Long-Term Project.

An Ancient Egyptian Building

♦♦♦ group   🕒 30 minutes

Materials: poster board or large sheet of paper, pencils, colored pencils

Groups make three architectural drawings for a proposed Egyptian palace, temple, or other building. The first one shows the floor plan for the building complex (including outer buildings, lakes, canals, trees, plazas, etc.). The second shows the front relief of the main building. Both drawings should include dimensions of the buildings measured in cubits, an ancient measurement of approximately twenty inches. Encourage the students to use symbols to represent items in their drawings, such as small circles for columns and triangles for trees, and to include a key. The third drawing is an artist's rendition of the completed complex in use, integrated into the daily life of the city.

A List for the Afterlife

♦♦ partners   🕒 20 minutes

Materials: paper and pencils

Egyptian rulers did not pack light! They were buried with everything they would need in the afterlife, and that means *everything!* Ask students to make a list of all the kinds of things that have been found in Egyptian tombs or what they suppose may have been found. Encourage them to make their lists as comprehensive as possible. They should also be able to say why the items on their lists were included and what they were needed for in the afterlife.

Chapter 3 Writing Projects

Researching the Rosetta stone, imagining the daily life of a worker, writing a biography of a pharaoh—students learn more as they write and reflect on life in ancient Egypt.

A Summary of Research on the Rosetta Stone

Have the students use the library or maybe the Internet to research the Rosetta stone. They should look into why it is so important, who helped to unlock its secrets, and the difficulties those men faced when trying to use the Rosetta stone to decode Egyptian hieroglyphs. Once they have done this research, invite students to write a summary of what they have learned.

Once There Lived a Noble Ruler

Have students write a biography of one of the following Egyptian or Nubian rulers: Tutankhamen, Hatshepsut, Menes, Khufu, Mentuhotep II, Amenemhet, Kashta, or Ashurbanipal. They will have to use the library or perhaps the Internet to get information for their biographies.

O Mighty Nile

Invite students to suppose that they are living in ancient Egypt, and have them write a long poem of praise to the Nile. Remind them that the Nile was considered a source not only of water, but of all life—of fish, animals to be hunted, and papyrus reeds to make paper. The regular flooding of the Nile provided rich soil for farming and water for irrigation. It was a principal means of transportation, and, of course, swimming and boating were popular forms of recreation at that time. Student poems do not have to rhyme, but they should be filled with vivid images and details of life in ancient Egypt.

Another Day on the Job

Invite students to suppose that they are Egyptians working on the construction of a pyramid. Have each choose if he or she is a laborer (slave, prisoner of war, convict, or, most likely, peasant farmer), a skilled craftsman (stonemason, surveyor, carpenter, metalworker, scribe, stone carver, or painter), a foreman, an overseer, or a director. Students should decide what work they are doing and how far along the construction is. Once students have chosen their roles, invite them to write detailed journal entries about their day of work on the construction site.

See the Wonders of Egypt and the Sudan!

Have students write a modern-day travel brochure for tours to Egypt and the Sudan. The aim of the brochure is to entice people to visit these countries and tour their spectacular archaeological sites. The students should include descriptions of archaeological attractions that can be visited, as well as details of tour lengths and options. One tour option includes traveling in a boat down the Nile and viewing the ancient Egyptian structures from the river. Ask students to describe choices in accommodation (from tents to luxury hotels). Encourage students to make their brochures lively and to include prices and details for getting more information.

Two Letters Home

Probably the most spectacular archaeological discovery ever was on November 26, 1922, when Howard Carter, a British archaeologist, first looked into the tomb of the pharaoh Tutankhamen. This was the first and only tomb from ancient Egypt ever discovered "intact"—that is, before tomb robbers had struck. Carter wrote, "As my eyes grew accustomed to the light... I was struck dumb with amazement." The room was full of "gold—everywhere the glint of gold."

Invite students to suppose they are Howard Carter. Have them write two letters home: one, a month before his discovery when he is discouraged and thinking of giving up his lifelong search for the tomb; a second, a month after the discovery, when an inventory of the tomb has been made and Carter knows the full value of what he has found.

Chapter 3 Citizenship

Courage

Workers in ancient Egypt had no choice but to be courageous. Today, we have safety measures and workman's compensation. But many jobs still require courage. Students think, discuss, and write about different occupations.

The tomb builders of ancient Egypt showed courage, working in dangerous conditions for months and years on end as the pyramids were built. What about other people who have worked in the construction industry throughout history? What building projects can the students think of that would have been dangerous and challenging to work on and required a lot of courage?

Have groups of students discuss the following questions. Have one person in each group write down a few notes about the group's response to each question. After the groups have discussed the questions, their answers can be compared in the whole class.

1. What jobs can you think of that exist today that can still be dangerous?

2. Who do you know who works in one of these jobs? What does he or she do? Do you think he or she is courageous?

3. Do you think jobs today are generally safer or more dangerous than jobs were in ancient Egypt? Explain your answer. Can you think of any exceptions to your rule?

4. What kinds of safety protections are used today that did not exist in the past? What further safety measures should be put in place?

5. Do you think that people who do dangerous jobs should be paid extra? Explain your answer.

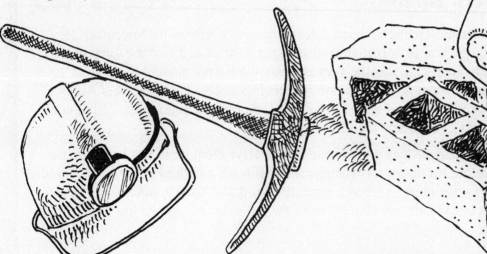

38 Unit 2 Citizenship Project

Social Studies Plus!

Name _____   Date _____

A Hieroglyphic Alphabet

Use this simplified Egyptian hieroglyphic alphabet to write out a message to someone in your class. Trade messages and see if you can understand what the other person wrote!

letter	hieroglyph	sound
A		cat, sat, around
		table, may
B		big, better
C/K		care, cousin, also kid, kick
CH		church, choose
D		delta, dime
E		reed, read and Mary
		earn, over, elf and bet
F or PH		fist, fair, also set, met
G		girl, go
		George, gentle
H		hit, who and behind
I		bit, bite
J		jam, jinx
K		kite, cat, back, Chris, school

letter	hieroglyph	sound
L		late, loaf
M		many, mango
N		none, never
O		loot, toot, also boat, look
		rot, hot, also thought, caught
P		pen, jump
R		ring, train
S		see, mist, also nice, cinder
SH		share, machine
T		time, rent
TH		thing, sloth
		then, mother
U		hut, rut, also bull, wool
V		very, clever
W		weary, worry, why
Y		young, yellow
Z		Zoe, crazy, also faces, girls, surprise

Social Studies Plus!   Unit 2 Blackline Master 39

Chapter 4: Short-Term Projects

A wide variety of hands-on projects increase students' involvement in the world of ancient China, from the production of silk to the wisdom of Confucius.

The Story of Silk

individual • 30–40 minutes

Materials: poster board, colored pencils, colored pencils or markers

Ask students to do some research to find out how silk cloth is made. What is it made of? What are the steps in the process that go into creating the finished product? The research should include something about the following topics: moths, eggs, worms, mulberry leaves, cocoons, boiling, reeling, weaving, and dyeing. Once the students learn how silk is made, they can present their findings in a series of labeled diagrams.

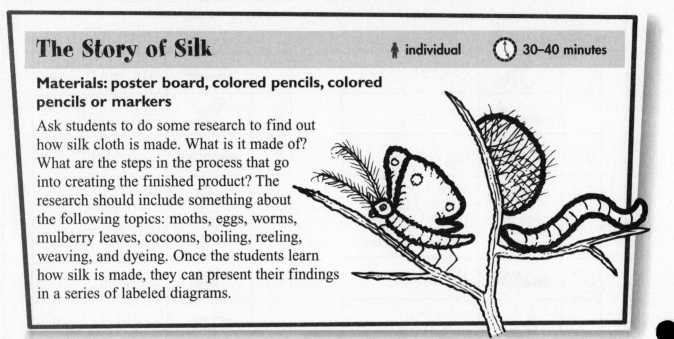

Words of Wisdom

individual • 30–45 minutes

Materials: paper, black pens, thin dowels, string or yarn

Confucius offered words of wisdom to the people of his country and his time. Many of his sayings, collected by his disciples, are still meaningful today. Here are three: "A person of true wisdom knows what he knows and what he does not know." "A man who commits a mistake without correcting it commits another mistake." "Don't criticize other people's mistakes. Criticize your own."

Ask students to come up with a wise saying that they think will be helpful to people in a thousand years. Have them write out the saying in beautiful handwriting on a piece of paper. If they want, they can make a decorative border. Attach one dowel or chopstick to the top and one to the bottom of the paper, and attach a length of string or yarn at the top to make a wall hanging.

A Watercolor Painting

individual — **30 minutes**

Materials: paper (preferably watercolor paper), black ink or watercolor paint, paintbrushes

Have the students make a watercolor painting after the Chinese style. Suggest they include mountains, waterfalls, trees, birds, horses, or anything else from nature. Students will use only black paint or ink, but should try to paint with the full range of shades of gray.

Make and Compare Climographs

partners — **20–30 minutes**

Materials: pencils and paper, colored pencils or markers

Using information found in the library or possibly on the Internet, students make climographs for Dallas (Texas), Seattle (Washington), and Boston (Massachusetts), plotting levels of precipitation and average temperatures by month. When they have completed their graphs, they should be able to answer questions, such as: Which of the three states has the most precipitation? Which has the least variation in temperature over the course of the year? Which has the highest average temperature? How do the climographs for these three cities compare to the one for Beijing?

Remember! Keep working on that Long-Term Project.

Equivalency Charts

individual/partners — **20–30 minutes**

Materials: paper and pencils

Not having a standard currency or system of measurement can make trade and commence difficult. In the United States today, we use feet and inches, pounds and ounces, and the metric system as well. Have students make a conversion chart, changing each of the following measurements into its metric equivalent: 1 inch, 6 inches, 1 foot, 2 feet, 1 yard, 10 yards; 1 ounce, 8 ounces, 1 pound, 100 pounds; 1 cup, 2 cups, 1 pint, 1 quart, 1 gallon. Ask students to think about Fahrenheit and Celsius measurements. What is 56 degrees Fahrenheit in degrees Celsius? What is 56 degrees Celsius in degrees Fahrenheit?

Chapter 4: Writing Projects

A decree from an emperor, a report about bronze, a letter home from an aspiring civil servant—these and other writing prompts add breadth and depth to students' study of ancient China.

A Decree from the Emperor

Construction of the Great Wall of China was begun by the emperor Qin Shi Huangdi. He ordered the wall to be eight horses wide at the bottom, six horses wide at the top, and as tall as five men. Every one hundred yards there was a watchtower two stories high. The wall was built with the labor of hundreds of thousands of prisoners, soldiers, and ordinary people forced into work gangs.

Invite students to write a decree from the emperor, going out to all the provinces in northern China, commanding them to begin work on this project by rounding up workers. Encourage them to make the decree sound both ancient and fierce.

Short Biography of a Famous Man

Have the students use the library or Internet to research any of these important people: Qin Shi Huangdi, the first emperor of the Qin dynasty; Han Gaozu, the first ruler of the Han dynasty; Wu Di, another Han emperor; Sima Qian, an ancient Chinese historian; Lao-tzu, founder of Taoism; Mencius, a follower of Confucius. Invite students to write a short summary about the person.

A Journal of the Day

Ask students to write as if they were laborers working on the construction of the Great Wall; a worker in a silk-making "factory"; a goldsmith, stone carver, or painter employed by the emperor; or a soldier fighting in Qin Shi Huangdi's army. Invite them to write a detailed journal entry for a long day of hard work.

A Letter Home

Invite students to imagine that they are students in China during the time of the Han dynasty emperor Wu Di. They are staying in a town many miles from their parents, studying to become scholars. Each student writes a letter home explaining the wish to take the entrance exam for the civil service. The letter should be polite and respectful and ask for permission and approval. It should give details to explain why the student wants to join the civil service and what will be achieved.

When Heroes Made Inventions

During the Xia period in Chinese history, from about 2000 to 700 B.C., people told tales or legends about ancient superheroes and how they invented things that were useful to people and made life easier—things such as irrigation, farming, and the domestication of animals. Have students think of an invention that made life better for ancient peoples, such as coins, writing, roads, the wheel, or baskets. Have the students write a legend explaining how one of these useful tools or ideas was invented.

Bronze: Research and Summarize

From the Shang dynasty onward, the people of China used bronze. What is bronze? How is it made? What did the people in early China use bronze for? Why was bronze a big improvement over stone, wood, or clay for making tools and weapons? What other metals did early civilizations learn to use, and in what order?

Have students do research in the library or possibly on the Internet to find out about bronze and answer these questions. Then ask them to summarize what they have found out in a short written report.

Citizenship

Respect

Students discuss the importance of respect in early China, and its importance today. Groups tackle questions of how respect can be shown between individuals, groups, nations, cultures, and religions.

Respect for elders has been an important part of Chinese culture from the time of Confucius. It continues to be important today. How do you think Chinese children from the Qin or Han dynasty showed respect for their parents and elders? How do you think children today in China show respect for their parents? How has it changed?

Is respect still important today here in the United States? How is respect a part of the students' lives? When do they want respect? When do they show respect? Ask them to think how their lives would change for the better if there was more respect in the world.

In groups, have students discuss respect between the pairs shown below. Explain that the double-sided arrows indicate that the respect should go in both directions—so, for example, when they see "children ⟷ adults," they should discuss both how *children* can show respect for *adults* and how *adults* can show respect for *children*. After talking about each pair, they should write down ways that respect between the two groups can be shown. These lists can be read aloud or posted. Students may also use these ideas to complete the blackline master on page 45.

children ⟷ children

adults ⟷ adults

children ⟷ adults

governments ⟷ citizens

countries ⟷ other countries

one religion ⟷ another religion

one culture ⟷ another culture

Name _____ Date _____

Use the letters below to write a reminder about the importance of respect. Use each letter to start a sentence. Write your sentences on the page.

R _____

E _____

S _____

P _____

E _____

C _____

T _____

Social Studies Plus! Unit 2 Blackline Master

Chapter 5: Short-Term Projects

Individually, in pairs, and in groups, students tackle a variety of fun activities that increase their understanding of the ancient civilizations they have been learning about. Something for everyone!

A Map of the City of Mohenjo-Daro 👤 individual 🕐 30 minutes

Materials: paper, pencils, colored pencils

Mohenjo-Daro and Harappa were two cities of the ancient Indus River Valley civilization that began to flourish around 2500 B.C. and then disappeared by about 1700 B.C. Archaeologists have found that both cities were well planned: the streets were laid out on a grid, and complicated drainage systems existed to take away the wastewater from the houses.

Have students create a city map for Mohenjo-Daro. Remind them that the streets crossed at right angles, forming city blocks. They should include private houses, workshops for craftsmen, public areas including public wells and baths, areas for public religious festivals to be celebrated, as well as a palace. Encourage students to explore Web sites about the excavations, if possible.

Remember! Keep working on that Long-Term Project.

Ashoka's Columns 👤 individual 🕐 20 minutes

Materials: construction paper, pens or markers, rubber bands, paper clips

Ashoka used inscriptions on columns to convey important information to the people of the empire. Have students make "rock markers" by taking a piece of construction paper (8½ by 11) and marking a one-inch margin down the left and right sides and a two-inch margin at the top and bottom. In the center, they should write out their "inscription"—a proclamation, important news, or a message about tolerance and nonviolence. The top and bottom margins should be used for decorations. Create the column by gluing the side margins together. Hold the column with a rubber band around the middle and paper clips over top and bottom ends until glue dries.

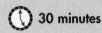

VIOLENCE BEGETS VIOLENCE

Numbering Systems

partners · **20 minutes**

Materials: paper, pencils

Many ancient people had numbering systems, but none was as efficient as the Arabic numerals we use today. "Arabic" numerals were in fact developed in India around two thousand years ago. This ancient numbering system, which included a zero and introduced the idea of "place value," was known as "Arabic" because it was brought west by Muslims around eleven hundred years ago.

Have students discuss the importance of place value in our numbering system. Where would we be without a zero? Remind students that we use base ten. How do you count to ten in a base four numbering system? What are the advantages of a base ten numbering system?

Ask students to write out the following information in three numbering systems, Arabic, Roman, and base four: the current year, their age, their height in inches.

Empire

 group · **30–45 minutes**

Materials: large piece of heavy paper or cardboard, pens, markers or colored pencils, dice, small objects to be game pieces

Students invent a board game called Empire! The players are the Indus River Valley people, the Aryans, the Persians, the Mauryan people, and the Guptas. Each group tries to gain territory while spreading its culture and accumulating wealth. Players are helped or hindered by wars, natural disasters, agricultural development, successful trade, technological growth, and other obstacles and advances.

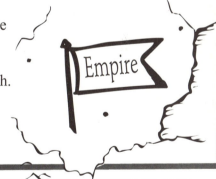

A Time Line of History

partners · **30 minutes**

Materials: paper, pencils

Students draw a time line of the history of the Indian subcontinent. The time line should include the dates for the earliest known civilizations, the approximate dates of invasions, the times associated with important rulers and groups of rulers, developments in religion, and other important details.

Writing Projects

Students use their research skills and imaginations to make the early history of India come alive!

A Hindu Festival

The Hindu calendar is filled with festivals such as Divali, Holi, Navaratri, and Raksha. Have students use the library or the Internet to find out about one festival and write a report about what they find. What gods, goddesses, or other deities are honored during the festival? Is there a story about why the festival is celebrated? Are there particular foods, games, costumes, decorations, activities, or songs associated with the festival? How long does the festival last? Is it celebrated throughout India or in one region? Do Hindus living outside India still celebrate this festival?

An Animal Story

Buddha told stories of animals to teach about morality, wisdom, and spirituality. In these stories, Buddha becomes an animal and learns a lesson about how to live, and how to treat others. At the end of a story, Buddha explained to his disciples what he learned.

Invite students to write an animal story. Remind them that in the story, they *become* the main animal character. The story should start something like, "Once, when I was a rabbit..." and end with a lesson about life.

The Death of a Civilization

Nobody knows for sure why the Indus River Valley civilization died away around 1700 B.C. The cities of Mohenjo-Daro and Harappa were not lived in after that time, and no one knows whether they were abandoned gradually or suddenly. Invite students to write about possible explanations for the demise of this ancient civilization.

Research and a Report

Science, mathematics, medicine, and philosophy in ancient India were remarkably advanced. Ask the students to research and write a report on one of the following people or topics: Sushruta, an ancient Indian surgeon; Chaharaka, a doctor for King Kanishka; Kashyapa (also known as Kanada), a philosopher; Brahmagupta, a mathematician and scientist; Ayurvedic medicine; yoga.

A New God or Goddess

Many Hindu gods and goddesses have special attributes such as extra arms or heads or eyes, or body parts from different animals. Often they are pictured holding symbolic objects in their hands. For example, Lord Ganesh, the god of wisdom, has the head of an elephant (symbolizing wisdom and strength) and the body of a man, with a big potbelly (symbolizing the abundance of nature). He has four arms. The hand of one holds a rope (to carry devotees to the truth), another an ax (to cut devotees' attachments), another a sweet dessert ball (to show the sweetness of spiritual life), and the fourth hand is extended out in a symbol of blessing.

Invite students to make up and write about a new god, one with several special attributes and holding symbolic objects. For example, they might make up the "god of mathematical insight" who has an extra eye to see below the surface of things, the wings of an eagle to soar over the problem, and four hands holding a calculator, a ruler, a pencil, and an eraser!

Buddhism and Hinduism

Hinduism and Buddhism are two important religions practiced in India. Ask students to write a short report that compares and contrasts Hinduism and Buddhism. The report should start with a summary of the basic principles, deities, and beliefs of each religion. The report should then move on to discuss how these two religions are similar and how they are different.

Chapter 5 Citizenship

Caring

Caring for others is an important part of good citizenship. Ask students to recall Buddha's concern about human suffering. Then ask them how caring for others affects their own lives.

Buddha left his life as a wealthy prince because he was so upset thinking about human suffering in the world. He had everything he needed for himself, but he was concerned about others. He spent his life trying to teach others how to live so that they could be free of suffering.

Ask students what they think of Buddha's ideas. Is it true that people suffer when they want too many things? Is one way to feel better to free yourself from wanting things you don't have?

In every period of history there have been poor people, sick people, and people who needed help for one reason or another. Different religions and governments have had many approaches to caring about and for those people and helping them to have better lives. In our society, caring for others is a part of good citizenship. Ask students to form groups and discuss the following questions about caring, then report their answers to the class:

1. What things can *you* do to help or care for others?
2. How can your class or your school show concern for others?
3. What are some ways that churches, synagogues, mosques, and other religious institutions help others?
4. What nonreligious organizations and groups do you know that try to help others?
5. What can governments do to try to improve people's lives?
6. What do people mean when they talk about "helping people to help themselves"?

A Rangoli Pattern

A rangoli is a Hindu sign of welcome. During the festival of Divali, people welcome the goddess Lakshmi into their homes by drawing a rangoli pattern at the entrance. Rangoli patterns are square, circular, rectangular, or a combination of shapes. They also sometimes include a drawing of a lotus flower. Cut out and color this rangoli pattern, and then color another of your own design.

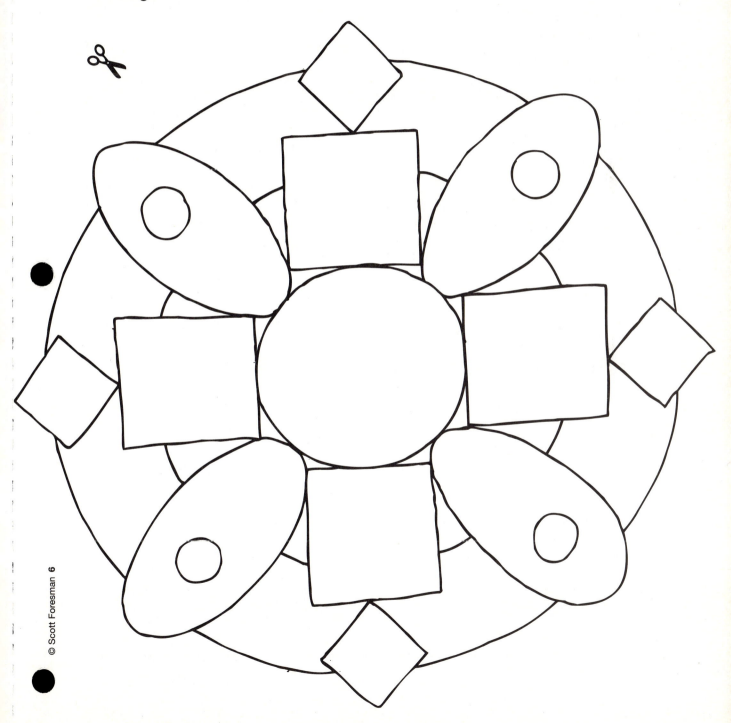

Social Studies Plus! Unit 2 Blackline Master

Teacher Planner

Long-Term Project pages 54–55	Materials	⏱	Lesson Link
A Scale Model of Machu Picchu, Tenochtitlan, or Pueblo Bonito Students produce a scale model of theses cities using plans they find through research.			Lessons 1–3
Week 1 whole class/group Students brainstorm how their models will be built.	paper, pencils	1 session 2 hrs.	
Week 2 group Students draw the plan for their city and construct houses, public buildings, and other necessary structures.	poster board or cardboard, pencils, pens, art supplies	1 session 1–2 hrs.	
Week 3 group Students add details such as people, animals, and vegetation to their city models.	various art supplies	1 session 1–2 hrs.	
Week 4 group Students prepare "guided tours" of their cities, explaining the structures and providing information about the city.	various art supplies	1 session 1 hr.	

Unit Drama pages 56–61			
Scenarios: Then and Now group Students role-play skits about North, South, and Central America from across the ages.	props (optional)	6 sessions 30 min. each	Lessons 1–3
Play: Moctezuma and Cortés group Students perform a play about the ruler Moctezuma and Cortés, the Spanish explorer.	props, costumes (optional)	1 session 2–2 1/2 hrs.	Lesson 3

Chapter 6 Short-Term Projects pages 62–63			
Everyday: Corn, Beans, Squash partners Students create a menu using only dishes that have corn, beans, and squash as the main ingredients.	markers, paper	1 session 20–30 min.	Lesson 1
A Mesoamerican Creation Myth group Students tell about creation myths that they research.	none	1 session 30–40 min.	Lessons 1–2
A Scene from Mayan Daily Life individual Students draw scenes depicting Mayan farmers, craftsmen, nobles, priests, and/or children going about a task.	paper, pencil, markers or colored pencils	1 session 20–30 min.	Lesson 2
Making a Codex individual Students make a codex, including a combination of pictures and symbols.	white paper, pencils, markers or colored pencils	1 session 30 min.	Lesson 3
An Aztec Metal Pendant individual Students create original Aztec metal pendants.	thin cardboard, scissors, foil, clay, rolling pin, pencil, string	1 session 20 min.	Lesson 3

Chapter 6 Writing Projects pages 64–65	Materials	⏱	Lesson Link
Astronomy 👤 individual Students write reports on the uses of astronomy in ancient civilizations.	paper, pencils	1 session 20 min.	Lesson 2
A New Legend 👤 individual Students write new myths, involving the gods and goddesses studies in the Aztec and Mayan legends.	paper, pencils	1 session 30 min.	Lessons 2–3
What if . . . ? 👤 individual Students write essays speculating on questions such as: What might have happened if the Spanish had encountered people with the same technology as they had?	paper, pencils	1 session 20 min.	Lesson 3
A Biography 👤 individual Students research and write a biography on one of the key figures studied in the chapter.	paper, pencils	1 session 30 min.	Lesson 3
Compare and Contrast: Equipment and Tactics 👤 individual Students compare the fighting equipment and tactics of the Aztecs and the Spanish.	paper, pencils	1 session 20 min.	Lesson 3
A Message from a Friend 👤 individual Students write messages from a local person describing the new arrivals to someone who has not seen them yet.	paper, pencils	1 session 20 min.	Lesson 3

Chapter 6 Citizenship Project page 66			
Honesty 👥👥👥 whole class Students examine how honesty and dishonesty can affect relationships between people and countries.	paper, pencils	1 session 40 min.	Lesson 3

Chapter 7 Short-Term Projects pages 68–69			
Longitude and Latitude 👥 partners Students find the approximate longitude and latitude coordinates for certain places.	paper, pencils, globe or atlas	1 session 20–30 min.	Lesson 1
No Telephone or Computers? 👤 individual/partners 👥 Students calculate how long it would take to get messages between your school and other locations.	paper, pencils	1 session 20 min.	Lesson 1
Potato Mania 👥 partners Students write out the recipes for favorite dishes including potatoes.	paper, pencils	1 session 20–30 min.	Lesson 3
Making a Quipu 👤 individual Students make a quipu to record information about the class, the school, the weather, or other topics.	string or yarn in different colors	1 session 30–40 min.	Lesson 3
Society Pyramid Chart 👥 partners/group 👥👥👥 Students make pyramid charts showing what they learned about the chain of command in the Incan system.	poster board, pencils, colored pencils or markers	1 session 20 min.	Lesson 3

Unit 3 Teacher Planner

Chapter 7 Writing Projects pages 70–71	Materials	🕐	Lesson Link
A Letter to a Bishop individual Students write letters from the priest to his bishop in Spain complaining about how the local people are treated.	paper, pencils	1 session 20 min.	Lesson 2
From Moctezuma to Atahualpa individual Students write letters from Moctezuma to Atahualpa, warning the Incan leader not to trust the Spanish.	paper, pencils	1 session 30 min.	Lesson 2
National Service: For or Against individual Students write essays saying whether they think a required year of military service would be good for the U.S.	paper, pencils	1 session 20 min.	Lesson 2–3
A Newly Domesticated Animal individual Students pick an animal to domesticate and write about their choice.	paper, pencils	1 session 25 min.	Lesson 3
Compare and Contrast: Conqueror and Conquered individual Students compare being conquered by the Inca and being conquered by the Spanish.	paper, pencils	1 session 20 min.	Lesson 3

Chapter 7 Citizenship Project page 72			
Caring whole class Students write about people who have cared enough to fight for the rights of others.	paper, pencils	1 session 45 min.	Lessons 1–3

Chapter 8 Short-Term Projects pages 74–75			
Experiment with Oral History group Students play Telephone to see how accurately information was passed down along the generations.	none	1 session 20 min.	Lesson 1
Being Self-Sufficient individual/partners Students make a list of the foods they eat, and decide which foods they could grow and harvest themselves.	paper, pencils	1 session 20 min.	Lessons 1–4
Real Estate Advertisement individual/partners Students write real estate ads for a Native American dwelling available for rent or purchase.	paper, pens and pencils, markers or colored pencils	1 session 30 min.	Lessons 2–4
An Iroquois "False Face" Mask individual Students make frightening-looking masks to drive away evil spirits.	cardboard, construction paper, various art supplies	1 session 30 min.	Lesson 3
Ancient and Modern group Students make a list of Native American objects and their modern equivalents.	paper, pencils	1 session 20 min.	Lesson 3

Chapter 8 Writing Projects pages 76–77	Materials	🕐	Lesson Link
Deganawidah and Hiawatha: A Speech 👤 individual Students write a speech that Hiawatha will give to one of the Iroquois-speaking tribes to persuade them to join the confederacy.	paper, pencils	1 session 25 min.	Lesson 1
Living Life as a Native American 👤 individual Students write essays speculating on how it would be to live life as a Native American.	paper, pencils	1 session 25 min.	Lessons 1–3
Why Cultures Vanish 👤 individual Students write explanations of why they think many Native American cultures disappeared.	paper, pencils	1 session 20 min.	Lessons 1–4
Native American Groups 👤 individual Students write about a Native American group that lived in their area of the country.	paper, pencils	1 session 20 min.	Lessons 1–4
Compare and Contrast: Inuit and Iroquois 👤 individual Students write essays comparing the environments and lives of the Inuit and the Iroquois.	paper, pencils	1 session 20 min.	Lessons 3–4
The Great Serpent Mound: A Legend 👤 individual Students write myths or legends explaining how the burial mound came to be.	paper, pencils	1 session 30 min.	Lesson 3
Chapter 8 Citizenship Project page 78			
Courage 👥👥👥 whole class Students examine how and when courage and other qualities were needed in earlier times.	paper, pencils	1 session 35 min.	Lessons 1–4

Long-Term Project

Unit 3

A Scale Model of Machu Picchu, Tenochtitlan, or Pueblo Bonito

The class works to produce a scale model of Machu Picchu, Tenochtitlan, or Pueblo Bonito, using plans of the city that they find through their research.

Week 1 — Choosing a City

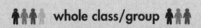 whole class/group 2 hours

Materials: pencils and paper

Explain to the students that they are going to build a scale model of an ancient city. Break the class into three groups to do research at the library or on the Internet on one of three cities: Machu Picchu, Tenochtitlan, or Pueblo Bonito. When groups have completed their research, ask a spokesman for each group to present whatever the group has found. Then have the class vote on the city it wants to build.

Brainstorm with the class on how the model will be built. What scale will be used? What material will be used to make buildings look made of stone or adobe? How will they show the lake and canals for Tenochtitlan? What will they use for people, animals, plants? Make a list of easy to find materials and assign each student items to bring in to school (or assign in groups).

Week 2 — A Base to Build On

group   1–2 hours

Materials: cardboard or poster board for base of model (about 4 feet by 4 feet), pencils and pens, materials decided upon in Week 1

Divide the class into five groups. The first group will draw the overall plan for the city, basing its work on maps and plans found from research. Plans should include some areas where crops were grown (for Machu Picchu and Pueblo Bonito) and, for Tenochtitlan, canals, lake, and causeways leading to the shore. Meanwhile, the other four groups begin construction (detailed) of houses, public buildings, boats (if necessary), and other structures. At the end of the work period, the class should decide what other materials are needed to finish the project. Individuals (or groups) will be responsible for bringing the materials to class.

Week 3 — A City Under Construction

 group   1–2 hours

Materials: as needed to finish the project

The five groups continue work on the city. The group that drew the plans can place, on the base, the houses that the other four groups made. The second group can finish the construction of any larger structures (including city walls) that are still needed. The third group can concentrate on adding details such as people, animals, and vegetation. The fourth group can place goods in the marketplace, sculptures and idols in the temples, pots and baskets in the houses, grain and treasures in the storehouses, and so on. The fifth group can make any ornaments needed for the buildings, and make sure the roads, canals, and fields look as realistic as possible. Assign individuals to gather materials, if more are needed.

Week 4 — The Finishing Touches and a Guided Tour

 group   1 hour

Materials: as determined in the previous week

All five groups work to finish the model city. The class then prepares a "guided tour" of the city: one representative from each group will "guide" visitors through an area of the city, explaining the structures and giving information about the city, the people who built it, their lives, their culture, and their civilization. Invite other classes and teachers to come for their guided tour!

Then and Now

By acting out scenes from North, South, and Central America from across the ages, students have a chance to think and feel like the people they are studying.

Incan Officials at the Palace of a Conquered Leader

A group of Incan officials is at the palace of a local king who has just surrendered and accepted Incan rule. The officials explain what it will mean to be a part of the Inca Empire, what the locals can expect and what will be expected of them. The king and his councilors can ask questions, but they must remember that the Incas are their new rulers.

Archaeologists Make a Discovery

A group of archaeologists walking in the jungle near the border of present-day Colombia and Panama come across some impressive stone ruins. While all of the archaeologists agree that the structures are pre-Columbian, they disagree on which ancient culture was most likely to have built them. Act out the conversation among the archaeologists, explaining why each person thinks his or her theory is correct.

The Explorers and the King

A group of Spanish explorers and adventurers have an audience with the Spanish king and his most important advisors (including a representative of the church). The explorers are heading for South America and want financial backing from the king. In return, they promise to add new lands to the king's dominion. The king and his advisors are skeptical. Act out the whole meeting.

Lessons from an Inuit Grandparent

An Inuit grandparent sits with a group of grandchildren and great-grandchildren. He or she is telling the children how everything has changed now that the Inuit people live in modern towns, buy their food in stores, and work in factories and other businesses. The grandparent talks about the old days: what people wore, what tools they used, how they traveled, how they hunted, what kind of houses they lived in, how they used the different parts of the animals they caught, how children learned what they needed to know, and what sorts of things they did for fun. The children ask questions. Make up the dialogue.

The Incan Farmers, the Spaniard, and the Potato

A Spanish explorer comes across a group of Incan farmers who are harvesting potatoes. The Spaniard asks what the potato is and how it is used. He may ask some pretty funny questions since he has never seen a potato before. The Incan farmers explain what a good crop it is, and all the ways they use it. They also explain the different ways they store the potato, including their special technique of "freeze-drying" – mashing it and letting it freeze overnight, then putting it in the sun during the day so that the water evaporates, and repeating the process until all the water has evaporated. Potatoes "freeze-dried" in this manner could be stored for up to a year.

An Argument: How Best to Use the Rain Forest

A group of miners, businessmen and some natives of the Amazon are discussing the rain forest. The businessmen argue that there is plenty of forest, and that there is no harm in clear-cutting areas for mining and other uses. What would the arguments of the Amazonian people be? Each side tries to support its views with economic reasons, and examples. Perhaps some scientists join the discussion. What do they say about preserving the rain forest?

Moctezuma and Cortés

Students act out the historic meeting between Cortés, the Spanish conquistador, and Moctezuma, the leader of the Aztec people. The fate of a great civilization is in the balance!

The Parts (8 players)
- Narrator
- Cortés
- Moctezuma
- Two Spanish Officers
- 2 Aztec Nobles
- Cuitlahuac (Moctezuma's younger brother)

Director's Notes: When Cortés met Moctezuma, tension and drama were in the air. Both sides sought to impress each other, but also to appear friendly. The players should remember this tension at all times. For the sake of speed and simplicity, the play does not use interpreters.

Scene 1 Outside the Gates of Tenochtitlan

(The narrator talks to the audience as Cortés and his men approach the gates of the city. The Aztecs watch closely.)

Narrator: At long last, Cortés and his men are about to enter Tenochtitlan. He wants the treasure of the great Aztec city, and will stop at nothing to get it! He has been invited into the city as a friend and guest, and he knows his small army is greatly outnumbered, and that these Aztec warriors could turn against him in an instant.

Cortés: *(to his men under his breath)* Do not show fear. Watch your sides. Keep your swords ready. Smile.

Sp. Off. 1: This stone causeway going from the lakeshore to the island city is amazing! It must be over two miles long!

Sp. Off. 2: I can't wait to see inside the city! It looks so beautiful! Look! These must be the nobles. Look at the headdresses, the gold and jewelry! I can't believe this is all real. It's like a dream.

Cortés: We stop here to acknowledge the nobles. Bow, smile, be wary...

Sp. Off. 1: Oh look! Four nobles carrying a golden litter. That must be their king, Moctezuma. Look at him!

Sp. Off. 2: We will be rich! Rich!

Cortés: If we live. Keep vigilant, do not show fear. I will meet Moctezuma. *(Moctezuma appears on stage, looking proudly royal. The Aztec nobles act out spreading cloth for him to walk on so that his feet never touch the ground, then stand protectively around him.)*

Moctezuma: Your Lord, the prophecy has been fulfilled: the great god has come from the East to take his throne. I have guarded the throne for you, and now you will take it and rule over this beautiful city. Come inside the gates, rest yourself. Visit your palace. All is yours...

Cortés: Moctezuma does not need to fear. All is well. We wish him to know that our hearts are satisfied with what he has said. We have brought this gift for the mighty king.

(Cortés takes a necklace of beads out of his pocket and reaches up to put it over Moctezuma's head but is blocked by the guards. Moctezuma takes the necklace and puts it over his own head. Then he claps his hands and a noble hands Moctezuma a heavy necklace which he gives to Cortés.)

Moctezuma: This small token is for you, our god. Many more treasures await you within our city. Come inside and rest.

Cortés: *(pleased with the necklace, putting it on)* It is good. We will enter.

(Moctezuma leads the way, then Cortés and the Spanish officers follow. All exit.)

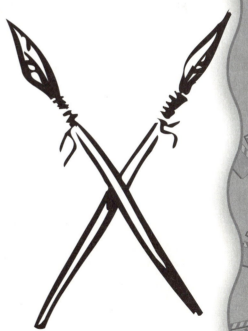

Moctezuma and Cortés *continued*

Scene 2 Inside Moctezuma's Palace

Narrator: Cortés and his men have been taken to a palace where they can rest. No one knows what to think of these visitors. Are they gods or men? In Moctezuma's palace, the king's brother and two nobles discuss the situation.

Cuitlahuac: What has happened to my brother? He believes this Spanish demon is our god! I believe in the prophecy, but anyone can see this is not a god!

Az. Nob. 1: How can he give our city to a stranger?

Az. Nob. 2: It looks to me like all these people want is gold!

Cuitlahuac: Our true gods will desert us if they see us bowing down to this stranger. We must fight!

Az. Nob. 1: Our soldiers outnumber them ten to one! Now is the time to fight.

Az. Nob. 2: But how can we go against our leader? It is impossible. Here he comes!

(Moctezuma enters and sits. The others bow their heads.)

Moctezuma: Our visitors wish to see the city. We will show them all the great wealth that is now theirs. You three come with me.

Cuitlahuac: Yes, Brother, my king. But do you think it is safe to show them around? What if they are planning to attack us? Do you really believe that Cortés is Quetzalcoatl, returning to earth to fulfill the prophecy? What if he isn't?

Moctezuma: No mortal could have fought against such odds on his way here. And look at the gods they ride, and the lightning and thunder sticks they control. Truly, these are not men, but gods who have come to take their city. Let us go.
(All rise and exit.)

Scene 3 At the Temple

(As the narrator talks, Moctezuma and the nobles are showing the Spanish around the town. The Spanish look amazed and pleased. Cortés whispers to his men.)

Narrator: Moctezuma and his nobles show Cortés around the city. The Spanish are astonished by the city with its stone streets, canals, whitewashed buildings, and huge marketplace.

Moctezuma: We will climb up to the top of the temple. My nobles will help you.

Cortés: That will not be necessary. The Spanish never get tired! *(Cortés and his men walk up the steep steps to the top unaided while the Aztec nobles assist Moctezuma to the top.)*

Cortés: *(to his men)* Look at the view from here. See the drawbridges and the soldiers' barracks. Study the layout of this city and prepare well for battle. *(to Moctezuma)* It is an honor to be shown such a beautiful city. And now, we would like to see the inside of the temple.

Az. Nob. 1: *(talking to Noble 1):* He can't go in there! That is sacred!

Az. Nob. 2: *(answering Noble 1):* His presence will anger the gods!

Moctezuma: It shall be as you wish. *(gestures)* Enter.

Sp. Off. 1: Oh, the smell! I'm choking!

Sp. Off. 2: See, there *(pointing)*–proof of human sacrifice! I can't bear it!

Cortés: What bloody slaughterhouse is this? It is not a temple! It is a place of evil! You worship false idols.

Moctezuma: How dare you insult our gods? Leave this place immediately, for you have caused it to become unclean. The gods will be very angry! *(Cortés and the Spanish exit. Moctezuma turns and speaks to Cuitlahuac.)* Instruct the priests to purify the temple and pacify our angry gods!

Cuitlahuac: It shall be done, my brother! *(He and the noblemen exit.)*

Moctezuma: This is a bad day indeed for the city of Tenochtitlan and the Aztec people! Surely war will now follow. A bad day indeed. *(Exits.)*

Chapter 6: Short-Term Projects

Creating an Aztec pendant, drawing a scene from Mayan life, building a model of a pyramid, making an Aztec codex, and other hands-on activities will spark the students' interest.

Everyday: Corn, Beans, Squash

 partners   20–30 minutes

Materials: colored markers and paper

The ancient peoples of Mesoamerica depended on corn, beans, and squash as the foundation of their diet. Ask the students what they like to eat that is made mostly from one or more of these ingredients. Challenge them to create a full day's menu using dishes that have corn, beans, and squash as the main ingredients. Have them write out the day's menu on paper and decorate it.

Making a Codex

individual   30 minutes

Materials: plain white paper; pencils, markers, or colored pencils

The Aztecs recorded information in a special book known as a "codex," a long strip of paper (up to forty feet), folded in a zigzag, made from fig tree bark. Scribes used pointed sticks and soot to make the outlines of their pictures, then colored them using paints made from plants.

Aztec "writing" was made up of a combination of pictures and symbols that represented both ideas (such as a picture of footsteps to represent travel) and sounds.

Have students make a codex by cutting two pieces of paper in half lengthwise, and attaching them together to form a long strip. Have them write on the strip, using pictures and symbols outlined in pencil then colored in. Ask them to make a key explaining their symbols.

An Aztec Metal Pendant

individual   **20 minutes**

Materials: thin cardboard, scissors, aluminum foil, modeling clay, rolling pin (if possible), pencil with a dull point, string or yarn

1. Students cut a circle from the cardboard and a circle of foil at least one inch larger than the cardboard circle.
2. Students roll out a piece of modeling clay a little bigger than the foil circle, then lay the foil on the clay, shiny side down.
3. Students draw a design on the foil with the pencil, gently pressing the foil into the clay. When they are finished, they carefully lift the foil from the clay.
4. Students lay the foil on top of the cardboard circle and fold back the edges. They can pierce a hole in the pendant, and thread through the string or yarn.

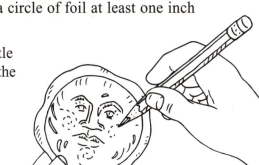

A Mesoamerican Creation Myth

group   **30–40 minutes**

Materials: none

Ask students to use books or Internet sources to research creation myths from the Maya, Aztecs, or other Mesoamerican people. Then have individual students tell about the myths they studied to their groups. Encourage them to be dramatic and descriptive like elders telling the stories around a fire at night.

Remember! Keep working on that Long-Term Project.

A Scene from Mayan Daily Life

individual   **20–30 minutes**

Materials: paper, pencil, markers, or colored pencils

Students have learned about the impressive structures—the palaces, plazas, baths, artificial lakes, aqueducts, observatories, and pyramids—left behind by the Maya. They have learned about their calendars, writing, and mathematics. Have each student think of how the Maya lived and then draw a scene carefully, with great detail. The scene can depict farmers, craftsmen, nobles, royals, priests, builders, children, and women, each going about a task that depicts how the Maya lived.

Chapter 6 Writing Projects

Students research the importance of astronomy in early civilizations, create myths about ancient gods and goddesses, and ponder what might have happened if the Aztecs and Spanish had the same technology.

Astronomy

Archaeologists have speculated that a tall, round tower discovered in the ancient Mayan city of Chichén Itzá was an observatory for watching the stars. They have evidence that the Maya were knowledgeable about astronomy and made accurate calculations of the length of the solar year. Clearly, studying astronomy was important to the Mayan people.

In fact, astronomy was important to all ancient peoples and civilizations. Why is this so? Ask students to research and write a report on uses of astronomy in ancient civilizations.

What if . . . ?

The Aztec had a very highly developed civilization but, when attacked by the Spanish, their huge empire crumbled. Have students consider why they were so easily defeated.

What if the Spanish had encountered people with the exact same technology as they had? Would the attitudes of the Aztec have been different toward the Spanish, and vice versa? Ask students to write an essay speculating on these questions.

A Biography

Invite students to research and write a biography of one of the following people:

Moctezuma 1: ruler of the Aztec Empire from 1440–1469
Hernando Cortés: Spanish conquistador
Doña Marina: interpreter for Cortés
Diego Velázquez: governor of Cuba, friend and later rival of Cortés
Charles 1: king of Spain 1516–1556

Compare and Contrast: Equipment and Tactics

Ask students to compare and contrast the fighting equipment and tactics of the Aztec and the Spaniards. They can research the kinds of weapons, armor, and fighting tactics of both groups. Remind them that when they compare and contrast, they need to write about what was the same *and* what was different.

A Message from a Friend

Cortés and the Spaniards were in other parts of Mesoamerica before they came to Tenochtitlan and defeated Moctezuma. Ask the students to write a message from a local person who has already encountered the Spaniards, describing the new arrivals to someone in Tenochtitlan who has not seen them yet. The students should include descriptions of the Spaniards' metal armor, their horses, the guns, the large ships, and perhaps certain items of clothing. Remind students to write from the perspective of someone observing things for the first time.

A New Legend

Invite students to read Aztec and Mayan myths and legends. They should be able to find these in the library or on the Internet. In these stories, they will encounter gods and goddesses, including some of the following: (Aztec) Huitzilopochtli, Quetzalcoatl, Tlaloc, Chalchihuitlicue, Chicomecoatl; (Mayan) Itzamná, Kinich Ahau, Chac, Yum Caax, Kulkulcán. Invite the students to write a new myth, involving these same gods and goddesses, in the style of the myths they have read.

Social Studies Plus! Unit 3 Writing Projects

Citizenship

Honesty

Students examine how honesty and dishonesty can affect relationships between people and countries. Dishonesty may lead to short-term gains, but honesty is a better foundation for the long term.

Hernando Cortés and his soldiers did not reveal their real intentions to the Aztec. They actively used trickery and deceit to take advantage of the local people. Cortés used the peoples' superstitions and unfamiliarity with items the Spaniards had (such as horses and cannons) to frighten, bully, and intimidate them.

Ask students to discuss the following questions:

1. Given Cortés's goals—the plunder of gold and other treasures and the acquisition of land—would it have made any sense for him to be honest with the Aztec? What might have happened if the local people knew what he was really trying to do?

2. The Spaniards conquered the Aztec and other groups of native people in South America, and then they tried to extract as much wealth as they could from them and their land. The short-term gains for the Spaniards were huge, but what about the long term gains? What alternatives might there have been? Do you think that the Spaniards and local peoples could each have benefited from trade? What would have been the advantages and disadvantages of honest interaction?

> When it came to dealing with native peoples, Cortés had no scruples.
>
> What does the expression "no scruples" mean?
>
> Can you give an example?

3. What happens when one person or group is dishonest and tries to take advantage of another person or group? Can both sides benefit from this dishonest relationship? Have students explain their answers.

4. Ask students to write about a situation in their lives where they or someone they know tried to get something through dishonesty. What was the result? Would being honest in the first place have been a better idea? Have students explain their answers.

66 Unit 3 Citizenship Project

Social Studies Plus!

Name _____ Date _____

A Day in Tenochtitlan

You are an Aztec living in Tenochtitlan. Tell what kind of person you are? Tell what kind of work you do. Next, take a walk through the city, going from place to place, doing errands, visiting friends, or carrying out important business. Draw a map and mark your journey on the map, with an X at places where you stopped. Use the pictures on pages 176–177 of the text as a guide. Write a story to accompany this map telling about your day in the city, the places you visited, and the things you did.

Social Studies Plus!   Unit 3 **Blackline Master** 67

Chapter 7 Short-Term Projects

Writing about potatoes, making a quipu, drawing plans for an Incan city, finding map coordinates for different locations—here are a wide variety of projects for students to enjoy.

Potato Mania

 partners 20–30 minutes

Materials: paper and pencil

Potatoes were an important crop for the Inca. After the Spaniards brought potatoes back over the Atlantic, they became an important crop for Europe and many places throughout the world. Ask students to come up with a list of different ways to prepare potatoes. Each student should choose his or her favorite potato dish and write out the recipe. Last but not least, the partners should collaborate on a "praise poem" for the potato.

Making a Quipu

individual 30–40 minutes

Materials: string or yarn in a variety of colors or textures (if possible)

The Inca had no writing system, but they used an ingenious device called a *quipu* to record things such as births and deaths, numbers of people of various ages in villages across the land, and the kinds and amounts of crops stored away.

The quipu was a collection of strings, each with knots tied into it to record a number. Each string recorded a different thing. The strings were color-coded. Knots at the bottom of the string showed the number of units; after a gap, the next set of knots showed the number of tens, followed by another gap and knots for hundreds, and so on up to hundred thousands! The quipus were a clever and accurate way of keeping track of everything in the empire, but someone had to know what each string represented!

Invite students to make a quipu of at least a dozen strings with tallies of a dozen different things. Students can write out a key for their quipo on paper. Things students might record: number of girls in the class with sisters, or with in-line skates; rainy days in the past three months; books about archaeology in the school library. Be creative!

68 Unit 3 Short-Term Projects

Social Studies Plus!

No Telephone or Computers?

individual/partners — 20 minutes

Materials: pencil and paper

If we no longer had telephones or computers, could we go back to a message-delivery system such as the one the Inca used? Incan runners waited in small huts every $1\frac{1}{2}$ miles along the highways, ready to jump up when they saw another runner coming. The runners averaged one mile every six and a half minutes. Messages could make the 1,250-mile journey between Cuzco and Quito in just five days! Ask students to calculate how many runners, and how long, it would take to get messages between your school and (a) the nearest town hall, (b) the state capital, and (c) the nation's capital.

Remember! Keep working on that Long-Term Project.

Society Pyramid Chart

partners/group — 20 minutes

Materials: poster board or large sheet of paper; pencil, colored pencils or markers

Invite students to research how the Inca effectively governed their enormous empire. Have students make a pyramid chart showing what they learned about the chain of command in the Incan system of government. At the top of the pyramid will be the *Sapa Inca*—the supreme leader.

Longitude and Latitude

partners — 20–30 minutes

Materials: paper and pencil, globe or atlas

Ask each pair of students to look at a globe or atlas and find the approximate longitude and latitude coordinates for certain places such as Lake Titicaca, the Andes mountains, the modern capital of Peru, Cuzco, Machu Picchu, Mexico City, and the location of your school. (Note that some coordinates may be a range.) Ask students to record their findings.

Social Studies Plus!

Unit 3 Short-Term Projects

Chapter 7: Writing Projects

Writing opportunities help students expand their knowledge of the Inca and other early peoples of South America and help them think creatively about related topics.

A Newly Domesticated Animal

The Inca domesticated llamas—a perfect animal for the climate and terrain in the Andes. Llamas were used as pack animals, for wool, for leather, and for food. Invite students to pick an animal to domesticate that has not been domesticated before, and write about their choice. Students should include the purpose for domesticating the animal and how it would be trained. Encourage them to be creative. Give the following example: Train bats to catch mosquitoes buzzing around people's heads!

A Letter to a Bishop

Invite students to research the *encomienda* system set up by the Spaniards to rule the conquered people of Central and South America. Ask students to imagine that they are a Spanish priest living in Peru in the 1500s. The priest witnesses the life of the local people under the encomienda system, and is very troubled by it. Invite students to write a letter to a bishop in Spain complaining about how the local people are treated.

Compare and Contrast: Conqueror and Conquered

What happened to local leaders and people when they were conquered by the Inca? How does that compare to how local people were treated when they were conquered by the Spaniards? Ask students to compare and contrast being conquered by the Inca, and being conquered by the Spaniards. Encourage students to include as many details as possible.

From Moctezuma to Atahualpa

The Aztec at Technotitlan were completely conquered by Hernando Cortés in 1521, and their leader, Moctezuma II, was killed. Eleven years later, in 1532, Francisco Pizarro defeated the Incas, and executed their emperor, Atahualpa. Both Moctezuma and Atahualpa made a similar mistake by allowing the Spaniards into their empires.

Invite students to write as if Moctezuma were still alive in 1532 when Pizarro entered Peru. Have them write a letter from Moctezuma to Atahualpa, warning the Incan leader not to trust the Spaniards, and telling him what happened to the Aztec at Technotitlan. They might want to include warnings about the Spaniards' guns, cannons, horses, and other items the Inca were unlikely to have seen before.

National Service: For or Against

In the Inca Empire, men over 25 years old had to pay taxes (nobles, officers in the army, local leaders, and women were exempt). The taxpayer frequently had to do as much as five years' work in the army, the mines, or on a public works crew. Often, groups of local people worked together to "pay taxes" by doing things such as constructing buildings or repairing roads.

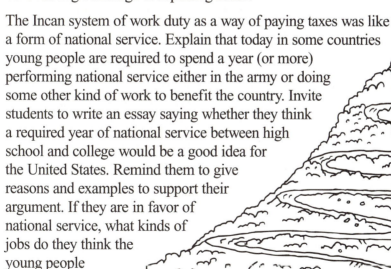

The Incan system of work duty as a way of paying taxes was like a form of national service. Explain that today in some countries young people are required to spend a year (or more) performing national service either in the army or doing some other kind of work to benefit the country. Invite students to write an essay saying whether they think a required year of national service between high school and college would be a good idea for the United States. Remind them to give reasons and examples to support their argument. If they are in favor of national service, what kinds of jobs do they think the young people should do?

Chapter 7 Citizenship

Caring

Students learn about Bartolomé de Las Casas, and then use his example to talk and write about other people who have cared enough to fight for the rights of others.

The Spaniard Bartolomé de Las Casas (1474–1566) first traveled to the New World in 1502, where he worked for the Spanish colonial government. Las Casas was troubled by what he saw of Spanish treatment of the local people. In 1512, he became a priest and began a lifelong fight for the rights of the native peoples. Las Casas wrote many books exposing the behavior of Spanish colonial officials and adventurers. His books informed (and shocked) people in Spain. They are still an important source of information about the cruelties of life under Spanish rule in the 1500s.

Ask students to discuss the following questions and then choose one of the items and write a short essay.

1. Why do you think Bartolomé de Las Casas fought for the rights of the native people? What were his objectives?

2. What other people can you think of who fought for the rights of others, even when they were not directly affected by the injustices they witnessed. Give examples.

3. Pick one campaigner for justice and write a short biography. Make sure to include information on any successes the person had, even if the successes came after the person's lifetime.

"I must confess that if I were to set down on paper each and every unforgivable violent crime committed against God, the King and the innocent people of the province by the Spanish in Santa Maria—every murder, every injustice, every atrocity, every attempt at genocide—they would make a very lengthy chronicle indeed...May God grant enlightenment to those who are in a position to do something about what has been happening."

This excerpt is from a book by Las Casas, A Short Account of the Destruction of the Indies.

Name _____   Date _____

The Tomb of the Lord of Sipan

Take a good look at the items in the tomb on page 192 of your text. Using what you know of ancient South American civilizations—and your best guesswork—decide what the items were for, and why they were put there. In the space below, write down a list of the items. Add a brief explanation of what each was and why you think it was there.

Item	Explanation

Chapter 8: Short-Term Projects

An experiment in oral history, a real estate ad for an igloo, an Iroquois "false face" mask, a diagram of a cliff town, and other projects will get students thinking!

Experiment with Oral History

group   **20 minutes**

Materials: none

Each group member in turn thinks of something he or she knows how to do that has at least six separate steps, for example, how to make a particular recipe. The first person carefully whispers the instructions to the next person, and so on around the group. The last person says the instructions out loud. Ask how accurately the information was "passed down along the generations"? Give one negative and one positive trait of oral history.

Being Self-Sufficient

individual/partners   **20 minutes**

Materials: paper and pencil

Invite students to make a list of the foods they eat most often for breakfast, lunch, and dinner, including all the separate ingredients in each food they list. If they had been living in a self-sufficient culture in your area one thousand years ago, which of the items on their lists would they have been able to hunt or catch, grow, harvest, produce, or find locally? Approximately what percentage of their modern diet does this represent? What are the sources of the other foods on the list?

Real Estate Advertisement

individual/partners   **30 minutes**

Materials: paper, pens and pencils, markers or colored pencils

Invite students to write a real estate ad for an Inuit igloo or sod house, a Hohokam pit house, an Anasazi pueblo or cliff dwelling, an Adena circular house, a Hopewell "wigwam," or an apartment in an Iroquois longhouse. Remind the students to include a picture and a list of details about the dwelling such as the general description and dimensions; number of rooms; storage space; heating and cooking facilities; proximity to water, fields, other houses, religious centers, roads, and other amenities. Like good real estate agents, try to make the place sound irresistible!

74   Unit 3   Short-Term Projects   Social Studies Plus!

An Iroquois "False Face" Mask   individual 30 minutes

Materials: cardboard; construction paper; scissors; string or yarn; buttons, shells, or other objects for decoration; markers; paste

Iroquois "false face" masks were carved out of a living tree, and used to drive out evil spirits and cure people of illnesses. Have students make a frightening-looking mask following the directions below. They may want to do some library research for ideas.

1. Cut out a piece of cardboard a little larger than your face with openings for the mouth and eyes. Cut out pieces of cardboard for ears, lips, and eyelids, and attach these with glue or staples.

2. Color the cardboard. If you have buttons, shells, or other objects to use as features or decorations, glue them to the mask.

3. Make small holes at the top, and thread through yarn for hair.

4. To wear it, attach two strips of cardboard to the mask with a stapler, the first strip fitting snugly around the back of your head, and the second one going from the top of the head and attaching to the middle of the first strip.

Ancient and Modern   group 20 minutes

Materials: pencil and paper

Have groups make a list of Native American objects and their modern equivalents, for example, a Native American birch bark canoe and a fiberglass canoe; an Iroquois longhouse and an apartment building. They can start with the four items below, then add items of their own: an Inuit seal-intestine jacket, a dogsled, a string of wampum, a cradleboard.

Remember! Keep working on that Long-Term Project.

Social Studies Plus!   Unit 3 Short-Term Projects 75

Chapter 8: Writing Projects

Students write about the lives of Native Americans, create a new legend, and think about why cultures sometimes disappear.

Native American Groups

Invite students to research a Native American group that lived in your area of the country. What is the name of the group? What language did the people speak? When did they first live in the area? What was their way of life? How did their way of life change after the Europeans arrived? Give examples. Where are members of this group today?

Compare and Contrast: Inuit and Iroquois

The Inuit lived in the snowy North; the Iroquois lived in the area around the eastern Great Lakes. Ask students to write an essay comparing and contrasting the environments and ways of life of these two groups. They should include some discussion of housing, diet, their religions and rituals, their tools, and clothing. Remind students that they need to discuss things that were *similar* between the two groups as well as things that were *different*.

The Great Serpent Mound

The Adena culture thrived from about 700 B.C. to about A.D. 100 when it mysteriously disappeared. The Adena people built burial mounds, the most spectacular being the Great Serpent Mound located in present-day Ohio. Invite students to suppose they are pioneers exploring the area where the Adena lived. They come across the Great Serpent Mound and draw their own conclusions about of how it got there and what it represents. Have students write an explanation of how the mound came to be.

Living Life as a Native American

Ask students to think about the various ways of life of early Native American peoples. Would they like to have lived in a traditional Native American society before the arrival of the Europeans? Which tribe or culture would they choose? What about that culture is particularly appealing? Which things in Native American life would they particularly enjoy? What things about their current life would they miss? Have students reflect on the questions, and then write an essay explaining their answers.

Deganawidah and Hiawatha: A Speech

Invite students to do some additional research about Deganawidah and Hiawatha, the two visionary leaders who worked together to found the Iroquois Confederacy. Why did they feel that a confederacy was so important? How do students think they managed to persuade the five tribes that it was in their interest to join the confederacy?

Have students write a speech that the two leaders will give to one of the Iroquois-speaking tribes to try to persuade them to join the confederacy. The speech emphasizes their joint determination to see the Iroquois prosper through peace.

Why Cultures Vanish

Several North American Native cultures flourished at various periods in North American history, then vanished without trace. Cultures from Central and South America also disappeared mysteriously. What do the students think happened to these cultures, and to the people in them? Ask the students to think of, and write about, three or more possible explanations for why these cultures disappeared.

Chapter 8 Citizenship

Courage

Early Native Americans needed courage every day. Students examine how and when courage and other qualities were needed, then give examples from their own lives.

Daily life for many traditional Native American peoples took a lot of courage: Can you see yourself going out to hunt an enormous whale in a small boat made from seal skin, or tracking down and killing a bear with nothing more than a spear? Native Americans required other qualities as well, such as endurance and physical strength.

With students working in groups, ask them to write a definition of each of the qualities listed below. They should then give two or more examples of how each quality was needed by Native Americans. Finally, each group should think of an example of how this trait is needed today. If possible, students should give examples from their own lives. Have them compare and contrast their examples.

Courage
Endurance
Perseverance
Patience
Faith
Obedience
Ingenuity
Physical strength

78 Unit 3 Citizenship Project

Social Studies Plus!

Symbols and Geometric Patterns

The Anasazi people of the Southwest are particularly known for the beautiful geometric designs they made on their pottery. Use the geometric patterns on this page, and/or others of your own design, to make a decorative book cover, a bookmark, or a picture frame.

SOCIAL STUDIES PLUS! Unit 3 Blackline Master **79**

Teacher Planner

Long-Term Project pages 82–83	Materials	⏱	Lesson Link
The People, Places, and Cultures of the Roman Empire Students explore peoples and cultures under the banner of Rome.			Lessons 1–5
Week 1 group — Students brainstorm a list of the Roman names of some of the areas that were part of the early Roman Empire.	one or more maps of the Roman Empire	1 session 1–2 hrs.	
Week 2 group — Students begin research for "time tours" of their region.	pencils, paper	1 session 1–2 hrs.	
Week 3 group — Students work on their presentations, focusing on how the area changed over time.	various art supplies, charts, maps	1 session 1–2 hrs.	
Week 4 group — Students make their presentations to the class, displaying "artifacts," models, maps, and charts.	as needed for demonstrations	1 session 1–2 hrs.	

Unit Drama pages 84–89

	Materials	⏱	Lesson Link
Scenarios: As It Was in Greece Long Ago group — Students role-play skits about classical Greece and Greek myths.	props (optional)	5 sessions 25 min. each	Lessons 1–4
Play: Jason and the Argonauts group — Students perform a play about a famous Greek myth.	props, costumes (optional)	1 session 40 min.	Lessons 1–4
Scenarios: All Roads Lead to Rome group — Students role-play skits about Julius Caesar, a Roman general, Caligula, and Regulus.	props (optional)	4 sessions 25 min. each	Lessons 1–5

Chapter 9 Short-Term Projects pages 90–91

	Materials	⏱	Lesson Link
The Labyrinth of Knossos individual — Students design a labyrinth with the Minotaur at its center.	paper, pencils, markers or colored pencils	1 session 30 min.	Lesson 1
A Painted Plate individual — Students create painted plates in the Greek style.	white paper plates, paints and brushes, pencils, black markers	1 session 45 min.	Lessons 1–4
A Recitation of Homer individual — Students memorize a poem from the *Iliad* and the *Odyssey*.	Homer's *Iliad* and/or *Odyssey*	1 session 30–45 min.	Lesson 2
Olympic Events group — Students brainstorm a list of events recently added to the Olympics.	paper, pencils	1 session 20 min.	Lesson 2
Inventions and Discoveries partners — Students find out about an important invention and draw a diagram of it.	construction paper, pen, markers	1 session 20–30 min.	Lesson 4

Chapter 9 Writing Projects pages 92–93	Materials	🕐	Lesson Link
A Greek God or Goddess individual Students rewrite a myth in a more modern context.	paper, pencils	1 session 20 min.	Lesson 1
The Greek Theater individual Students write newspaper reviews for a theater.	paper, pencils	1 session 25 min.	Lesson 2
A Favorite Olympic Sport individual Students write essays explaining special equipment and/or terminology used in their favorite Olympic sport.	paper, pencils	1 session 20 min.	Lesson 2
A Speech to the Assembly of Athens individual Students write a speech that a woman living in Athens will give to the Athenian assembly.	paper, pencils	1 session 20 min.	Lesson 3
Letter from India individual Students write letters home from a soldier traveling with Alexander the Great.	paper, pencils	1 session 20 min.	Lesson 3
A Young Scholar in Alexandria individual Students write journal entries about a day of study, debate, and discussion.	paper, pencils	1 session 20 min.	Lesson 4

Chapter 9 Citizenship Project page 94			
Fairness whole class Students think of a story that involves some kind of punishment.	paper, pencils	1 session 45 min.	Lessons 1–4

Chapter 10 Short-Term Projects pages 96–97			
Old English, Greek, and Latin Roots partners Students write words and their roots.	paper, pencils, dictionaries	1 session 30 min.	Lessons 1–5
A Roman Soldier partners Students draw a fully equipped Roman soldier.	paper, pencils, colored pencils	1 session 30–45 min.	Lesson 2
Friends, Romans, Countrymen! individual Students memorize Mark Antony's famous speech.	*Julius Caesar*, or copy of Antony's speech	1 session 20–30 min.	Lesson 2
An Advertising Flyer partners Students make advertising flyers for a spectacle to be held at the Colosseum.	paper, pencils, markers or colored pencils	1 session 20–30 min.	Lesson 3
The Bad Emperor: A Cartoon individual Students make up cartoon strips about a bad emperor.	paper, pencils, markers or colored pencils	1 session 30–45 min.	Lesson 3

Chapter 10 Writing Projects pages 98–99			
Mount Vesuvius and the Volcanoes of Italy individual Students write a research report on the volcanoes of Italy.	paper, pencils	1 session 25 min.	Lesson 1
Raised by a Wolf? individual Students make up stories about a child raised as an animal.	paper, pencils	1 session 20 min.	Lesson 1
A Roman Emperor individual Students write the biography of a Roman emperor.	paper, pencils	2 sessions 20 min. each	Lesson 1

Teacher Planner

Chapter 10 Writing Projects *continued*	Materials	🕐	Lesson Link
Which Would You Want to Be? individual Students write essays saying which person they would have liked to be during the height of the Roman Empire.	paper, pencils	1 session 25 min.	Lessons 1–5
The Five Principles of Roman Law individual Students write essays explaining why each of the Roman principles is important.	paper, pencils	1 session 20 min.	Lesson 2
In Defense of Joining the Empire individual Students write speeches explaining why the king has decided to welcome the Roman army.	paper, pencils	1 session 20 min.	Lesson 2
Chapter 10 Citizenship Project page 100			
Responsibility whole class Students discuss what citizens can and should do when they see leaders abusing their power.	none	1 session 40 min.	Lessons 1–5

NOTES

Long-Term Project

The People, Places, and Cultures of the Roman Empire

At its greatest, the Roman Empire stretched from modern-day Portugal to the Persian Gulf. Students explore peoples and cultures under the banner of Rome and give exciting presentations.

Territory of the Roman Empire

Week 1 group 1–2 hours

Materials: one or more maps of the Roman Empire

Begin by looking at a map of the Roman Empire with the whole class. Make a list with the class of the Roman names of some of the areas (outside present-day Italy) that were part of the empire. Then, with a *modern* map, have students try to figure out the modern-day names of these areas.

Break the class into six groups. Explain that each group will research a part of the Roman Empire, and will make a class presentation. Have each group claim a part of the Empire.

Learning More About the Local Culture

Week 2 group 1–2 hours

Materials: pencils and paper

Tell groups to begin research for "time tours" of their region: before, during, and after the Roman Empire. Using library and Internet resources, groups should look into all aspects of life in their regions—religion, culture, trade, art and architecture, wars, language, clothing, agriculture, and science and technology.

Tell students that, in addition to an oral report, the presentations will include at least two of the following: an "artifact"; a model; a map; a time line; a traditional costume; a traditional folktale; a skit, song, or other performance. Have the groups decide what they are going to do, and make plans for bringing in any materials that will be needed.

Week 3 — Getting Ready!

 group   1–2 hours

Materials: as needed to make "artifacts," charts and maps, and so on

As the groups continue to work on their presentations, remind students that their emphasis should be on how the area changed over time. What was life like before the Romans arrived? How was it different when the area was part of the empire? Was the area also a part of Alexander's empire? What other invasions and wars have there been? What are some of the different names that have been used for the area?

Once the groups have organized their information, they can begin to work on the "special" parts of their presentations such as maps, time lines, charts, and so forth. Ask if students know what languages are spoken in the area today. Can they say a few words in one of those languages? What about regional food specialties? Do any of the groups want to prepare some food samples? Encourage groups to be creative, and to be sure that each group member has something to contribute to the presentation.

Week 4 — Time Travel to the Roman Empire

 group   1–2 hours

Materials: as needed for demonstrations

Time for the presentations! Arrange the room so that there is plenty of space for the groups to make their presentations, and "audience" chairs available for any visitors. Give each group the same amount of time—but make sure it is not too long—15–20 minutes at the most. Leave some time for questions and answers at the end of each presentation. Arrange for a place to display "artifacts," models, maps, and charts after all the presentations have been given.

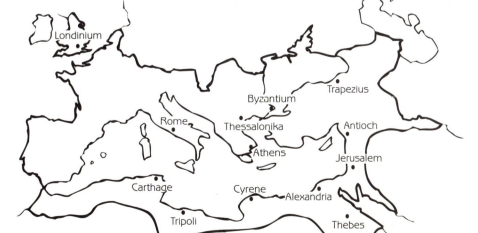

As It Was in Greece Long Ago

Through dramatic interpretations of Greek myths, reenactments of debates from the Athenian assembly, and a famous incident with Archimedes and King Hiero, students bring classical Greece to life through these simulations.

Theseus and the Minotaur

Athens is forced to send a tribute of fourteen young men and women to the island of Crete every nine years. There, they are sent into a horrible labyrinth to be killed by the Minotaur, a beast with the head of a bull and the body of a man. Theseus sails to Crete to try to kill the monster. Ariadne, the daughter of King Minos of Crete, helps Theseus by giving him a sword and a ball of thread (to find his way out of the labyrinth). Theseus kills the Minotaur, then he and the other Athenians return home. Act it out! Be dramatic!

Perseus and Medusa

King Polydectes wants to marry Danae, and he wants to get rid of her son Perseus. He tells Perseus to bring his mother a wedding present, the head of Medusa, one of the Gorgons—horrible monsters with the bodies of birds and heads covered with thousands of living snakes. He assumes Perseus will die.

But Zeus sends his messenger Hermes to help Perseus and give him winged sandals so he can fly, a helmet of invisibility, and a bag that can hold anything. Athena gives him her shield and tells him never to look directly at Medusa; he must look only at her image in the shield. Perseus cuts off Medusa's head, and, after many adventures, returns home. He shows the head to the evil king, who immediately turns to stone. Have students play out the story with gusto!

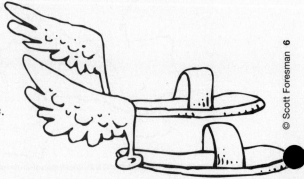

A Debate in the Assembly

The men of the Athenian assembly are gathered to debate the fate of Socrates, the great philosopher and teacher. Some say he is a bad influence on the young people of Athens and must be put to death. Others say he is a great teacher and should be respected. The assembly debates what to do, and finally decides on a trial. Have students act out the trial and decide Socrates' fate.

Archimedes, the King, and the Ship

Archimedes said that there was no weight on earth that he could not move by himself, with the help of mathematics. King Hiero of Syracuse challenged him to prove this by moving a heavy ship, stuck in the harbor. Archimedes accepted.

On the agreed day, the harbor was crowded with spectators. The king had put additional freight on the ship, plus passengers. Archimedes set up a system of pulleys attached to a hand crank. When the signal was given, he turned the handle of the crank. Inch by inch, the ship began to move toward the shore. The crowd roared! The king issued a proclamation that from that day forward that, Archimedes was to be believed in everything he said! Invite students to enact this myth using homemade props and costumes.

A Debate About Rebuilding Athens

Pericles wants to rebuild Athens now that Greece is no longer at war with Persia. He says that unused money set aside for the war should be used for the rebuilding projects. Some in the assembly agree. Others warn that the Persians may fight again, and that the money should be saved. Still others wonder if Sparta, and other Greek cities, will support the use of the money to benefit only Athens. Have students make up dialogue for the debate and act it out.

Social Studies Plus! Unit 4 Drama Scenarios

All Roads Lead to Rome

"Close your eyes and suppose you are in Rome two thousand years ago." Students become Roman senators, engineers, generals, foot soldiers, and emperors, and let us listen in on their lives!

Julius Caesar's Last Day

Julius Caesar was a successful general who eventually won control of the Roman Empire. He was made ruler for life. Some senators in Rome were afraid that if Caesar had so much power he would make himself king. If he were king, he might end the republic—take away the power from the senate and rule without seeking the consent of the citizens. Invite students to act out a scene in which the Senators express their concerns to Caesar. What is Caesar's reaction? Students may also play ordinary citizens, who respond to both Caesar and the Senators.

A Roman General and a Conquered King

A Roman general and some of his top commanders talk with the king of a newly defeated region. The king has several of *his* top advisors present. The general explains what the Roman government will require from the king. The king asks whether the people will be allowed to continue to worship their traditional gods.

The king's advisors ask about taxes, tributes, and slaves. Will local men be required to join the army? What construction will the Romans begin? Who will be allowed to issue orders and laws for the population? Even though this is a discussion, remember that the Romans have just defeated the others in battle.

Caligula and His Horse

The emperor Caligula ruled from A.D. 37 to 41. He was a good leader for the first six months, but then, after a serious illness, he became a vicious and cruel tyrant. Historians have guessed that his illness must have caused some kind of mental instability. He declared himself a god and had temples erected to himself. He had his horse proclaimed a consul, and tried to have it named a senator.

Imagine the debate on the senate floor on that day. What do senators think about the idea of having a horse join their ranks? Remember, they most likely do not feel free to say what they really think: Caligula was ruthless and sure to punish anyone who seemed to be opposing him. How can they vote against the idea without seeming to contradict Caligula?

Regulus at the Senate

The Roman general Regulus was captured in the war against Carthage. The leaders of Carthage thought they had the upper hand in the war, and wanted Rome to agree to their terms for peace. They sent envoys to Rome with their proposals.

Regulus was allowed to accompany the envoys, saying that he would urge his countrymen to agree to the peace terms. But when he rose to speak at the Roman senate, he did the exact opposite: he urged the Romans to fight on, never to surrender! He told the senate he had disgraced Rome by being captured and was willing to pay the price. Bravely, he returned to Carthage with the envoys, where he was put to death. Act out the scene in the senate.

Unit 4 Drama Play

Jason and the Argonauts

Students ham it up as Aphrodite, Eros, Jason, Medea, and King Aeëtes in this short version of the classic tale.

The Parts: (6–7 players)
- Narrator
- Jason
- Aphrodite
- Eros
- Medea
- King Aeëtes
- Serpent

Narrator: Jason and the Argonauts have arrived in Colchis, where the Golden Fleece is kept in a temple, guarded by a huge serpent. Our hero stops to pray to Aphrodite, goddess of love and beauty.

Jason: Oh, immortal Aphrodite, more lovely than any creature here on earth or in the heavens! Help us attain the prize we seek!

Aphrodite: Wow! I love being flattered! Of course I'll help you. Go to the king and ask him for the fleece. I will find a way to make him give you what you want.

(Aphrodite and Eros mime as the narrator speaks.)

Narrator: Aphrodite went to see her son, Eros, the god of love. Aphrodite bribed the lazy boy with a beautiful gift to get him to help her aid Jason. Eros went and hid behind a pillar in the king's palace and waited for the right time to strike...

(Jason comes and bows before King Aeëtes. Medea is sitting on the side, not paying much attention.)

Jason: O, Great King I have traveled many weary leagues in order to reach the place where the Golden Fleece is kept. I ask you most humbly and politely to give it to me. In return for this favor, I will conquer all your enemies!

King Aeëtes: Get out of here! I'll never let you take that fleece, no matter what you promise me!

Eros: I think that's *my* cue to *do* something! *(He shoots his arrow into Medea, who sees Jason and falls in love. Eros exits.)*

Medea: Oh Father! Do not be so hasty, and so cruel! Think what this beautiful young prince might be able to do for me, I mean, you. Assign him any task! Give him a chance, I beg you!

King Aeëtes: Oh, all right, but just as a favor to you, my child. Now, look here, Prince. Yoke my two fire-breathing bulls, plow a four-acre field, and sow it with dragon's teeth. Got it? Good. Now get out!

Jason: It shall be done! *(Medea and Jason walk to one side of the stage, and King Aeëtes exits.)* Thank you for pleading my case, fair maid. Is there anything I can do to thank you?

Medea: Yes. Swear by all the gods to be my husband for as long as you live!

Jason: OK. I swear. Now, how am I going to yoke these fire-breathing bulls? Sounds tricky.

Medea: Don't worry. I have some magic crocus juice here, and I will sprinkle it all over your body, and this will protect you from the bulls' fiery breath. *(Pretends to sprinkle juice on him.)* Go yoke those bulls and plow that field! *(Medea exits. Jason mimes as the narrator talks.)*

Narrator: Jason yoked the bulls, plowed the field, sowed the dragon's teeth, and, when dangerous soldiers sprang up from the teeth that were sown, he threw a stone among them which caused them to fight each other until they were all dead! He then returned to the palace and told the king the tasks were done. *(King enters.)*

King Aeëtes: You cheated! You were covered with magic crocus juice! The deal's off! *(King exits. Jason and Medea mime as the narrator talks.)*

Narrator: Jason was very disappointed, but Medea told him not to worry—she had a plan. That night, Medea took Jason into the temple. She dropped poppy juice into the serpent's eyes and sang it to sleep.

Serpent: I'm feeling very sleepy! *(Yawns and goes to sleep.)*

Medea: It's asleep! Grab the fleece! Let's get out of here!

Narrator: Jason and Medea ran off and sailed away with the Argonauts, but their adventures—and *mis*adventures—were far from over. Read the whole story of Jason and the Argonauts to find out what happened next!

Social Studies Plus!   Unit 4 Drama Play   89

Chapter 9: Short-Term Projects

A plate painted after the Greek style, a list of Olympic events, a recitation of Homer, a labyrinth, an exploration of Alexander's empire, a diagram of an invention—let's do all!

A Painted Plate

 individual   45 minutes

Materials: white paper plates (not plastic or foam), paints and paintbrushes, pencils, black markers

The Greeks painted vases and plates with scenes from battles, daily life, and athletic competitions. Have the students follow the directions below to create a "Greek" plate.

1. Paint a paper plate light orange or tan.

2. While the plate dries, think of a design for the center of the plate. It could be people playing a sport, musicians, local heroes, or just people going about their daily tasks.

3. Paint a decorative pattern onto the outside border of the plate using dark brown and black paint. Draw a line with black paint around the outside edge of the plate.

4. Copy or trace your design onto the center of the plate. Outline the figures with a fine permanent marker or thin line of black paint. Do not fill in the figures—they will look better just as outlines!

Olympic Events

 group   20 minutes

Materials: paper, pencils

Ask students to make a list of events held at the ancient Olympics. Ask them to discuss how these events might have helped develop and promote skills needed in ancient times. How many are still part of the Olympic games today? Now have students write a list of ten events recently added to the Olympics. Why were these events not a part of the ancient Olympics?

90   Unit 4   Short-Term Projects   Social Studies Plus!

The Labyrinth of Knossos

individual — 30 minutes

Materials: paper, pencils, markers or colored pencils

The labyrinth underneath the Minoan palace at Knossos (on the island of Crete) was supposedly so complicated that no one could ever find the way out. Only Theseus, with his silken thread from Ariadne, managed to come out alive. At the center of the maze was the dreaded Minotaur, the monster with the head of a bull and body of a man.

Ask students to design a labyrinth and draw the awful Minotaur at its center. Around the edges of the page, they can make geometric designs or draw scenes of bull jumping or other details of life at the palace. Afterwards, students can exchange drawings and time each other for how long it takes to reach the Minotaur.

Remember! Keep working on that Long-Term Project.

A Recitation of Homer

individual — 30–45 minutes

Materials: Homer's *Iliad* and/or *Odyssey*

The *Iliad* and the *Odyssey* have been favorites for over twenty-five hundred years. Versions of the stories were told as part of the oral tradition of Greece and surrounding areas. School children in ancient Greece memorized and recited long sections of the poems. Ask students to pick a section to memorize and recite to the class.

Inventions and Discoveries

partners — 20–30 minutes

Materials: construction paper, pens, markers

Archimedes, Pythagorus, Eratosthenes, and Euclid: these were some of the greatest mathematicians of the ancient world. Each contributed important ideas to the development of mathematics. Invite students to find out about one invention or important mathematical idea developed by one of these mathematicians. Have the students draw diagrams and give a short talk explaining the idea or invention.

Chapter 9: Writing Projects

A speech to the Athenian assembly, a letter home from India, a report on Greek theater, and other writing activities help students expand their understanding of life in ancient Greece.

A Speech to the Assembly of Athens

Ask students to imagine a woman living in Athens during the Athenian golden age. The woman is educated and intelligent, and she is a very good public speaker. She believes that both women and slaves should be citizens and participate in the democracy in the same way as men. Invite students to write a speech for her to give to the Athenian assembly. In each paragraph she will state one main idea and then support it with details.

Letter from India

The soldiers who fought with Alexander the Great traveled (mostly on foot) from Greece to India, and almost all the way back, in about thirteen years. Along the way they saw amazing wonders, from the pyramids of Egypt to elephants trained to fight in battles in India.

Ask students to suppose that they are soldiers traveling with Alexander and they have just arrived in India. Have them write a letter home telling about the journey, and about the strange and wonderful things they have seen.

A Greek God or Goddess

The Greek gods and goddesses were a colorful group. Ask the students each to choose a god or goddess and do some research on him or her. When they have read a number of myths involving their god or goddess, have them choose one myth and rewrite it in a more modern context.

The Greek Theater

Invite students to do some research on the theater in ancient Greece. What were the names of some of the most popular playwrights, and what were the titles of their most famous plays? What was the role of the "chorus" in the play? What different kinds of plays were there? What is the origin of the word *tragedy*? Have students suppose they are theater critics reviewing a performance in ancient Greece. Make sure they answer the Who? What? When? Where? Why? How? questions.

A Favorite Olympic Sport

There are many Olympic sports, and new events are added all the time. Ask students to pick a favorite sport or event and do some research on it. What is its history? What kinds of training do the athletes need? Which countries do well in the sport or event? Which athletes are considered the best in the world? What special equipment and/or terminology is used? Ask students to write a brief essay.

A Young Scholar in Alexandria

In the time of Archimedes, young Greek scholars were often sent to Alexandria in Egypt to study at the "museum" there. The museum was actually more like a university. There the greatest scientists, mathematicians, and philosophers of the times taught astronomy, architecture, anatomy, engineering, medicine, and philosophy.

Invite students to suppose that they are a Greek student living in Alexandria and studying at the museum. Have them write a journal entry about a day of study, debate, and discussion. What do they study? What are some of the questions that the student is trying to answer? What scientific mysteries and puzzles is the student trying to figure out?

Citizenship

Fairness

Gods in Greek myths dole out punishments all the time. Why? What is the purpose of imposing a punishment? When is imposing a punishment fair? Unfair?

In Greek myth, Arachne is known as the best weaver in all the land. But she is so boastful, she claims her weaving is better than that of the goddess Athena. Athena and Arachne compete to see who can weave the most beautiful designs. Athena wins and decides to teach the proud woman a lesson: she turns her into a spider so that she will weave forever!

In many Greek myths, gods and goddesses hand out punishments when they want to teach a lesson to a wayward mortal. They also reward good behavior!

Invite groups to discuss the following questions:

1. What is meant by the expression "Make the punishment fit the crime"? Give examples.

2. Is imposing a punishment for negative behavior fair? Explain your answer.

3. Did you ever receive a punishment you thought was unfair and later realized it was fair? Explain your answer.

Have each student in the group think of a story that involves some kind of punishment. It could be a real story, a folktale, or an invented story. Have each student tell what happened, then have the group decide if the punishment in the story was fair or unfair. If the group decides it was unfair, have the group create a fair solution.

Crossword on the Greek

Use the clues to fill in this crossword with names and places you have learned about in your study of ancient Greece.

Clues Across

1. It was fought between Athens and Sparta
2. Story about a god or goddess
3. God of war
4. A leader of Athens
5. A famous philosopher
6. City known for military discipline
7. Period of time after Alexander the Great
8. Writer of geometry books
9. Author of the *Iliad*

Clues Down

1. God of the sea
2. What winners in the Olympics put on their heads
3. Mountain where the gods lived
4. _____ "The Great"
5. A story about a human hero
6. A helot
7. People from the island where King Minos ruled
8. Paintings made on wet plaster
9. King of the gods

Chapter 10: Short-Term Projects

Friends, Romans, classmates, come do these fun activities!
Make a mosaic, study word families, memorize a famous speech,
draw a cartoon, and design a flyer for the Colosseum.

Old English, Greek, and Latin Roots partners — 30 minutes

Materials: paper and pencil, dictionaries that show word roots

English is made up of words with roots from Greek, Latin, Old English, and many other languages. Sometimes there are many ways in English to say the same thing. For example, *rotten* (from Old English), *putrid* (from Latin), and *septic* (from Greek) mean about the same thing, but they have different roots.

In each group below, there are three words and/or prefixes with related meanings but different roots. Have the students look up each of the words (or roots) in the dictionary. How many related words can they find with the same root? Have partners make a list of all the related words they can find for each of the words below.

1. geo- (Greek), terra (Latin), earth (Old English)
2. hygienic (Greek), sanitary (Latin), healthy (Old English)
3. hydra- (Greek), aqua- (Latin), water (Old English)
4. graph (Greek), script (Latin), write (Old English)

Remember! Keep working on that Long-Term Project.

The Bad Emperor: A Cartoon individual — 30–45 minutes

Materials: paper, pencils, markers or colored pencils

Ancient Rome was notorious for having some eccentric and, at times, unsavory emperors. Two famous ones were Caligula and Nero, but there were many others. Bad emperors often lived luxurious lives, ignoring the problems in Rome and all over the empire. They usually were not shy about having themselves proclaimed gods, or otherwise making themselves the objects of admiration and applause. They often had many enemies, both real and imagined. Invite students to make up a cartoon strip about a bad emperor (real or fictional), and some of the things he does.

A Roman Soldier

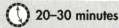 partners 30–45 minutes

Materials: paper, pencils, colored pencils

Have students draw a fully equipped Roman soldier (legionary). They may have to use the library or the Internet to get information on the kind of gear Roman soldiers wore and carried. They should include weapons, armor, clothing, shoes, tools, backpack (and contents), and any decorative items or insignia. Have them label their diagrams.

An Advertising Flyer

partners 20–30 minutes

Materials: paper, pencils, markers or colored pencils

Have students make an advertising flyer for a spectacle at the Colosseum. The flyer should use dramatic language and include a drawing of the main attraction, the date and time, the name of emperor sponsoring the event, and names of any famous gladiators who will be taking part.

Are there slaves from a newly conquered part of the empire who will be fighting? What kinds of animals will be part of the spectacle? Encourage students to make their flyers exciting, like previews for a movie or TV show.

Friends, Romans, Countrymen!

individual 20–30 minutes

Materials: a copy of Shakespeare's *Julius Caesar,* or a copy of Antony's speech

Julius Caesar's fame and notoriety did not end with his assassination in 44 B.C.. More than sixteen hundred years later, the English playwright William Shakespeare wrote a historical play about him, which, four hundred years after *that*, is still studied and performed. There is a famous speech in the play (act 3, scene 2) by Mark Antony, a friend of Caesar's, after Caesar's death. The speech begins "Friends, Romans, countrymen, lend me your ears."

Have students read the speech. What is Antony really saying about Caesar? Invite students to memorize as much of the speech as they can in a set period of time, then, let the recitations begin!

Chapter 10 Writing Projects

Here's a chance for students to go into more depth in their examination of life in the Roman Empire. In different exercises, students research, debate, proclaim, justify, and explain!

Mount Vesuvius and the Volcanoes of Italy

In A.D. 79, the Roman city of Pompeii was completely buried in ash from the erupting volcano Mount Vesuvius. It was only in 1709 that the buried city was discovered. Since then, much of the town has been excavated, and visitors today can see a two-thousand-year-old Roman town. Invite students to write a research report on one of the following topics: Pompeii and Vesuvius, the volcanoes of the Mediterranean, or famous volcanic eruptions in history. Encourage them to make their reports explosively interesting!

Raised by a Wolf?

According to legend, Romulus and Remus—the twins who founded Rome—were raised by a wolf. Atalanta, a figure in Greek mythology, was said to have been raised by a bear. Ask if students know any other stories about human children raised by animals? (Tarzan, Mowgli in *The Jungle Book*) Invite them to write their own story about a child raised by a wild animal.

A Roman Emperor

Invite students to research and write the biography of a Roman emperor. They can choose one of the emperors listed below, or an other of their own selection: Augustus; Tiberius; Caligula; Claudius; Nero; Vespasian; Trajan; Hadrian; Marcus Aurelius; Commodius; Diocletian.

In Defense of Joining the Empire

Have the students suppose that they are the king in an area soon to come under attack from the advancing Roman army. Some of the king's advisors say that it is better to fight to the death than be ruled by the Romans. But the king knows that his army cannot defeat the Roman war machine. Besides, he has heard that there are many benefits to becoming part of the empire.

Invite students to write a speech explaining why the king has decided to welcome the Roman army rather than fight it. The speech must anticipate and counter the argument that it is not noble to surrender, and convincingly argue that opening the city's gates to the Roman army is the best choice to make.

The Five Principles of Roman Law

The Romans developed a code of laws for all the people in their empire to follow. Much of the legal system in the United States today is based on these basic principles:

- All free people have equal rights before the law.
- A person must be considered innocent until he or she is proven guilty.
- Accused people should be allowed to face their accusers and defend themselves.
- Judges must interpret the law and make decisions fairly.
- People have rights that no government can take away.

Have students write an essay explaining why each of these five principles is important.

Which Would You Want to Be?

For the rich and powerful, life was good during the height of the Roman Empire. But for many people, life was hard even in the good times. Ask students to consider the following people: a gladiator, a soldier, a slave in a rich household, a slave on a farm in the countryside. Ask students to think about their daily lives, and the deprivations, dangers, and difficulties they would have faced. Have students write an essay saying which of those four people they would prefer to have been, and why.

Chapter 10 Citizenship

Responsibility

In a democracy, leaders have a duty to govern well, but citizens also have responsibilities. Students discuss what citizens can and should do when they see leaders abusing their power.

Marcus Aurelius was a just and responsible ruler who took the job of leading the empire very seriously. Caligula was an irresponsible ruler who was not only corrupt, but also cruel.

Have students think about and discuss the following questions:

1. As representatives of the people, do you think Roman senators should have had rulers such as Caligula removed from office?

2. Do you think it was the senators' duty and responsibility to speak out against tyranny and madness, even if that meant risking their own safety?

3. Did the Roman government have a system of checks and balances to ensure that bad leaders could be overruled or impeached? What about our own system? What checks and balances are in place to remove incompetent or corrupt public officials?

4. What can citizens today do against corruption? What examples can you think of where citizens have taken effective action against corruption? What did they do?

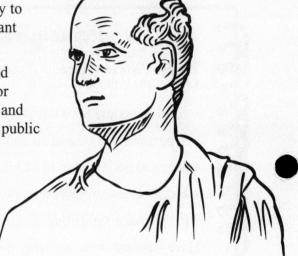

"Caligula, an irresponsible emperor"

"Marcus Aurelius, a responsible emperor"

100 Unit 4 Citizenship Project Social Studies Plus!

Name _____ Date _____

A. Unscramble the Words

Unscramble the words and write the answers in the blanks. Place the numbered letters in the blanks at the bottom to find out what this is all about!

1. A supposed founder of Rome
   (smolruu)   __ __ __ __ __ __ __
                 10   3

2. Opposite of patrician
   (eenabilp)   __ __ __ __ __ __ __ __
                  8   6   5

3. What was fought against Carthage
   (upicn rswa) __ __ __ __ __ __ __ __
                         9   4 1

4. A place where gladiators fought
   (usolomces)   __ __ __ __ __ __ __ __ __
                    2   11   7

Answer: __ __ __ __ __   __ __ __ __ __ __ __
         1 2 3 4 5   6 7 8 9 8 9 10 11

B. Word Puzzle

Answer the questions and fill in the blanks using the letters in the words "final days" as an extra hint.

1. Orestes _____ to give power.   __ __ F __ __ __ __

2. Here, the highest bidder wins.   __ __ __ __ I __ __

3. A German tribe.   __ __ N __ __ __

4. A famous Visigoth.   __ __ A __ __ __

5. Rob during a war.   __ __ __ L __ __

6. What Diocletian did to the empire.   __ __ __ D __ __

7. Modern name of Byzantium.   __ __ __ A __ __ __

8. Greek name for Constantinople.   __ Y __ __ __ __ __ __

9. The _____ part of the Empire declined. __ __ S __ __ __ __

Unit 5 Teacher Planner

Long-Term Project pages 104–105	Materials	🕐	Lesson Link
Wall Painting Students make a wall painting of medieval life.			Lessons 1–4
Week 1 whole class Students decide which area of the medieval world they would like to paint.	none	1 session 30–45 min.	
Week 2 group Students begin research for their panels, looking for scenes from daily life or historical events.	research materials, paper, pencils	1 session 30–45 min.	
Week 3 group Students sketch out the final design for their wall panel.	butcher paper, pencils or chalk, paints and brushes	1 session 30–45 min.	
Week 4 group Students create and finish their panels, including a title for each panel.	tempera paints and brushes	1 session 30–45 min.	
Unit Drama pages 106–111			
Scenarios: Rulers, Travelers, and Serfs group Students role-play skits that bring to life people and legends from the vast world of the Middle Ages in Asia, Africa, and Europe.	props (optional)	4 sessions 35 min. each	Lessons 1–4
Play: Sundiata: The Hungering Lion group Students perform a play about Sundiata leading his army against Sumanguru.	props, costumes (optional)	1 session 1½ hr.	Lessons 1–4
Chapter 11 Short-Term Projects pages 112–113			
Make a Diorama: The Hippodrome individual Students make dioramas of the arena where chariot racing took place.	shoebox, milk cartons, clay, small figures, art supplies	1 session 30 min.	Lesson 1
Portolan Chart individual Students make up a chart of a seaport.	paper, markers or pencils	1 session 30 min.	Lesson 1
Make a Mosaic individual/group Students make a mosaic using small pieces of different materials.	small pieces of materials, various art supplies	1 session 30 min.	Lesson 2
Paint an Icon individual Students paint scenes from their own lives for an icon.	paper, watercolor paper, paints and brushes	1 session 30 min.	Lesson 2
Illuminated Manuscript individual Students choose a page from a favorite book to copy and decorate.	paper, pens, markers or colored pencils	1 session 30 min.	Lesson 3
Water Clock individual Students draw a picture of a water clock, decorating the surface in the ornate style of medieval Muslim artists.	paper, pens or markers	1 session 45 min.	Lesson 4
Chapter 11 Writing Projects pages 114–115			
A Visit to the Byzantine Capital individual Students write letters praising the glory of the emperor and the empire.	paper, pencils	1 session 20 min.	Lesson 1

Chapter 11 **Writing Projects** continued	Materials	🕐	Lesson Link
A Justinian Code for Today 👤 individual Students write their own version of a code of law for students.	paper, pencils	1 session 20 min.	Lesson 2
Journal Entry: Pilgrimage to Mecca 👤 individual Students write about the experience of making a pilgrimage to Mecca.	paper, pencils	1 session 20 min.	Lesson 3
Arabic Innovations 👤 individual Students write about the many scientific innovations of the early Arab world.	paper, pencils	1 session 25 min.	Lesson 4
Journal Entry: Ibn Battuta's Escape from Delhi 👤 individual Students write an entry in the journal of the intrepid traveler of the medieval Arab world.	paper, pencils	1 session 20 min.	Lesson 4

Chapter 11 **Citizenship Project** page 116

Respect 👥👥 whole class Students envision themselves as documentary filmmakers, creating a film to teach respect for another culture.	paper, pencils, BLM p. 117	1 session 45 min.	Lesson 4

Chapter 12 **Short-Term Projects** pages 118–119

The Land of Genghis Khan 👤 individual/group 👥 Students draw and label a map of the thirteenth century Mongol Empire.	atlas, paper, pens or markers	1 session 30–45 min.	Lesson 2
A Dragon for Good Luck 👤 individual Students paint a dragon to symbolize good luck, strength, and wisdom.	poster paper, markers or paints and brushes	1 session 30–45 min.	Lesson 2
Go Fly a Kite 👤 individual Students make and paint their own kites.	paper, string, paints and brushes	1 session 30–45 min.	Lesson 2
The Flowery Kingdom 👤 individual Students create a book of flowers.	paper, watercolors, paintbrushes, colored pencils	1 session 40 min.	Lesson 2
Chinese Calligraphy 👤 individual Students try their hand at calligraphy.	watercolor paper, tempera paints and brushes	1 session 30 min.	Lesson 2
Make a Good Impression 👤 individual Students make their own seal.	potatoes, blunt cutting instruments, paints and brushes	1 session 30 min.	Lesson 2

Chapter 12 **Writing Projects** pages 120–121

Contradictions of an Empire 👤 individual Students write about the contradictions in the nature of the Mongol Empire.	paper, pencils	1 session 20 min.	Lessons 1–4
Travel Journal: The Great Wall of China 👤 individual Students write travel journal entries about the sights they see in Beijing.	paper, pencils	1 session 20 min.	Lesson 2
Letter to the Emperor 👤 individual Students write letters to the emperor disagreeing with the policy of sending envoys to foreign lands.	paper, pencils	1 session 20 min.	Lesson 2
Absolute Power! 👤 individual Students write about absolute power, justifying its use from the point of view of a *deva-raja*.	paper, pencils	1 session 25 min.	Lesson 2

Unit 5 Teacher Planner

Chapter 12 Writing Projects continued	Materials	🕐	Lesson Link
Biography: Lady Murasaki Shikibu 👤 individual Students write biographies of this poet and writer of long ago.	paper, pencils	1 session 30 min.	Lesson 3
Compare and Contrast: Hinduism and Buddhism 👤 individual Students compare two religions that are a major force in India and Asia.	paper, pencils	1 session 20 min.	Lesson 4
Citizenship Project pages 122			
Honesty 👥 whole class Students research people who had the courage to be honest about important issues.	paper, pencils, BLM p. 123	1 session 40 min.	Lesson 3
Chapter 13 Short-Term Projects pages 124–125			
Mapmaking: People and Climate 👤 individual Students make a map of Africa showing the different climate zones.	paper, pens or markers, research materials	1 session 30 min.	Lessons 1–3
Ghana: The Silent Salt-Gold Trade 👤 individual Students draw a storyboard of the silent barter for salt and gold along a riverbank.	paper, colored pencils, markers or paints and brushes	1 session 30–45 min.	Lesson 2
How Do You Say "Student" in Swahili? 👤 individual Students make a chart showing basic words in Swahili, and their English counterparts.	paper, pens, research materials	1 session 30 min.	Lesson 3
Mancala—Game of Strategy 👥 partners Students make a Mancala board, and play the game.	BLM p. 129, oaktag, various art supplies	1 session 30 min.	Lesson 3
Chapter 13 Writing Projects pages 126–127			
Sequence for a Kingdom 👤 individual Students write about the sequence of events that led to the rise and fall of one or more of the ancient African kingdoms.	paper, pencils	1 session 20 min.	Lessons 1–3
A Day in the Life of a Middleman 👤 individual Students write entries in the journal of a middleman in the ancient capital of Ghana.	paper, pencils	1 session 25 min.	Lessons 1–3
On the Move with Royal Solomonids 👤 individual Students write entries in the journal of a member of the Solomonid court on the move.	paper, pencils	1 session 25 min.	Lesson 2
Journal Entry: Life in Great Zimbabwe 👤 individual Students imagine what life would have been like in Great Zimbabwe.	paper, pencils	1 session 20 min.	Lesson 3
Investment Report 👤 individual Students write reports on trade in ancient Africa, and write persuasively in favor of foreign trade.	paper, pencils	1 session 25 min.	Lesson 3

Chapter 13 Citizenship Project page 128	Materials	⏲	Lesson Link
Responsibility 👥 whole class Students research environmental problems in Africa today, and what people are doing about them.	paper, pencils	1 session 45 min.	Lesson 3

Chapter 14 Short-Term Projects page 130–131			
Domesday Book for Our Time 👥 group Students create a Domesday Book for our time.	pictures from magazines, markers, paper	1 session 20 min.	Lesson 2
Design a Stained-Glass Window 👥 group Students make a design for a stained-glass window featuring scenes from their daily lives.	paper, colored pencils, markers, paints and brushes	1 session 20 min.	Lesson 3
Castle Drawing 👤 individual Students research and draw a medieval castle.	research materials, paper, pens or markers	1 session 30 min.	Lesson 3
Book of Hours 👤 individual/group 👥 Students create a book of hours illustrating the months of the year or showing their own activities for each month of the year.	paper, colored pencils, markers, paints and brushes	1 session 30–45 min.	Lesson 3
Guild Signs 👤 individual Students make signs for different craft guilds.	paper, colored pencils, markers, paints and brushes	1 session 30 min.	Lesson 3
Diorama of a Manor 👤 individual Students make a diorama of a medieval manor, showing each part of the manor.	shoebox, milk cartons, various art supplies	1 session 30 min.	Lesson 3

Chapter 14 Writing Projects pages 132–133			
The King Signs the Magna Carta 👤 individual Students write letters to a fellow nobleman or noblewoman telling about the signing of the Magna Carta.	paper, pencils	1 session 20 min.	Lesson 2
A Scribe's Job 👤 individual Students write letters describing the siege of the lord's castle.	paper, pencils	1 session 20 min.	Lesson 2
Tournament Day 👤 individual Students write an account of a tournament day in a medieval town or manor.	paper, pencils	1 session 20 min.	Lesson 3
Journal Entry: Christine de Pisan 👤 individual Students write journal entries of a medieval woman who was ahead of her time.	paper, pencils	1 session 20 min.	Lesson 3
An Account of the Plague 👤 individual Students write journal entries of a doctor who is treating people during the plague.	paper, pencils	1 session 25 min.	Lesson 4
Eight Crusades 👤 individual Students write about the sequence of the eight crusades.	paper, pencils	1 session 30 min.	Lesson 4

Chapter 14 Citizenship Project pages 134			
Courage and Fairness 👥 whole class Students research the code of chivalry and discuss how the values of chivalry apply to modern-day life.	paper, pencils, copy of the King Arthur Legend	1 session 40 min.	Lesson 3

Social Studies Plus!

Long-Term Project

Wall Painting

Caravans crossed the desert. Warriors clashed. Kings and queens decided the fates of entire nations. Lords and ladies hunted while serfs worked the fields. Students get into the act as they make a wall painting of life in the medieval world.

Preview and Choose

Week 1 — whole class — 30–45 minutes

Materials: none

Introduce your students to the four major areas of the medieval world covered in this unit. The Byzantine Empire—concentrated around the Mediterranean Sea—gradually gave way to the Islamic or Arabian Empire. The ancient Asian cultures in India, China, Cambodia, and Japan flourished during this period. African empires included those of Ghana, Mali, and Songhai. Europe, meanwhile, went through a period of feudalism. Each of the cultures left behind a tremendous legacy in sculpture, paintings, and art.

Explain that the class will make a wall painting in four panels. Each panel will represent one of the four parts of the medieval world covered in this unit. Divide the class into four groups.

Research and Sketch

Week 2 — group — 30–45 minutes

Materials: research materials, paper, pencils

Invite the groups to begin research for their panels. Encourage them to look for scenes from daily life or historical events. Also suggest they look at examples of the arts typical for each culture, including sculptures, paintings, tapestries, books, and charts. Ask groups to create a sketch for their mural panel.

104   Unit 5   Long-Term Project   Social Studies Plus!

Week 3 — Sketch and Paint

 group   30–45 minutes

Materials: large pieces of butcher paper, pencils or chalk, tempera paints, paintbrushes

Invite each group to sketch out its final design for a wall panel on a large piece of butcher paper. Then invite groups to begin painting their panels. Remind them that medieval paintings and illustrations were often very lively and colorful. Encourage them to pay attention to details such as dress, historical accuracy, and architectural details (they may want to show part of a city or part of a building, such as a cathedral or mosque, in the background). Remind them of the different parts of a painting: the foreground (in the front), the background (behind), and the center of the painting, which is usually the main focus.

Week 4 — Finish and Exhibit

 group   30–45 minutes

Materials: tempera paints, paintbrushes

Encourage the groups to finish their wall panels. Find a place in the classroom to hang and exhibit them. Each group should create a title for its panel and paint it above or under the panel. Suggest to the students that they may use the wall paintings as backdrops for the scenarios and plays they create for this unit.

Rulers, Travelers, and Serfs

History is a story of bit players and starring roles. Use these scenarios to bring to life people and legends from the vast world of the Middle Ages in Asia, Africa, and Europe.

Theodora Advises Her Husband, the Emperor

Theodora, the wife of Justinian I, was a strong-willed woman. The daughter of a bear trainer who worked at the hippodrome in Constantinople, she worked as a mime and an actress. When she was twenty, she met Justinian, who fell in love with her. They married in 525. In 527 Emperor Justin, Justinian's father, died. Justinian and Theodora assumed the throne together. Theodora took an active part in all decision making.

Create a scenario about the revolt in Constantinople in 532. Justinian was ready to flee the city. Theodora made a persuasive speech to the emperor and his advisors, convincing them to stay and fight. Her rousing speech saved the day.

A Lost Love, A Terrible Betrayal

Shah Jahan is walking through the gardens around the Taj Mahal, the magnificent palace he built in memory of his wife, Mumtaz. The gardens include four water channels that represent the four rivers of Paradise according to the Muslim religion. He is thinking about his beloved wife.

Meanwhile, in another palace, his three sons are arguing over who will succeed their father to the throne. Suddenly, Shah Jahan becomes ill. One of the sons, Aurangzeb, sees his chance. He imprisons his father and takes over the empire. Soon his harsh rule will lead to his own downfall, and that of the Mogul Empire too. Stage some scenes from the story of this family that ruled India from approximately 1526 to 1707.

Ibn Battuta Tells the Story of His Travels

The year is 1354. Ibn Battuta has returned to Fez after almost thirty years of travel. The sultan of Morocco listens to his report on Mali and many other stories. Intrigued by all these tales, the sultan orders Battuta to dictate his stories to a scribe. Ibn Juzayy, a young man, is hired to write down the tales. Stage the scene among the traveler, the scribe, and the sultan. What does Battuta remember about the beginning of his journey so long ago? Are his stories truthful, or is he exaggerating? The sultan and the scribe are not always so sure.

And the Serfs Work the Land

Today is a special day in the castle. A lord will swear his loyalty to the king and receive a land grant in return. The lord will present the king with the service of a knight to show his military support. Many nobles, barons, and bishops will also attend the ceremony. The lord will then give *seisin*, or a clod of earth, to a tenant to represent his right to work the land for the lord. In return, the tenant will proclaim his allegiance to the lord.

Meanwhile, the servants have a lot to do, preparing the feasts. The serfs are also hard at work, bringing in the harvest from the fields. Are they grumbling? What's in it for them? Stage a scene that shows the relationships among the different tiers of people in the feudal system in medieval Europe.

Sundiata: The Hungering Lion

The story of Sundiata makes compelling drama as students act out one of the great folktales of Africa.

The Parts: (9 players)
- Griot
- Villager
- Sundiata
- Drummer
- Sumanguru, the king of Sosso
- Maghan, Sundiata's father
- Sogolon, Sundiata's mother
- Buffalo Woman, Sundiata's grandmother
- Sassouma (and her eleven cutout sons)

 Director's Notes: This play is based on a folktale from Mali, kept alive by the griots of West Africa. A griot (GREE oat) is a traditional African storyteller. Here the griot's name is Balla Fasseke (bah lah fah SEE kay). Wassa, Wassa, Aye (WAH sah, WAH, sah, Eye ay) is a Mandinka cry of joy.

Griot: O people, hear my story! I am Balla Fasseke, a griot of ancient Mali. In my mind rest the stories of my people and the history of our land. Listen now to the story of Sundiata, the Hungering Lion, who brought peace and prosperity to the great land of ancient Mali.

(Maghan enters wearing or carrying the picture of a lion.) This is the king of the Mandinka people. He has brought the rule of *barika,* or law and progress, to human society. His totem is the lion. He is looking for a wife.

(Sogolon and Buffalo Woman enter.) This is Sogolon, and her mother, Buffalo Woman. They are said to have the powers of *nyama*—the ancient powers of our people.

Villager: *(stepping forward)* We respect these ancient powers. But sometimes they are very frightening. For example, if Buffalo Woman gets angry at you, she changes into an animal and attacks!

(Buffalo Woman slips a mask over her face.)

108 Unit 5 Drama Play Social Studies Plus!

Griot: Wait! Our tale has not yet begun. *(Buffalo Woman slips off the mask.)* The king took Sogolon as a wife. *(Maghan and Sogolon stand side by side facing audience.)* Their marriage was blessed when Sogolon gave birth to a little boy—Sundiata. *(Maghan and Sogolon turn their backs to the audience. When they turn around again, Sundiata enters and stands between them. They sit him down on the ground and take care of him as if he is a baby.)*

Villager: When Sundiata was born, the king rejoiced! The great royal drums carried the news all over the kingdom. *(Drummer drums on a drum or desk.)*

Sogolon: But we soon despaired, for Sundiata could not walk or speak. *(Sundiata tries to get up on his feet, but cannot.)*

Maghan: Sundiata, my son, what is wrong? *(Sundiata looks at his father but cannot speak.)*

Sassouma: *(holding her eleven sons)* It's a joke. This boy will never be king. He cannot walk or talk. And anyway, the king already has eleven heirs. One of my sons will be king.

Griot: One day, after Maghan had grown old, he felt death approach. *(Villager brings a chair for him to sit on.)* He called his child.

Maghan: Sundiata! I shall give you the gift each king gives to his heir. I shall give you a griot.

Griot: And on that day, the king gave *me*, Balla Fasseke, to be his son's griot. And on that day, for the first time, Sundiata spoke.

Sundiata: Balla, you shall be my griot.

Griot: And Maghan died peacefully, knowing that his son—the son of the lion and the buffalo—was worthy to be king.

(Drummer drums. Villager covers the king with a cloth and helps him walk off playing area covered from audience.)

Griot: But when the king died, Sassouma put her own son on the throne. *(Sassouma puts one of her cut-out figures on the chair.)* And she sent us far away. *(Sogolon helps Sundiata across stage. Griot, Sogolon, and Sundiata go off. Villager waves good-bye.)*

Sundiata: The Hungering Lion *continued*

Villager: Many years passed and Sassouma's son ruled upon the throne. But her other sons quarreled among themselves, and the people were unhappy. That was when Sumanguru, the king of neighboring Sosso, saw his opportunity.

Sumanguru: For a long while I have been watching the Mandinka people. Now that the old king is dead, their power is weak. His sons fight among themselves. If I get rid of them, their kingdom is mine. *(Takes a spear and marches to the throne. He sweeps Sassouma's son off the throne and sits in it himself. He addresses Villager.)* Take them away.

(Villager takes Sassouma and her sons offstage.)

Villager: *(running back to Sundiata, Sogolon, and Griot)* Sumanguru has invaded Mali! The king and his mother, Sassouma, have fled. Only you can save our people! Return, young lion, and reclaim your throne!

Sundiata: Today I will walk. *(to the Griot.)* Balla, tell the smiths to make me the sturdiest iron rod possible. Iron is the work of man. An iron rod will help me walk. *(Griot goes off and returns with a strong "iron" stick. He gives it to Sundiata. Sogolon helps him. He stands for a moment, but the rod slips and he falls down.)*

Buffalo Woman: *(enters wearing her mask)* An iron rod alone is not enough to support a lion. The work of man must be united with the forces of nature. Sogolon, my daughter, fetch a supple branch from the sun sun tree. *(Sogolon goes off and returns with a branch. She gives it to Buffalo Woman who gives it to Sundiata. He holds it in one hand. Griot gives him the iron rod again. He holds it in the other hand. Slowly he stands steady.)* The sun sun tree holds the ancient power of nyama.

Griot: With the iron rod—the symbol of man's technology—in one hand, and the sun sun branch—the symbol of the ancient ways—in the other hand, Sundiata walked!

(Sundiata takes a step or two, slowly, but powerfully. By the third step he lets the two sticks drop away and can walk on his own.)

Sogolon, Buffalo Woman, Griot, and Villager: Wassa, Wassa, Ayé!

(Sundiata takes his place at the head of a procession. Behind him are Sogolon, Buffalo Woman, Griot, and Villager. He walks to the throne.)

Griot: And so it was. Sundiata led his army against Sumanguru and defeated him. And the great kingdom of Mali was born. *(Sundiata moves Sumanguru off the throne and takes it for himself.)* Listen, my people, and remember this tale. How the great king Sundiata—the Lion King—harnessed his great hunger, and came to take his rightful place on the throne of his father.

All: Wassa, Wassa, Ayé!

(Drumming and dancing end the play.)

Chapter 11: Short-Term Projects

How do we know so much about the people from long ago? To a great extent, we know them through the art and architecture they left behind. Get students working on projects that re-create some of the glories of the past.

Make a Diorama: The Hippodrome

individual   30 minutes

Materials: shoe box, milk cartons, modeling clay, small figures (horses), pipe cleaners, bits of fabric, glue, tempera paints, paintbrushes

What do you do for entertainment in the Byzantine Empire? You go to the hippodrome—to watch some horse and chariot racing. Seating sixty thousand people, the tradition came out of the Greek and Roman cultures. Invite your students to make a diorama of the hippodrome.

Portolan Chart

individual   30 minutes

Materials: paper, markers or pencils

Italian navigators developed the *portolan*, a book that listed seaways, ports, harbors, anchorages, and borders. Challenge your students to make up a chart or map of a seaport. Ask them to include the border of the area, and geographical features such as bodies of water, mountains, and plains, or other features they feel are important. Remind them to label all features on the map.

Make a Mosaic

individual/group   30 minutes

Materials: small pieces of materials such as beads, ceramics, pebbles; or colored oaktag cut into small squares and other shapes; cardboard; glue

Mosaics, pictures made of small pieces of stone, glass, or wood, were the leading art form of the Byzantine Empire. They decorated the walls of churches and cathedrals, such as the Hagia Sophia in Istanbul. Invite your students to make their own mosaic.

Paint an Icon

 individual   30 minutes

Materials: paper, watercolor paper, tempera paints, gold or silver colors, paintbrushes

Icons—hand-painted pictures with religious themes—were popular during the Byzantine Empire. These pictures, usually painted on wood, were often highlighted with gold paint. Your students can make their own icons. Invite them to paint a scene from their own lives— or choose a scene or event from their book, such as Ibn-Jubay's entrance into Mecca.

Illuminated Manuscript

 individual   30 minutes

Materials: paper; pens, markers, or colored pencils; gold and silver colors

Medieval Muslim artists used elaborate artwork and calligraphy to decorate the pages of hand-copied books. Invite your students to choose a page from a favorite book, copy it and decorate the page. Challenge them to take the first letter on the page and weave their artwork into the letter.

Water Clock

 individual   45 minutes

Materials: paper, pens or markers

Sundials are the oldest clocks, but how could you tell the time when the sun wasn't shining? Muslim engineers built water clocks. The timekeeping was governed by the rate that water dripped into a jar.

Challenge your students to do some research and then draw a picture of a water clock. Invite them to decorate the surface of the clock in the ornate style of medieval Muslim artists.

Remember! Keep working on that Long-Term Project.

Chapter 11 Writing Projects

Get ready for some time travel! Your writers travel back to the Byzantine and Arabic Empires, and write from the point of view of emperors, pilgrims, travelers, and merchants.

A Visit to the Byzantine Capital

Invite your students to put themselves in the shoes of a son or daughter of a noble family of the Byzantine empire who has been summoned to Constantinople. There he or she will have an audience with the emperor, who plans to appoint a new governor of a province. Your students want the job! Challenge them to write letters praising the glory of the emperor, talking about some of the political, economic, and cultural accomplishments that make this empire great.

A Justinian Code for Today

Emperor Justinian commanded Byzantine scholars to collect and organize the laws of the Romans into a code. This became known as the Justinian Code, and is the basis of many legal systems even today. It stressed efficiency and fairness in all dealings. What would a new Justinian Code for your school include? Invite students to write their own version of a code of law for students.

Journal Entry: Pilgrimage to Mecca

Invite students to write an entry in a journal of a Muslim pilgrim, making a pilgrimage to Mecca. This city (the birthplace of Islam's founder, Muhammad) is considered holy by Muslims. Every year hundreds of thousands of people make the journey, today as in ancient times. Challenge students to write about this experience. What is it like to be in the middle of such a huge crowd? What is the city like? What is the purpose of your pilgrimage?

Arabic Innovations

In the Middle Ages, the Muslim world made significant contributions to the advancement of science and technology. Muslim engineers built water clocks and complex irrigation systems. They invented branch banking, algebra and trigonometry, and calculated the distance around the world. They developed instruments for making accurate calculations in astronomy, navigation, and mapmaking. Invite students to research and write about some of the many scientific innovations of the early Arab world.

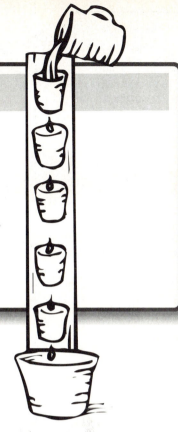

Journal Entry: Ibn Battuta's Escape from Delhi

The Sultan of India sends Ibn Battuta as an ambassador to the Mongol court of China with one thousand soldiers; two hundred slaves, singers, and dancers; fifteen pages; one hundred horses; and mountains of gifts. But a few days outside of Delhi, the company is attacked by four thousand Hindu rebels. Battuta's forces defeat the rebels, but they are attacked again. Battuta escapes only to be captured by robbers who keep him prisoner in a cave. Since he has nothing left of any worth, he convinces them to let him go. Challenge your students to write an entry in the journal of the intrepid traveler of the medieval Arab world. They can research and read Battuta's adventures first.

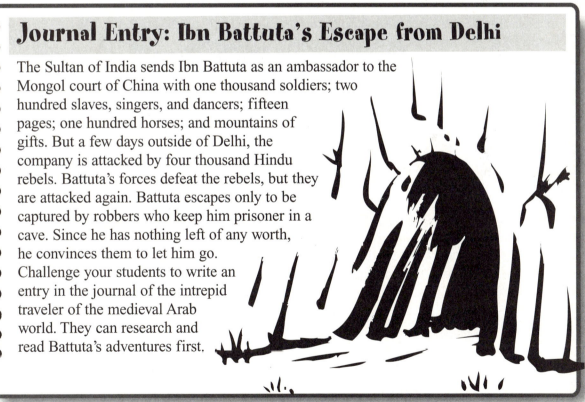

Chapter 11 Citizenship

Respect

In the course of his life, Ibn Battuta traveled some seventy-five thousand miles and visited nearly every Islamic kingdom in the world of his time. He also visited cultures very different from his own. His writings show that he had great respect for other peoples' ways of life.

Advance Preparation: *Copy and pass out the blackline master on page 117.*

Respect for cultures other than our own is as important today as it was then. People from different cultures often live side by side in the same neighborhoods, cities, and countries. Understanding and respecting each other's traditions can help reduce thinking of others as stereotypes.

Challenge your class to research the activities of grassroots peace organizations from both sides of the Israeli-Palestinian conflict. In particular, have them look into the making of the film, *Promises*, interviews with Israeli and Palestinian children on their lives and their feelings about each other. Filmmaker Justine Shapiro says about the film, "We are used to the three-minute news stories on [television] and we desperately want international conflict (as well as conflicts in our own cities and in our own homes) to be simple, reducible to who is wrong and who is right. . . . I hope that people who see the film, will feel connected to human beings that are growing up in places of conflict all over."

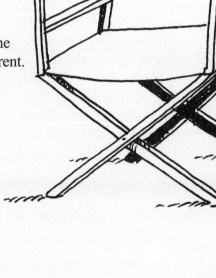

Invite your students to envision themselves as documentary filmmakers. How could they use film to teach respect for another culture? What would they make a film about? Ask them to brainstorm ideas for the film including ways the other culture is similar to their own and ways that it is different.

116 Unit 5 Citizenship Project

Social Studies Plus!

Name _____ Date _____

Respect for Another Culture

How Are We Alike	How Are We Different

Chapter 12: Short-Term Projects

Conquerors and empires came and went. But in times of peace, the arts in Asia flourished. Invite your students to join in making a panoply of ancient creative forms.

The Land of Genghis Khan

 individual/group   30–45 minutes

Materials: atlas, paper, pens or markers

Genghis Khan and his hordes swept across the plains of central Asia in a fury, conquering as they went. At its height, the Mongol Empire was the largest the world has ever seen, stretching from China to present-day Hungary and Syria! Have your students draw a map of the Mongol Empire in the thirteenth century. Ask them to label as many features as they can and to show the scale.

A Dragon for Good Luck

 individual   30–45 minutes

Materials: poster paper, markers or tempera paints and paintbrushes

In the Chinese tradition, the dragon is considered a symbol of good luck. It is supposed to represent wisdom, strength, and goodness. It also symbolized the life-giving force of water. The Chinese believed that dragons lived in every body of water, and also among the rain clouds. Invite your students to paint a dragon to symbolize good luck, strength and wisdom. Hang up these good luck symbols in the classroom.

Go Fly a Kite

 individual   30–45 minutes

Materials: paper, string, tempera paints, paintbrushes

The Manchu emperors introduced an autumn kite-flying festival called Tengkao, or "Mounting the Height." They believed flying kites brought them good luck. The kites were often decorated with mythological creatures. Invite your students to make kites, and paint them. They can research Chinese kites or make up their own design. Display the kites in the classroom.

118   Unit 5   Short-Term Projects   Social Studies Plus!

The Flowery Kingdom

individual   40 minutes

Materials: paper, watercolors, paintbrushes, colored pencils

Many flowers had symbolic meanings for the Chinese. For example, the lotus flower was a symbol of purity; the peony symbolized spring and rebirth; the chrysanthemum, flower of autumn, was a symbol of long life; the narcissus, which bloomed at the New Year, was a symbol of good luck.

Invite your students to make a book of flowers. Each page presents a flower and an explanation of what it represents. Your students can draw real flowers, or invent their own. Bind the books and display them in the classroom.

Chinese Calligraphy

individual   30 minutes

Materials: watercolor paper, tempera paints, paintbrushes

According to legend, Chinese writing was invented over four thousand years ago by Cang Jie, an official of the mythical Yellow Emperor. He created written characters based on the tracks left by birds and animals. Chinese writing, or calligraphy, developed over centuries into an art form. To become a master required years of training and practice. With more than forty thousand characters in the Chinese language, you can see why it took so long to learn! Invite your students to try their hand at calligraphy. They may copy the brush strokes of a Chinese symbol or invent their own characters. Have them experiment!

Make a Good Impression

individual   30 minutes

Materials: potatoes, blunt cutting instruments, tempera paints, paper

How did artists sign their names to paintings in ancient China? They used a seal to identify their work. Seal impressions were always printed in red ink. Invite your students to make their own seal. After cutting out their design in a potato half, they can use red paint, or other colors, to print their design on paper.

Remember! Keep working on that Long-Term Project.

Chapter 12 Writing Projects

Medieval Asia was a place of contrasts! Ruthless tyrants conquered everything in their path. Peaceful explorers sailed the seas. Artists created masterpieces. Get your writers to work on themes from empires long past.

Contradictions of an Empire

Genghis Khan is remembered as a ruthless warrior who terrorized populations into submitting to him. Yet his grandson, Kublai Khan, fostered cultural and scientific advances. Invite your students to write about the contradictions in the nature of this empire. Do we still find these contradictions in today's world? Where do we find them? How can we understand them?

Travel Journal: The Great Wall of China

Ask students to suppose they have arrived in Beijing, the capital city of China, during the Ming dynasty. Renovation and new construction on the Great Wall is under way. Block printing of money and books is widespread. High-quality porcelain and ceramic goods catch their attention. Will they have an audience with the emperor in the Forbidden City? Invite them to write an entry in a travel journal about the sights they see.

Letter to the Emperor

During the Ming dynasty, the Chinese emperor financed the voyages of Zheng He. The emperor filled the ships with gold, silver, and silk to give out as gifts in Asia, India, and Africa. But now a new emperor closes China to foreigners and begins a period of isolation. Invite your students to write letters to the emperor disagreeing with this new policy. Why do they think it will be harmful to China? What is the advantage of maintaining good relations with your neighbors?

Absolute Power!

In the Khmer kingdom, the *deva-raja* (ruler) was considered to be a god king. He had absolute power over the realm. Challenge your students to write about absolute power, justifying its use from the point of view of a *deva-raja*. What will they do with power? Will it be used for the good of the kingdom? Explain.

Biography: Lady Murasaki Shikibu

Her book, *The Tale of the Genji,* tells the story of life at the royal court of Heian Japan around the year 1000. How did Lady Murasaki acquire skills at a time when many were discouraged from learning to read and write? How did she become the favorite of the Empress Akiko? Why did her stories shock the royal court? Challenge your students to do the research and write a short biography of this fascinating writer of long ago.

Compare and Contrast: Hinduism and Buddhism

The Buddhist religion was founded in northern India about two thousand five hundred years ago by a prince named Siddhartha Gautama. Hinduism developed over a thousand years ago, although its origins are said to be more ancient. Challenge your students to compare and contrast these two religions that are still a major force in India and many parts of modern Asia. What are the main beliefs of each? How are they similar to and different from each other?

Chapter 12 Citizenship

Honesty

Lady Murasaki Shikibu was critical of many practices of court life and wrote about them openly. She made enemies for being so outspoken. But she had the courage as a writer to tell the truth about her contemporaries and their weaknesses.

Advance Preparation: *Copy and use the blackline master on page 123 to get students started.*

We all know that "honesty is the best policy." But sometimes honesty comes with a price. Invite your students to discuss the courage it takes to be honest about issues that are difficult. Ask them to think of people who had the courage to be honest during difficult times or circumstances.

You could discuss Martin Luther King, Jr., who had the courage to be honest about the civil rights situation in this country in the 1960s.

Rachel Carson's honesty in writing about our natural resources and how they were being threatened also called for courage in a time when people did not think much about conservation or recycling.

Challenge students to research people who had the courage to be honest about important issues. What did they risk by being honest? What did they gain? What contributions did they make that we can appreciate today?

Name _____ Date _____

Use the space below to list the names of people you think spoke or wrote honestly about an important issue. Next to the name, write down the issue that was important to the person.

Name	Issue

Social Studies Plus!

Chapter 13 Short-Term Projects

Travel to the ancient kingdoms of Ghana, Mali and Songhai!
Use these short-term projects as a bridge to the legends, trade,
customs, language, and games of medieval Africa.

Mapmaking: People and Climate 👤 individual   30 minutes

Materials: paper, pens or markers, research materials

Invite your students to make a map of Africa showing the different climate zones, using different colors. Ask them to illustrate their maps to show how a climate zone determines the way people live. What kinds of clothes do they wear? What are the main occupations? What is the predominant way of life?

Ghana: The Silent Salt-Gold Trade   👤 individual   30–45 minutes

Materials: paper; colored pencils, markers, or tempera paints and paintbrushes

The salt-gold trade was the lifeblood of the ancient empire of Ghana. It was carried out in a most unusual manner—silently! Salt—essential in the human diet—was mined in Taghaza in the northeastern desert (modern-day Algeria.) But the location of the Wangara gold mines was kept secret by the kings of Ghana and the Wangara people, who knew their prosperity depended on this secrecy. However, the Wangara desperately lacked one thing—salt!

To trade gold for salt, the Wangara chose a trading site on the banks of a river. The merchants from Ghana brought their goods—animal skins, ivory, kola nuts, wool, silk, cotton, dates, and figs. They laid bars of salt on the ground near their goods. The traders then beat their drums to announce the market was open, and withdrew to a site several miles away. Then the Wangara came by boat to inspect the goods. Next to each pile of salt, they laid a bag of gold dust. They beat *their* drums to signal their withdrawal from sight. Then the Ghanians would return. If they were satisfied with the trade, they collected the gold and left. If not, they withdrew again, hoping for a better price. Challenge your students to draw a storyboard of the silent barter for salt and gold along a riverbank.

How do You Say "Student" in Swahili?   individual   30 minutes

Materials: paper, pens, research materials

As Islam spread in the seventh and eighth centuries, it came into contact with the cultures of East Africa. The mixing of African and Arabic cultures and languages produced Swahili, a new language. Swahili means "people of the coast" in Arabic. It is a language still spoken by many people in Africa today. Invite your students to use the Internet to find an interactive Swahili-English dictionary. Then challenge them to make a chart showing ten basic words in Swahili, and their counterparts in English. Challenge them to learn how to say the words in Swahili.

> Remember! Keep working on that Long-Term Project.

Mancala–Game of Strategy   partners   30 minutes

Materials: blackline master (page 129); oaktag; scissors; markers; 48 pebbles, buttons, beans, or other small markers

Mancala may well be the oldest game in the world. Stone Mancala boards were found carved into the roofs of temples in ancient Egypt. The game may have evolved from ancient boards used for accounting and stock taking. It is a wholly mathematical game. Its more complicated versions are as complex as chess. Invite your students to make a Mancala board using the blackline master as a reference and then follow the rules to play the game. They can also find Internet sites for interactive Mancala games, and variations on the game.

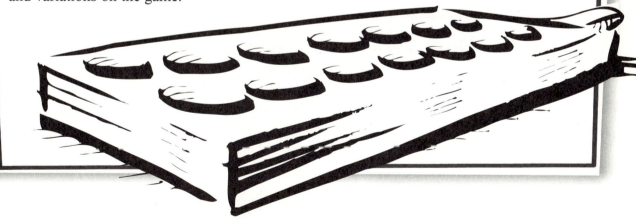

Chapter 13: Writing Projects

As ancient African kingdoms rise and fall, your writers are there, documenting the daily life of traders and royals, and taking a look at the big picture.

Sequence for a Kingdom

Challenge your students to write about the sequence of events that led to the rise and fall of one or more of the kingdoms of ancient Africa: Mali, Ghana, Songhai, Axum, Ethiopia, Great Zimbabwe, or Benin. How did one kingdom's fall make way for another kingdom's rise? Is there a pattern in the rise and fall of empires? Challenge your students to sequence the facts and then comment upon them.

A Day in the Life of a Middleman

The location of ancient Ghana's capital, Koumbi—between the salt mines in the Sahara and the gold mines of Wangara—made the middlemen wealthy. They traded gold, copper, and palm oil from the south for salt, glass, and ceramics from the north. Muslim traders from as far off as Baghdad came to do business. Challenge your students to write an entry in the journal of a middleman in the ancient capital of Ghana. Ask them to explain how they think business might have been done.

On the Move with the Royal Solomonids

When the Solomonid dynasty took over the ancient empire of Ethiopia, the king and his court began to move from place to place as often as two or three times a year. This helped him to stay in touch with all the regions of his kingdom. Invite your students to write an entry in the journal of a member of the Solomonid court on the move. Why is the court moving? Where is it going? Is this is a good practice? What is it like to be constantly on the move with a huge court of people?

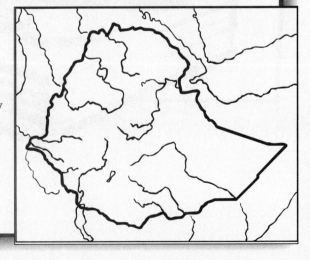

Journal Entry: Life in Great Zimbabwe

Invite your students to imagine what life would have been like in Great Zimbabwe. Remind them that *Zimbabwe* means "houses of stone" in the Shona language. Although gold was not actually mined in the area, Zimbabwe became one of the largest, and wealthiest of the ancient sub-Saharan cultures by taxing the trade goods that passed through it. About eleven thousand people lived in and around Great Zimbabwe by the early fifteenth century, before it began to decline. Challenge your students to write an entry in the journal of a boy or girl living in this ancient African kingdom. Ask them to consider what the cone-shaped towers were used for.

Investment Report

Invite your students to imagine that they are financial reporters for a newspaper covering ancient Africa. Their mission is to encourage foreign investors to trade on the continent. Assess the economic opportunities, risks, and dangers for traders. How accessible are the goods? What are the best trade routes? Challenge students to write a report on trade in ancient Africa and to write persuasively in favor of foreign trade.

Chapter 13 Citizenship

Responsibility

Today we understand the importance of our relationship with the environment. We know we have a responsibility to conserve resources. What about ancient peoples? Did they understand this delicate balance?

In about 1450, people abandoned Great Zimbabwe, the sub-Saharan kingdom, whose population had grown to about eleven thousand people. Scholars believe that the large population exhausted the natural resources of the area: trees for timber, soil for growing crops, and grasses for grazing farm animals.

Discuss with your class the responsibility of taking care of our environment. Challenge them to research environmental problems in Africa today and what people are doing about them. You may want to divide the class into groups to research different environmental issues such as water, desertification, wildlife, forestry, and sustainable development. Many sites exist on the Internet with information on these areas.

You may also want to research conservation issues in your own area. In what ways are they similar to the important issues in Africa? In what ways are they different? How can people make a difference around the world?

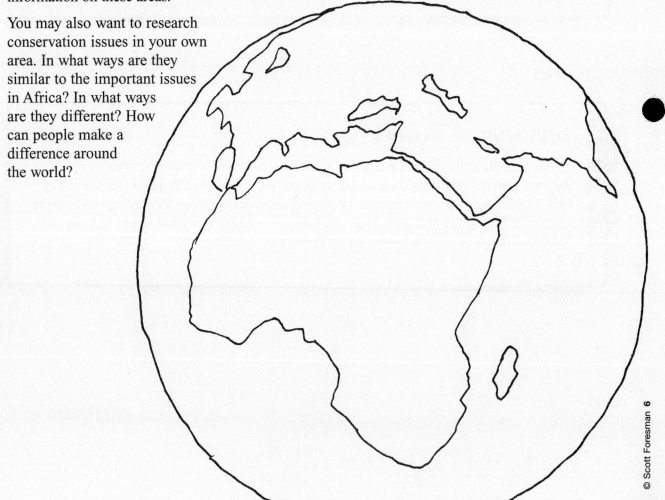

Name _____ Date _____

The Ancient Game of Mancala

For two players

How to Play

Purpose: To collect the most stones in your Mancala (Mancalas are the large bowls at each end of the board.)

Preparation: Cut out and enlarge the picture of the Mancala board below, or copy it onto a piece of oaktag. Make sure the bowls and Mancalas are large enough to hold ten or more pebbles.

Set Up: Place four stones in each small bowl. Leave the Mancalas empty. Place the board between the players, with the Mancalas on the left and right. Player 1's Mancala is on the right-hand side. At the bottom of the board are Player 1's six small bowls. Player 2's Mancala is on the left-hand side and his or her six small bowls are in a row on the top.

General Rules:

- Player 1 starts by scooping up all the stones from one of his or her small bowls.
- Moving counterclockwise, Player 1 drops one stone into the next bowl, a stone into the second bowl, and so forth until he or she has no more stones.
- Then Player 2 does the same.
- Players proceed in this way, taking turns.
- When a player reaches his or her own Mancala, he or she drops a stone into it. Players never drop stones into their opponents' Mancalas. They skip over them.
- If a player drops the last stone from his or her hand into the Mancala, he or she gets to move again.
- At the end of the game, players count the stones in their Mancalas. Whoever has the most stones wins.

Use the Internet or other sources to find more ways to play the game. There are many different variations.

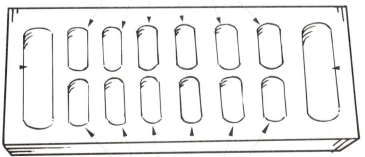

Chapter 14: Short-Term Projects

From the great cathedrals to the manor houses, people are active, making stained-glass windows, planting and harvesting, and working with their guilds. Students take on projects to learn more about medieval Europe.

Domesday Book for Our Time   group — 20 minutes

Materials: pictures from magazines, markers, paper

The Domesday Book was a kind of medieval census. But it also ended up being a portrait of medieval life in Europe. Challenge your students to create a Domesday Book for our time. Invite them to work in groups. They can create categories for different aspects of modern life such as sports, fashion, occupations, hobbies, and so forth. Encourage them to make a collage for each category, using pictures cut from magazines or drawing original pictures. Put the pages together and bind them to make a Domesday Book for Our Time.

Design a Stained-Glass Window   group — 20 minutes

Materials: paper; colored pencils, markers, or tempera paints and paintbrushes

As Christianity took hold in medieval Europe, the great period of cathedral building began. Entire towns worked to build these architectural wonders. Countless anonymous craftsmen and artists were employed to make statues, paintings, and stained glass windows to decorate the churches. Challenge your students to make a design for a stained-glass window. They may illustrate a scene from their own daily life or events at school. Remind them that the windows were made of small pieces of glass in different colors seamed together with lead.

Castle Drawing   individual — 30 minutes

Materials: research materials, paper, pens or markers

Challenge your students to research and draw a medieval castle. Invite them to label the parts of the castle. Challenge them to use terms such as *drawbridge, moat, flying buttress, fortifications,* and other descriptive words. They may want to draw a cross section of a castle, labeling the inside as well as the outside.

Book of Hours

individual/group **30–45 minutes**

Materials: paper; colored pencils, markers, or tempera paints and paintbrushes

A *book of hours* was a kind of medieval calendar that showed illustrations of manor life for each month of the year. Have students research the book of hours, then invite them to work in small groups to create one of their own. They may illustrate the months of the year on a medieval manor, or make a contemporary book of hours showing their own activities for each month of the year. Remind them that the books showed very detailed pictures of daily life. Bind the pictures together and make a title page: *Our Book of Hours*.

Guild Signs

individual **30 minutes**

Materials: paper; colored pencils, markers, or tempera paints and paintbrushes

Guilds were an important feature of medieval life. A guild was a group of people with the same craft. Groups that formed guilds included merchants, goldsmiths, bakers, tailors, weavers, and blacksmiths. Because most people could not read, each guild created a picture sign to represent its specialty. These signs hung outside the shops of the guild members. Invite students to research medieval crafts and guilds. Then challenge them to make signs for different guilds. What tool or instrument could they show to represent a craft?

Diorama of a Manor

individual **30 minutes**

Materials: shoe box; milk cartons; materials such as bits of fabric, pipe cleaners, small animal figures

Challenge your students to make a diorama of a medieval manor. Invite them to show the four parts of a manor: the manor house (of the lord) and village (of the serfs), farmland, meadowland, and wasteland. Most manors included a church, and a mill for grinding grain into flour. Serfs' cottages were made of mud bricks, and straw roofs. Where were the vegetable gardens of the serfs? Where did sheep and other animals graze?

Remember! Keep working on that Long-Term Project.

Chapter 14: Writing Projects

It's a feudal world, and most people cannot read and write. Somebody has got to keep track of rents and taxes, copy the old manuscripts, and prepare the documents for the king to sign. Turn your students into scribes to write about the lives of peasants and kings.

The King Signs the Magna Carta

On June 15, 1215, King John of England signed the Magna Carta, one of the first documents to limit the power of a king. One article stated that the king could not make special demands for money without the consent of the lords. Another said that no free man could be imprisoned, exiled, or deprived of property, except by law. The document is the basis of many legal codes today. Ask your students to write a letter to a fellow nobleman or noblewoman telling about the signing of the Magna Carta. Challenge them to say why they think this document is important.

Journal Entry: Christine de Pisan

Invite your students to write an entry in the journal of Christine de Pisan, a medieval woman who was ahead of her time. She wrote poetry and books protesting the way women were kept from decision making at all levels of medieval society. What observations do you think she would make about daily life in the Middle Ages? What kind of world do you think she would hope for in the future?

A Scribe's Job

The lord's castle is under siege. Since he cannot read or write, he employs a scribe. The lord commands the scribe to write a message to a neighboring castle asking for help. Invite your students to write letters describing the siege. Is the castle surrounded? Has it been attacked? How many casualties so far? How is the lord defending his castle? How many reinforcements are needed?

Tournament Day

Challenge your students to write an account of a tournament day in a medieval town or manor. Ask them to describe the events that take place, using colorful words to tell about the sights, sounds, smells, tastes, and feel of the day. What is the purpose of this event?

An Account of the Plague

The plague was a horrible epidemic that swept through medieval Europe from 1347 to 1352. By the time it was over, it had killed almost a third of Europe's population. People then did not know what caused the plague and, therefore, had no way to practice preventive measures. Challenge your students to write an entry in the journal of a doctor who is treating people during the plague. What were the symptoms? How did it affect different classes of people? Did quarantines help stop the spread of the disease? Where did people think it came from? Why did some people seem to be immune? Students may research the plague for first hand details from journals of the time.

Eight Crusades

Advance Preparation: *Copy and hand out the blackline master on page 135.*

Between 1095 and 1270, Christians in Western Europe organized eight crusades to liberate Jerusalem from the Turks and Muslims. However, the Crusades were also a struggle for land, power, and riches. And the Crusades had some unintended outcomes, such as increased trade and exchanges of ideas between European and Arabic lands. Invite your students to write about the sequence of the eight crusades. Encourage them to conduct some research. When did each happen? What was its goal? What did it accomplish?

Chapter 14 Citizenship

Courage and Fairness

The knights and soldiers of medieval Europe were often mercenaries. Mercy and gallantry frequently seemed more the exception than the rule. It was therefore an important development when the ideas of selflessness, service, and fairness took hold among many knights during the period of the Crusades.

This legacy—of the knights' code of honor—comes down to us through the legend of King Arthur and the Knights of the Round Table.

Challenge your students to research the code of chivalry. What does *chivalry* mean? Where does the idea come from? What were the main ideas of this code? Suggest that students research the King Arthur legend.

Invite them to discuss how the values of chivalry—specifically courage and fairness—apply to modern-day life. Are these values part of our military code today? How? In what ways?

Invite them to read aloud from a part of the King Arthur legend. Then discuss how chivalry was important to the Middle Ages.

Name _____ Date _____

Time Line

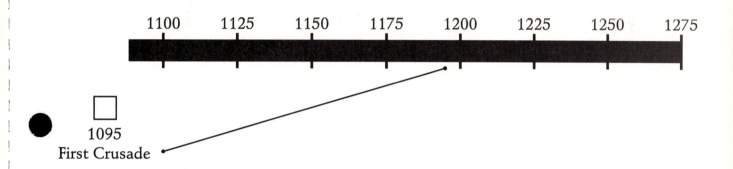

☐
1095
First Crusade

Teacher Planner

Long-Term Project pages 138–139	Materials	⏱	Lesson Link
Class Newspapers Students role-play reporters getting the facts about the big events in world history from inventions to revolutions.			Lessons 1–3
Week 1 whole class Students choose which time period they want to feature in their newspaper articles.	six clipboards, paper, pens	1 session 30–45 min.	
Week 2 group Students brainstorm ideas for stories.	clipboards, assignment sheets, folders, paper, pens, research materials	1 session 30–45 min.	
Week 3 group Students write articles based on the notes they took.	research notes, paper, pens	1 session 30–45 min.	
Week 4 group Students illustrate their stories or make a political cartoon for their newspaper.	first drafts, paper, pens, dictionaries	1 session 30–45 min.	
Week 5 whole class Students hold a roundtable discussion where "editors" and "reporters" from different eras discuss issues that are common to all times.	none	1 session 30–45 min.	
Unit Drama pages 140–145			
Play: Galileo Points His Telescope at the Stars group Students perform a play about Galileo Galilei's discoveries about the true nature of the world.	props, costumes (optional)	1 session 2 hrs.	Lesson 1
Scenarios: Making a Difference group Students role-play scenes in the lives of people who made a difference long ago.	props (optional)	6 sessions 25 min. each	Lessons 1–3
Chapter 15 Short-Term Projects pages 146–147			
Renaissance Perspective individual Students draw pictures using Renaissance techniques of perspective light and shadow.	paper, pencils	1 session 30–45 min.	Lesson 1
Pages from Leonardo's Notebook individual Students create their own sketchbook of ideas for new inventions based on Leonardo's work.	paper, pencils	1 session 30–45 min.	Lesson 1
Asian Renaissance individual Students draw or paint a picture of a Kabuki character.	research materials, paper, colored pencils or paints and brushes	1 session 30–40 min.	Lesson 1
Four Corners of the Globe individual Students make illustrated maps in the style of Renaissance mapmakers.	research materials, paper, pens, colored pencils or markers	1 session 30–40 min.	Lesson 1
Long Live the Queen! individual Students research and draw the fashions of Elizabethan times.	paper, colored pencils or markers	1 session 30–40 min.	Lesson 2

Chapter 15 Short-Term Projects continued	Materials	🕐	Lesson Link
The Middle Passage individual Students choose a character and create a storyboard from that character's perspective.	paper or oaktag, pens or markers	1 session 30–40 min.	Lesson 2
Chapter 15 Writing Projects pages 148–149			
Renaissance Achievements individual Students summarize the accomplishments of the Renaissance.	paper, pens	1 session 20 min.	Lesson 1
Printing Press vs. Home Computer individual Students write essays comparing two inventions that changed the world.	paper, pens	1 session 20 min.	Lesson 1
Counter Reformation? individual Students write reports from the Council of Trent about the changes it proposes.	paper, pens	1 session 20 min.	Lesson 1
Nine Weeks at Sea: A Pep Talk individual Students write a pep talk that Columbus could make to his men.	paper, pens	1 session 25 min.	Lesson 2
A Queen's Diary individual Students write entries in the journal of Queen Elizabeth I of England.	paper, pens	1 session 20 min.	Lesson 2
A Missionary with a Mind of His Own individual Students write a news article presenting las Casas' views, which were ahead of his time.	paper, pens	1 session 30 min.	Lesson 2
Chapter 15 Citizenship Project page 150			
Courage whole class Students discuss courage and explore its relevance in their own lives.	BLM p. 151, paper, pens	1 session 45 min.	Lessons 2–3
Chapter 16 Short-Term Projects pages 152–153			
Political Cartoon: Patriot or Loyalist? individual Students draw political cartoons about an issue or event in the American Revolution.	paper, pens or markers	1 session 30–40 min.	Lesson 1
Toussaint L'Ouverture: Haitian Hero individual Students make posters commemorating the leader of the Haitian revolution for independence.	poster paper, markers or colored pencils	1 session 30–40 min.	Lesson 1
Mural: Struggle for Independence group Students make murals about the struggle for independence in Latin America.	butcher paper, tempera paints and brushes	1 session 45 min.	Lesson 1
Music History: "1812 Overture" whole class Students listen to this piece of music and draw a picture in response.	recording of *1812 Overture*, tape or CD player, art supplies	1 session 30–45 min.	Lesson 2
Catalog of New Inventions individual Students create a catalog of new inventions of the first and second Industrial Revolutions.	paper, markers or pencils	1 session 30–40 min.	Lesson 3
Assembly-Line Production individual Students make a storyboard that illustrates how assembly-line production works.	paper, colored pencils or markers	1 session 30–40 min.	Lesson 4

Teacher Planner

Chapter 16 Writing Projects pages 154–155	Materials	🕐	Lesson Link
Eyewitness Account: The Boston Massacre — group Students write eyewitness accounts of this important event in the history of the Revolution.	paper, pens	1 session 25 min.	Lesson 1
Editorial: Taxation Without Representation? — individual Students write editorials for a newspaper about the issue of taxation.	paper, pens	1 session 30 min.	Lesson 1
All Men Are Created Equal? — individual Students write letters to a colonial newspaper about why the principle of equality should extend to everyone.	paper, pens	1 session 20 min.	Lesson 1
Journal Entry: The Storming of the Bastille — individual Students use descriptive words to write about the event.	paper, pens	1 session 20 min.	Lesson 2
Journal Entry: Napoléon in Exile — individual Students write an entry in the journal of the great French emperor Napoléon as he sits in exile.	paper, pens	1 session 20 min.	Lesson 2

Chapter 16 Citizenship Project page 156			
Fairness — whole class Students discuss their ideas of fairness and how they have evolved from earlier times.	BLM p. 157, paper, pens	1 session 40 min.	Lessons 1–4

Chapter 17 Short-Term Projects pages 158–159			
Political Cartoon: Berlin Conference — individual Students make political cartoons about the Berlin Conference in 1884.	paper, colored pencils or markers	1 session 30 min.	Lesson 1
Mary Kingsley: Victorian Adventurer — individual Students make comic books based on the real-life story of Mary Kingsley.	research materials, paper, pencils or markers	1 session 30–45 min.	Lesson 1
Queen Victoria's Diamond Jubilee — individual Students make pictures celebrating fifty years of Queen Victoria's reign.	research materials, paper, pens or markers	1 session 30–40 min.	Lesson 1
Nineteenth-Century Military Costumes — individual Students make catalogs of military uniforms of the nineteenth century.	research materials, paper, pens	1 session 30–45 min.	Lessons 1–3
Japanese-Style Watercolor — individual Students research the Japanese influence on American nineteenth-century art and create their own paintings.	research materials, watercolor paper, paints and brushes	1 session 30–40 min.	Lesson 2
Map of Italian Unification — individual Students make illustrated maps of Italy showing the different powers that reigned there before the *Risorgimento*.	paper, pens or markers	1 session 30–40 min.	Lesson 3

Chapter 17 Writing Projects pages 160–161	Materials	🕐	Lesson Link
Newspaper Editorial: For or Against Imperialism 👤 individual Students write newspaper editorials about imperialism.	paper, pens	1 session 30 min.	Lessons 1–3
Journal Entry: Lady-in-Waiting 👤 individual Students write journal entries about the challenges they observe Chinese Empress Ci Xi facing.	paper, pens	1 session 20 min.	Lesson 2
Open Door Policy 👤 individual Students write letters to the editor of a British newspaper either for or against the Open Door Policy in China.	paper, pens	1 session 20 min.	Lesson 2
Journal Entry: An Emperor's Thoughts 👤 individual Students write entries in the journal of the new Japanese ruler Emperor Meiji.	paper, pens	1 session 20 min.	Lesson 2
Compare and Contrast: Two New States 👤 individual Students write articles comparing the two new states of Germany and Italy.	paper, pens	1 session 25 min.	Lesson 3
From Colony to Dominion 👤 individual Students write speeches to be given in the parliament of a new dominion celebrating the country's change in status.	paper, pens	1 session 25 min.	Lesson 3
Chapter 17 Citizenship Project page 162			
Responsibility 👥 whole class Students discuss what they think are the responsibilities of a world power today.	BLM p. 163, paper, pens	1 session 45 min.	Lesson 2

Unit 6 Long-Term Project

Class Newspapers

Who? What? Where? When? How? And, above all, why? Hard-nosed student reporters get the facts about the big events in world history from inventions to revolutions!

Preview and Prepare

Week 1

 whole class 30–45 minutes

Materials: six clipboards, paper, pens

Explain to the students that this unit covers many different time periods, beginning with the Renaissance and the invention of the printing press. With greater availability of books, ideas spread more easily, and more people learned to read. Eventually, the printing press gave birth to the newspaper!

Invite students to sign up for one of the following six groups. Explain that each group will create a newspaper about one of the time periods covered in the unit.

Group 1: the Renaissance and Reformation
Group 2: the Age of Exploration and Early Colonization
Group 3: the first Industrial Revolution and mercantile system
Group 4: the Revolution (American, French, unification of Germany and Italy)
Group 5: the Imperialist era (nineteenth century)
Group 6: the second Industrial Revolution and the Age of Invention (late-nineteenth to early-twentieth century)

Reporters at Work

Week 2

 group 30–45 minutes

Materials: clipboards, assignment sheets, folders, paper, pens, research materials (books, the Internet)

Groups meet. Name an editor for each group who will record reporters' names and assignments on the group's assignment sheet. (The editor should also have a writing assignment.) Groups brainstorm ideas for stories. Then reporters get started researching their assignments and taking notes.

Meeting the Deadline

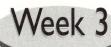 **Week 3**   group   30–45 minutes

Materials: research notes, paper, pens

Groups meet. Individuals write articles based on the notes they took. First drafts are due at the end of this session. Editors are responsible for collecting first drafts and keeping them in a group folder.

Final Drafts and "Layout"

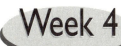 **Week 4**   group   30–45 minutes

Materials: first drafts, paper, pens, dictionaries

Groups meet. Individuals correct first drafts and prepare final drafts with headlines. Students may want to illustrate their stories or make a political cartoon for their newspaper. The editor collects all work. The group decides the "layout" or order of the stories. If it's possible, make several copies of each group's final work. Distribute the newspapers or make them available by displaying them in the classroom. Encourage students to read each other's newspapers.

Roundtable Discussion

 **Week 5**   whole class   30–45 minutes

Materials: none

Hold a roundtable discussion where "editors" and "reporters" from different eras discuss issues that are common to all times.

Making a Difference

What does it take to leave a mark on your time? Stage some scenes in the lives of people who made a difference long ago—and whom we still remember today.

Michelangelo Reflects

Michelangelo was recognized even in his own day as one of the greatest artists of all time. Stage a scene where he reflects back on his life and the people he has known (the Medicis, several popes, and stonecutters). Have him sketching a model as he reflects. Create characters for each of the persons he remembers, and have them appear.

Martin Luther Posts Articles on Church's Door

Martin Luther was very critical of many of the practices of the Roman Catholic Church of his day. In particular, he objected to the selling of indulgences, or pardons, for sins. Stage the scene where he posts his articles, criticisms of the church. The people from the town gather to discuss them. Meanwhile, an indulgence seller has arrived in town. He tries to make some sales. The people give him a piece of their minds.

Louis XVI Meets with the Estates-General

King Louis XVI of France and his wife, Marie Antoinette, have a problem: they need more money! The king calls a meeting of the Estates-General, a group that represents the three classes in France at that time— the priests, the nobles, and everyone else. The king explains he must raise taxes and calls for a vote. The first two estates support the king. The Third Estate representative calls the voting unfair. Have students form the three Estates and state their positions in front of the king and queen.

Father Hidalgo Rings the Bell for Freedom

It is 1810, and a priest named Father Miguel Hidalgo is calling the villagers together in the town square in Dolores, Mexico. As he rings the church bell, the villagers gather. Father Hidalgo encourages them to rise up against the Spanish who have colonized their land. He urges them to struggle for freedom in Mexico. The people raise their fears, and voice their support for his proposal. The word spreads throughout the land.

Roundtable Discussion: Women's Rights

Stage a roundtable discussion with women from the eighteenth century who struggled in different countries for equal rights for women: Marie-Olympe de Gouges (France), Mary Wollstonecraft (England), and Abigail Adams (United States). Have a moderator lead the discussion. Invite the ladies to compare notes. How have recent political events in each country affected the status of women?

Industrial Revolution: Manchester, England

An American journalist visits Manchester, England, during the Industrial Revolution. He or she reports on the "quality of life" in the streets: smoke from the factories, poor sanitation, overcrowded slums. The reporter takes a tour of a textile factory. The owner points out technological innovations in mass production. The reporter notes the poor conditions (light, space, sanitation) and the age of the workers (children). He or she questions the workers about working conditions. What conclusions does the reporter draw about the good and bad aspects of the Industrial Revolution? What will the reporter tell American readers?

Social Studies Plus!

Galileo Points His Telescope at the Stars

Unit 6 Drama Play

Galileo Galilei made some startling discoveries about the true nature of the world. But when he shared his findings he got into trouble with the authorities. Stage some scenes from the life of the great Renaissance scientist.

The Parts: (8 players)
- Galileo
- Brother Paolo Sarpi
- Three Church Fathers
- Father Clavius
- Young Helper

 Director's Notes: The narrator's lines are written in free verse. Practice saying them as naturally as possible.

Use a long paper tube to create a telescope. Mount it on a tripod if possible. On the blackboard, draw a full moon, the Milky Way, and Jupiter with its four moons.

Narrator: In the year of sixteen hundred and nine
A man named Galileo heard
Of a new instrument most fine
That could help the eye see far beyond
what normally an eye can see
on its own.
A clever man, he at once decided
to make his own telescope and to try it
on the stars—
for he had a theory that needed proof:
that the sun did *not* turn around the earth
as everyone believed.
He was quite sure it was the other way around.
The earth turns around the sun!
Let's watch. It will be fun.

(Galileo and Sarpi are climbing the stairs to the roof of Galileo's house.)

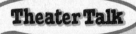 **Theater Talk**

Free verse: poetry that is written without a set rhyme scheme or set meter

142 Unit 6 Drama Play — Social Studies Plus!

Galileo: How are you tonight, Paolo? Can you still climb this many stairs?

Paolo: These old bones can still climb the stairs to see the stars, my friend, here in our independent republic of Venice, where we still allow people to speak and think freely.

Galileo: *(arriving at telescope)* Ah, here we are. Here is my new beauty. This telescope allows us to see what the eye cannot. What would you like to look at?

Paolo: Let's look at the full moon! *(Galileo trains the telescope on the moon, and then steps out of the way.)*

Paolo: *(looking and gasping)* That's amazing!

Galileo: What do you see?

Paolo: Mountains! There are mountains on the moon!

Galileo: *(nodding)* Exactly. The moon is not smooth and flat, as Aristotle says. It has mountains and valleys exactly like Earth has.

Paolo: It does not appear to be giving off its own light.

Galileo: Exactly. That is because the moon has no light of its own. It only reflects the light of the sun.

Paolo: *(looking up from the telescope)* But that means . . .

Galileo: *(nodding)* Exactly. Aristotle is wrong again. What do you see up there? *(Points to the Milky Way.)*

Paolo: *(looking with his eyes)* The Milky Way.

Galileo: And what does it consist of?

Paolo: No one really knows.

Galileo: Have a look. *(Adjusts the telescope and steps away.)*

Paolo: *(looking)* Fantastic!

Galileo: What do you see?

Paolo: Stars! Hundreds and hundreds . . . thousands of stars! It's unbelievable!

Galileo: *Not* unbelievable. How can you *not* believe the evidence of your own eyes? What's unbelievable are Aristotle's theories: that the planets are attached to spheres with fixed spaces between them; that all the planets revolve around Earth.

Social Studies Plus!   Unit 6 Drama Play

Galileo Points His Telescope at the Stars *continued*

Paolo: Be careful, Galileo. The church will criticize you for your ideas.

Galileo: Ideas! Ideas? These are not ideas, Paolo. These are truths. This is reason, supported by proof. Not superstition, or blind tradition based on the writings of an ancient who didn't know what he was talking about.

Paolo: Look, there's Jupiter. Let's have a look at her. *(Galileo adjusts the telescope and steps aside.)*

Paolo: *(looking through the telescope)* There are four points of light around her!

Galileo: Exactly. Jupiter has four moons that revolve around her, exactly as our moon revolves around Earth, just as Earth revolves around the sun. *(They exit.)*

Narrator: The Vatican is in an uproar.
New ideas are spreading that contradict its thought.
To try to stop the spread of this annoying controversy
The Collegio Romano asks Father Clavius
To look into the claims of Galileo.

(Three Church Fathers in a hall in the Vatican.)

Father 1: *(spinning)* Whee! I'm getting dizzy!

Father 2: *(spinning)* The earth is turning!

Father 3: If the earth were turning, don't you think we would feel it?

Father 1: How would we hold on? We'd be falling off!

Father 2: We'd all be sick to our stomachs! *(Fakes nausea.)*

Father 3: Anyway, it's clear. The stars are pinned to the sky. Aristotle said so.

Father 1: Why should we question the wisdom of the ancients?

Father 2: What purpose would it serve?

Clavius: *(enters)* It's true. Galileo's findings are true. I have seen it with my own eyes. *(He exits. The Church Fathers come together in a close circle and exit, speaking in an agitated manner.)*

Narrator: All his life he struggled
To find out the truth.
Then in his old age, he had to choose.
The Church forced him to sign a statement
Denying all his findings—it was that
Or imprisonment
or worse. What could he do?
Here we find Galileo still conducting experiments
With a young helper. He's been under house arrest.
But he doesn't take the time to rest.
There's still so much more to find out!

Galileo: *(old and partly blind, sitting at a table)* Where are those tables for the satellites of Jupiter?

Helper: Here they are, sir. *(Brings him papers.)*

Galileo: With these tables, I can calculate a system that will make it possible for sailors to determine longitude at sea.

Helper: A letter has come in the mail, sir. The Dutch are going to publish your *Discourse on the Two Sciences*.

Galileo: Ahhh, finally.

Helper: And everyone accepts your theory about the tides. About how they are moved by the gravitational force of the moon.

Galileo: Not the Church Fathers. Why else do I sit here confined to my house?

Helper: But the people in the streets know it. Every merchant in the square knows that the speed of falling bodies is proportional to their density, not their weight. You proved that by dropping two stones from the Tower of Pisa. They use your geometric compass to calculate many things. They use your thermoscope to measure temperature and your telescope to see things far away.

Galileo: *(putting down the paper and sighing)* Ah, you give me much hope, my young friend. Perhaps you are right. The world is changing, and it will go on changing, as it goes on turning. Others will follow after me. They will take up the challenge and make new discoveries!

Helper: Yes, we will.

Galileo: Who knows? One day people will even figure out how to fly!

Helper: One day maybe we'll even fly to the stars!

Chapter 15: Short-Term Projects

Painters use new techniques to make lifelike paintings! Explorers find new continents! New inventions and ideas abound! Students work on Renaissance projects that opened people's eyes to look at their world anew.

Renaissance Perspective

individual 30–45 minutes

Materials: paper, pencils

Renaissance painters began to use new techniques to portray people and nature realistically. They used perspective (making faraway objects smaller and closer objects bigger) to create the illusion of distance. They used light and shadow to make figures and objects appear to be three-dimensional. Challenge your students to draw a picture using Renaissance techniques of perspective and light and shadow. Have them explain how these techniques work.

Pages from Leonardo's Notebook

individual 30–45 minutes

Materials: paper, pencils

Leonardo da Vinci was a true Renaissance man. His interests ranged from painting to geometry, from flowers and insects to cannons, from human anatomy to flying machines. Whatever he was working on, he created sketches. Invite students to create their own Renaissance sketchbook of nature studies or new inventions.

Asian Renaissance

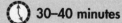

individual 30–40 minutes

Materials: research materials (books, the Internet), paper, colored pencils or tempera paints and paintbrushes

At the same time the Renaissance was spreading throughout Europe, China and Japan were experiencing a cultural renewal of their own. Invite your students to research Kabuki theater of Japan. Challenge them to draw or paint a picture of a Kabuki character. Encourage them to use bright colors and portray the elaborate costuming and stylized mask of a Kabuki performer.

146 Unit 6 Short-Term Projects Social Studies Plus!

Four Corners of the Globe

individual — 30–40 minutes

Materials: research materials, paper, pens, colored pencils or markers

Challenge your students to make an illustrated map in the style of Renaissance mapmakers—showing the four winds and sea monsters! Invite them to show the routes of the Portuguese sea expeditions of Bartholomeu Dias, Vasco da Gama, and Ferdinand Magellan. They may find library or Internet resources useful.

Long Live the Queen!

individual — 30–40 minutes

Materials: paper, colored pencils or markers

Elizabeth I was one of England's most successful rulers. During her long reign, England became one of Europe's major powers. In addition to being a clever judge of character, a political strategist, and a supporter of the arts, Elizabeth also appreciated the importance of wearing the right clothes. Invite your students to research and draw the fashions of Elizabethan times.

The Middle Passage

individual — 30–40 minutes

Materials: paper or oaktag, pens or markers

As colonies grew in North and South America, a large labor force was needed to work in them. People enslaved in Africa were shipped to the Colonies to do forced labor. The terrible sea journey from Africa to the New World was called the Middle Passage. Invite your students to make a storyboard for a movie about life aboard a ship sailing the Middle Passage. Students can choose a character and create the storyboard from the character's perspective.

Remember! Keep working on that Long-Term Project.

Chapter 15 Writing Projects

A variety of writing activities enhances students' appreciation of the Renaissance.

A Missionary with a Mind of His Own

Invite your students to suppose that they are reporters covering the New World for a newspaper back in Europe. Challenge them to accompany the Spanish missionary Bartolomé de las Casas as he makes the rounds on his mission. How is his view of the Native Americans different from the views of other Europeans? How does he put his views into practice? Students write a news article presenting this unusual man and his views that were ahead of his time.

Renaissance Achievements

Challenge your students to summarize the accomplishments of the Renaissance. Invite them to give examples of achievements in some of the following areas: arts and architecture, engineering, technology, politics, philosophy, and exploration. Challenge them to write about some of the consequences of these achievements.

Printing Press vs. Home Computer

Invite your students to compare and contrast two inventions that changed the world: Gutenberg's printing press and the home computer. Each, in its own time, changed the way information could be distributed. In what other ways did these inventions affect how people lived? In what ways are these inventions similar? In what ways are they different? Ask students to write a brief essay.

148 Unit 6 Writing Projects Social Studies Plus!

Counter-Reformation?

Tell your students that they are participating in the Council of Trent, a meeting called by the pope in 1545 to consider a number of reforms. The church is worried about this movement of reform begun by Martin Luther. A lot of people have been leaving the church and joining Luther in a new faith called Protestantism. The pope wants action. Write a report from the Council of Trent about the changes it proposes. Explain why you think these changes will be effective against Luther's movement.

Nine Weeks at Sea: A Pep Talk

It's been nine weeks at sea and still no land in sight. The sailors on the three ships are losing patience. They are afraid. They may encounter sea monsters. They may fall off the edge of the world. On top of all that, food supplies are running low. Invite your students to write a pep talk that Columbus could make to his men. How could he persuade them to keep up their courage—and discipline? What makes him feel sure that land is not far off?

A Queen's Diary

Challenge your students to write an entry in the journal of Queen Elizabeth I of England. Entries may include her private thoughts on the Spanish Armada, Francis Drake, her sister Mary and her Catholic supporters, that playwright William Shakespeare, and why she has chosen to remain single.

SOCIAL STUDIES PLUS! Unit 6 Writing Projects **149**

Chapter 15 Citizenship

Courage

**Courage is a quality shown by many throughout history.
Students discuss the trait and explore its relevance in their own lives.**

In every period, there have been people who have seen beyond the prejudices of their own time. In the Renaissance period, for example, Martin Luther had the courage to speak up against the corruption of the church. Galileo (and before him Copernicus and Giordano Bruno) had the courage to contest the prevailing view of his day that the earth was the center of the universe. Columbus had the courage to believe that the world was round. And in the New World, Las Casas had the courage to speak out for Native Americans and their right to freedom.

Discuss with your class the citizenship trait of courage as it relates to speaking up for what you believe is right, even when it is not a popular view. Have students give examples from history.

Discuss how this trait relates to the lives of your students. For example, students are often subject to peer pressure to dress or behave in a certain way. What does it take to stand up to a group opinion?

Have students find out if there are organizations or programs in your area for dealing with peer pressure. Discuss the information students gather. You may want to have the class act out situations where peer pressure is applied. Encourage your students to show how they can find support from family, teachers, and other students when resisting negative peer pressure. Emphasize that courage often involves finding others to help you deal with problems.

Pass out copies of the blackline master on page 151. Ask students to think of two people who are courageous and tell the class why.

150 Unit 6 Citizenship Project

Social Studies Plus!

The Courage Badge

Award badges of courage to two people. These can be famous people or simply people you know. Tell the class who you chose and why.

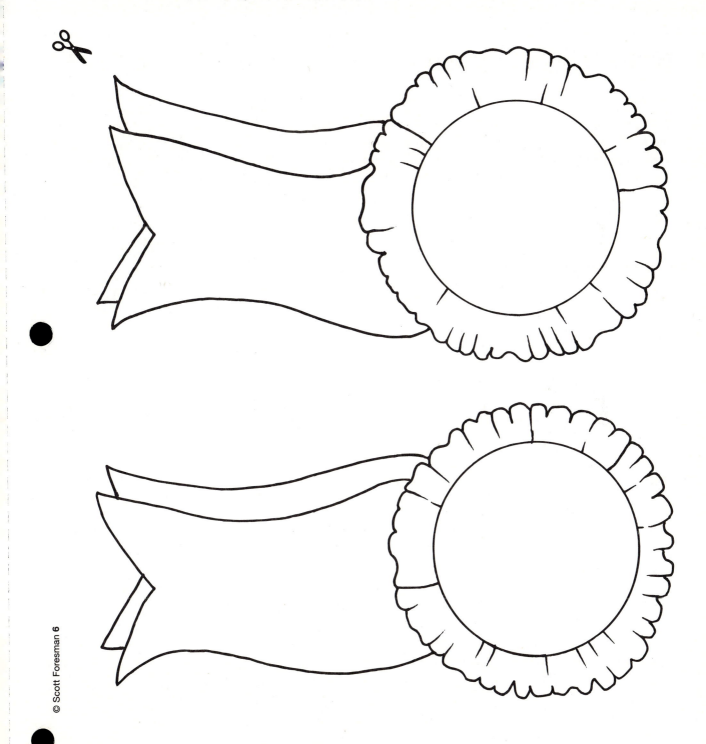

Chapter 16: Short-Term Projects

Political cartoons, posters, music, catalogs!
Students work with different media to portray the way it was—from the American Revolution through the Industrial Revolutions.

Political Cartoon: Patriot or Loyalist? 👤 individual 🕒 30–40 minutes

Materials: paper, pens or markers

Political cartoons—that criticized or made fun of politicians and policies—became a popular form of expressing opinions during the American Revolution. Invite students to draw their own political cartoon about an issue or event in the American Revolution. Remind them to include dialogue, a title, or labels for figures in the drawing so that its meaning is clear to the reader.

Toussaint L'Ouverture: Haitian Hero 👤 individual 🕒 30–40 minutes

Materials: poster paper, markers or colored pencils

Invite your students to make a poster commemorating Toussaint L'Ouverture, the leader of the Haitian revolution for independence from France. L'Ouverture, a former slave, struggled against the harsh colonial treatment of his people. He established the first independent republic in the Caribbean. Even though he was ultimately defeated, his struggle for freedom remains important. Students can use collage to include images from research sources.

Mural: Struggle for Independence 👥 group 🕒 45 minutes

Materials: butcher paper, tempera paints, paintbrushes

Mural art became popular in Latin America as a way of showing all the forces at work in a given historical moment. Usually large, colorful, and displayed in a public place, a mural is a form of storytelling about a people. Challenge students to make a mural about the struggle for independence in Latin America. They can show leaders who made a difference such as Simón Bolivar, José de San Martín, and Bernardo O'Higgins.

Music History: "1812 Overture" whole class 30–45 minutes

Materials: recording of Tchaikovsky's *1812 Overture*, tape or CD player, paper, colored pencils or markers

Napoléon's goal was to restore the Holy Roman Empire. This led him to conquer much of Europe. When his armies invaded Russia, however, the French met their match. French soldiers were not equipped for the harsh Russian winter, and Napoléon could not maintain supply lines across the huge Russian landmass. Russian composer Tchaikovsky commemorated the Russian victory over the French with his *1812 Overture*. Challenge your students to listen to this rousing piece of music and draw a picture in response. How would they portray the booming cannons at the end?

Catalog of New Inventions individual 30–40 minutes

Materials: paper, markers or pencils

Invite students to create a catalog of new inventions of the first and second Industrial Revolutions. Encourage them to label their pictures and give a short description of each invention. Remind students to make their items appear attractive and useful to the consumer. Challenge them to write about how each item can improve the consumer's daily life.

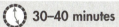

Remember! Keep working on that Long-Term Project.

Assembly-Line Production individual 30–40 minutes

Materials: paper, colored pencils or markers

Invite your students to make a storyboard that illustrates how assembly-line production works. Pioneered by Henry Ford, this technique made it possible to manufacture more items in a shorter period of time than had been possible earlier. (Previously, an item was made from scratch by one individual.) Challenge them to show the assembly line production of a Model T Ford!

Chapter 16: Writing Projects

From the Boston Massacre to Napoléon in exile, there's a lot to write about, and it's a reporter's job to do it. Your students become writers and editors as they cover events in history that changed the world.

Eyewitness Account: The Boston Massacre

What happened on that fateful day when British soldiers confronted an angry mob of colonists in Boston? What were the colonists protesting? What did the colonists do? How did the soldiers react? What was the result of this confrontation? Challenge your students to write an eyewitness account of this important event in the history of the American Revolution.

Editorial: Taxation Without Representation?

Challenge your students to write an editorial for a newspaper expressing either a Patriot or a Loyalist point of view about the issue of taxation. The editorial should express how the writer feels about the fairness of taxation without representation and how the money will be used by England. Invite your students to present a convincing argument to support the side they choose to represent.

All Men Are Created Equal?

The Declaration of Independence says "all men are created equal" and have the same rights to "Life, Liberty, and the Pursuit of Happiness." But were women included in that thought? Did enslaved men and Native American men have the same rights as colonial landholding men? Challenge your students to write a letter to a colonial newspaper explaining why they think the principle of equality described in the Declaration of Independence should extend to everyone.

"We hold these truths to be self-evident . . ."

Journal Entry: The Storming of the Bastille

Invite your students to suppose that they have witnessed the storming of the Bastille, the mob attack on the French prison in Paris in 1789. This event signaled the outbreak of the French Revolution. Challenge your students to choose a point of view to write from: French peasant, French nobleman or noblewoman, or British businessperson. Invite them to use descriptive words to write about the event. Also encourage them to say what they think the consequences of this event will be, from their chosen point of view.

Journal Entry: Napoléon in Exile

Challenge your students to write an entry in the journal of the great French emperor Napoléon as he sits in exile on the island of St. Helena in the Atlantic Ocean, far away from his former empire in Europe. What does he think about? What are his hopes? His fears? How does he occupy his time? What mistakes does he think he has made? What would he change if he could?

Chapter 16 Citizenship

Fairness

Fair treatment under the law: today we assume that we are all entitled to nothing less. But it was not always so.

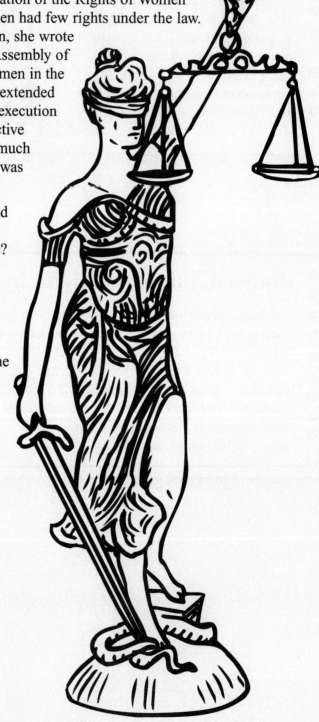

Marie-Olympe de Gouges wrote the Declaration of the Rights of Women and the Female Citizen in 1791, when women had few rights under the law. A strong supporter of the French Revolution, she wrote her own Declaration after the Constituent Assembly of France paid no attention to the rights of women in the Constitution of 1791. Her ideas of fairness extended even to the royal family! She protested the execution of Louis XVI and his family, and the vindictive bloodshed of the Revolution. This was too much for the reigning forces of the time, and she was sentenced to be executed as a traitor.

Discuss with your class ideas of fairness and how they have evolved from earlier times. What was considered fair in ancient Greece? In the Aztec culture? How does culture influence our idea of what is fair? What is considered fair today? Are our ideas of fairness universally accepted? Make copies of the blackline master on page 157 for students. Ask them which of the words in the center they associate with the boxed words.

Discuss these and other issues of fairness.

Name _____   Date _____

Law

Medicine

Fairness

Justice

Equality

Politics

Impartiality

Social Services

Sports

Chapter 17 Short-Term Projects

Imperialism is in full swing. The reigning powers are carving up the world to suit themselves. But new nations are also emerging. Students work on projects that show the scope of the age of imperialism.

Political Cartoon: Berlin Conference
individual   30 minutes

Materials: paper, colored pencils or markers

Challenge your students to make political cartoons about the Berlin Conference in 1884, where European nations divided up Africa among themselves. Remind them that political cartoons often use symbolism to represent nations and concepts. Ask students: How would you represent the European nations? How would you represent Africa? Remind them to label their cartoons or provide dialogue or captions.

Mary Kingsley: Victorian Adventurer
individual   30–45 minutes

Materials: research materials (books or the Internet), paper, pencils or markers

Invite your students to make a comic book based on the real-life story of Mary Kingsley, a Victorian woman who traveled alone through colonial Africa. Remind them that it was highly unusual for a woman to travel anywhere alone at that time. Have them research her life and represent some of her adventures, such as battling a crocodile! Ask them to include how Kingsley came to criticize Great Britain's imperialist policies in Africa in regard to the native people and the natural resources.

Queen Victoria's Diamond Jubilee
individual   30–40 minutes

Materials: research materials (books or the Internet), paper, pens or markers

Students make a picture book for Queen Victoria's Diamond Jubilee, celebrating fifty years of her reign. Students should include some of Victoria's triumphs and defeats during her reign. Challenge your students to portray the British in India during the Opium Wars and in China during the Boxer Rebellion. What were the conflicts about? What goods and products did the British export from the Far East that became common in British households?

158   Unit 6   Short-Term Projects   Social Studies Plus!

Japanese-Style Watercolor

individual   30–40 minutes

Materials: research materials (books, the Internet), watercolor paper, tempera paints, paintbrushes

When U.S. naval officer Matthew Perry sailed warships into a Japanese harbor in 1853, he demanded that Japan's leaders open their ports to trade. The opening of Japan to the West brought changes to both cultures. European and American art was highly influenced by the art of Japanese watercolor and woodcut. The American artist Winslow Homer incorporated some of these techniques into some of his paintings. The techniques included a flattening of perspective, and stylization of color and design. Challenge your students to research the Japanese influence on American nineteenth-century art and create a painting of their own in response.

Remember! Keep working on that Long-Term Project.

Map of Italian Unification

individual   30–40 minutes

Materials: paper, pens or markers

Challenge your students to make an illustrated map of Italy showing the different powers that reigned there before the *Risorgimento* (rising again, or unification). Invite them to use a color-coded system to represent the different powers that ruled over part of Italy. Encourage them to include portraits of the people who led the struggle for Italian unification.

Nineteenth-Century Military Costumes

individual   30–45 minutes

Materials: research materials (books, the Internet), paper, pens

Challenge your students to make a catalog of military uniforms of the nineteenth century. These could include Napoleonic, Prussian, British, Indian, and Italian uniforms. Encourage students to label their pictures.

Chapter 17 Writing Projects

Imperialism, westernization, nationalism, and unification—these ideas and others change the rules of the power game in the nineteenth and early-twentieth centuries. Find out what your writers have to say about these historical forces.

Newspaper Editorial: For or Against Imperialism

What's the scoop on nineteenth–century imperialism? Is it simply a way to satisfy supply and demand for products and raw materials? Is it the destiny of the weaker nations to submit to the stronger ones? Is it a question of who has the more advanced technology? Is it an unfair system that exploits people and nations? Challenge your students to choose sides in the debate about imperialism and write a newspaper editorial supporting their position.

Journal Entry: Lady-in-Waiting

Invite your students to suppose themselves to be a lady-in-waiting in the royal court of Chinese Empress Ci Xi. Invite them to write an entry in their journals about the challenges they observe the empress facing. It's well known that she wants to keep all foreigners out of China. But the Europeans have set up what they call an Open Door Policy. The empress is furious. She fears losing control of her own country. What do students think will happen next?

Open Door Policy

Invite your students to write a letter to the editor of a British newspaper either defending or opposing the Open Door Policy in China. Ask them to choose a point of view: British merchant or Chinese representative of the empress. What reasons can they give to support their position?

Journal Entry: An Emperor's Thoughts

The new Japanese ruler Emperor Meiji has just ascended to the throne. Unlike the rulers who came before him, Meiji is very interested in everything Western. He thinks Japan can benefit from modernizing and exchanging ideas with the West. Invite students to take on his point of view and write an entry in his journal. What kind of future does he foresee for his country? What steps is he planning to take to make changes in Japan? Why does he think change is necessary?

Compare and Contrast: Two New States

Invite students to suppose that they are the European foreign correspondent for a U.S. newspaper. Challenge them to write an article comparing the two new states of Germany and Italy. How were their struggles for unification similar? How were they different? What is similar about the new states that were created? What is different? What role do students think each of these states will play in the new Europe?

From Colony to Dominion

Great Britain is being pressured by its colonies for more self-rule. In 1867, the British parliament votes to change the status of Canada from a colony to a dominion. Canada can now elect its own legislature and rule itself. Australia becomes a dominion in 1901. New Zealand becomes one in 1907.
Challenge your students to write a speech to be given in the parliament of one of these new dominions celebrating that country's change in status. What does the change represent? What are the benefits? How will the country remain connected to Great Britain?

Chapter 17 Citizenship

Responsibility

In 1905, U.S. President Theodore Roosevelt brokered a peace treaty between Japan and Russia. He later won a Nobel Peace Prize for ending the war between those two countries. The United States was just beginning to understand its responsibility as a world power.

Challenge your students to discuss what they think are the responsibilities of a world power today. Make a list of student responses.

Establish a newspaper project. Invite the class to look for articles in the daily newspapers about ways in which the United States functions as a world power today. Invite students to bring in the articles, and discuss them with the class. Create an exhibition of these newspaper articles (on a bulletin board) labeled "Responsibilities of a World Power."

Discuss how the end of the cold war affected the role of the United States in the world. During the cold war, which two countries were the most powerful?

Discuss how smaller countries are working together today to pool their resources and power. How successful are they? Ask your students what new world powers might emerge in the future.

Most world powers of the past were empires ruled by conquerors, kings, or dictators. Discuss what makes a democratic world power different from, say, the Roman Empire, the empire established by Genghis Khan, or another of the empires the students have studied.

Use the blackline master on page 163 to point out that students have responsibilities too. Divide the class into groups. Cut out the blackline master categories, and put them into a bag (or box).

How to play (for small groups):

One person from each group pulls one category from the bag. Then each person in the group tells how he or she is responsible in the chosen category.

Social Studies Plus!   Unit 6   **Blackline Master**   **163**

Teacher Planner

Long-Term Project pages 166–167	Materials	⏱	Lesson Link
Face the Press Students call together some of the major players of the twentieth century and question them about their moments in history.			Lessons 1–3
Week 1 whole class Students brainstorm some of the major events and people from the twentieth century.	clipboard, paper, pens	1 session 30–45 min.	
Week 2 group Students research one figure or group from the twentieth century.	index cards, pens or pencils, research materials	1 session 30–45 min.	
Week 3 group Students use their notes to role-play a scene.	group note cards, pencils	1 session 30–45 min.	
Week 4 group Students go before the class and act out their scenes.	same as those for Week 3	1 session 30–45 min.	

Unit Drama pages 168–173			
Scenarios: A World in Opposition group Students role-play skits about the world in opposition during the twentieth century.	props (optional)	4 sessions 35 min. each	Lesson 2
Play: The Home Front group Students perform a play about the impact of World War II on family life.	props, costumes (optional)	1 session 1½ hr.	Lessons 2–3

Chapter 18 Short-Term Projects pages 174–175			
On the Eve of the Great War individual Students make world maps showing the colonial possessions of the European powers on the eve of World War I.	research materials, paper, various art supplies	1 session 30–45 min.	Lesson 1
European Royals individual Students make books about the European royal families on the eve of World War I.	research materials, paper, colored pencils, or markers	1 session 30–45 min.	Lesson 1
Parallel Time Lines individual Students make parallel time lines for Europe and the United States during World War I.	research materials; paper; pens, pencils, or markers	1 session 30–45 min.	Lesson 2
World War I Aircraft individual Students research and make a book about different kinds of aircraft used in World War I.	research materials; paper; pens, pencils, or markers	1 session 30–45 min.	Lesson 2
Poster Art: Comrades Unite! individual Students research early Soviet-style poster art and make their own posters about the Russian Revolution.	research materials, copier, various art supplies	1 session 30–45 min.	Lesson 2
League of Nations individual Students create emblems for the League of Nations.	paper, colored pencils or markers	1 session 30–45 min.	Lesson 3

Chapter 18 Writing Projects pages 176–177	Materials	🕐	Lesson Link
Target Skill: Cause and Effect 👤 individual Students write news analyses of the causes and effects of the assassination of the archduke and his wife in Sarajevo.	paper, pencils	1 session 30 min.	Lesson 1
Journal Entry: Soldier in the Trenches 👤 individual Students write entries in the journal of a World War I soldier.	paper, pencils	1 session 20 min.	Lesson 2
Letter Home 👤 individual Students write letters home from volunteer nurses in the war describing daily life.	paper, pencils	1 session 20 min.	Lesson 2
Newspaper Editorial: On the Sinking of the Lusitania 👤 individual Students write a newspaper editorial about the sinking of the British ship.	paper, pencils	1 session 30 min.	Lesson 2
Biography: Wilfred Owen, Poet 👤 individual Students write biographies of Wilfred Owen.	paper, pencils	1 session 30 min.	Lesson 2
Letter to the Editor 👤 individual Students write letters to the editor of a newspaper expressing their opinions on Woodrow Wilson's proposal.	paper, pencils	1 session 20 min.	Lesson 3

Chapter 18 Citizenship Project page 178			
Fairness 👤👤👤 whole class Students find out about the city of Geneva and its long history of promoting fairness.	paper, pencils, research materials	1 session 45 min.	Lesson 3

Chapter 19 Short-Term Projects pages 180–181			
Map Skills: Axis Invasion 👤 individual Students draw a map of Europe showing the lands conquered by the Axis powers.	research materials; paper; pens, pencils, or markers	1 session 30–40 min.	Lesson 1
Poster Art: Propaganda 👤👤👤 group Students create posters that use the techniques of propaganda to get across a positive message.	research materials, poster paper, colored pens or markers	1 session 30–40 min.	Lesson 2
Recruiting Poster 👤 individual Students make recruitment posters encouraging women to work in factories or join the United States war effort.	poster paper, colored markers or pencils	1 session 45 min.	Lesson 2
"Life" Magazine Cover 👤 individual Students draw pictures for the cover of *Life* magazine in realistic photographic style.	paper, colored pencils	1 session 30–40 min.	Lesson 2
World War II Memorial 👤 individual Students design memorials for people who died in World War II.	paper, colored pencils or markers	1 session 30–40 min.	Lesson 3
Universal Declaration of Rights 👤 individual Students document what they think are the basic human rights of all people.	BLM p. 185, paper, pens	1 session 30 min.	Lesson 3

Unit 7 Teacher Planner

Chapter 19 Writing Projects pages 182–183	Materials	⏱	Lesson Link
Letter to Anne Frank 👤 individual Students write letters to Anne Frank telling her how they feel about protests for peace in the world today.	paper, pencils	1 session 25 min.	Lesson 1
News Article: Stock Market Crash 👤 individual Students write eyewitness accounts from the floor of the stock market or the streets of New York on Black Tuesday.	paper, pencils	1 session 25 min.	Lesson 1
To Appease or Not to Appease? 👤 individual Students write letters to Chamberlain either supporting or criticizing appeasement.	paper, pencils	1 session 20 min.	Lesson 1
Journal Entry: The London Blitz 👤 individual Students write journal entries conveying the sights, sounds, and feelings of London during the Battle of Britain.	paper, pencils	1 session 20 min.	Lessons 1–2
Diplomatic Pouch 👤 individual Students write dispatches to the home office reporting on their observations.	paper, pencils	1 session 20 min.	Lesson 2
World War II: Effects and Causes 👤 individual Students write brief essays about the effects of World War II and what caused them.	paper, pencils	1 session 30 min.	Lesson 3

Chapter 19 Citizenship Project page 184			
Courage 👥👥 whole class Students write about Sadako's courage and what her story means to them.	paper, pencils	1 session 45 min.	Lesson 3

Chapter 20 Short-Term Projects pages 186–187			
Diorama: "Viking 1" 👤 individual Students create dioramas of the Mars landing of *Viking 1*.	shoe boxes, clay, pipe cleaners, tempera paints and brushes	1 session 30–40 min.	Lesson 1
Person of the Year 👤 individual Students choose a man or woman of the year for the cold war period and then create a magazine cover honoring him or her.	paper; colored pens, pencils, or markers	1 session 30–40 min.	Lessons 1–3
Cultural Revolution Comic Book 👤 individual Students create comic books about the Cultural Revolution in China.	paper, markers or pens	1 session 30–45 min.	Lesson 2
Two Sides of a Conflict: Vietnam 👤 individual Students make two-paneled posters that show the two sides of the Vietnam War debate.	collage materials, paper, colored pencils or markers	1 session 30–45 min.	Lesson 3
Energy Crisis Collage 👤 individual Students make a collage about the energy crisis and possible solutions.	pictures from magazines, paper, glue, scissors, markers	1 session 30–45 min.	Lesson 3
Health Craze Collage 👤 individual Students make collages about Americans' new concern for their health.	magazine pictures, scissors, glue, poster paper, markers	1 session 30–45 min.	Lesson 3

165A Unit 7 Teacher Planner Social Studies Plus!

Chapter 20 Writing Projects pages 188–189	Materials	🕐	Lesson Link
Eyewitness Report: The Cultural Revolution individual Students file a journalist's report from the midst of the Cultural Revolution in China.	paper, pencils	1 session 30 min.	Lesson 2
Cold War Biography individual Students research and write biographies of prominent people who defected from a Communist country.	paper, pencils	1 session 30 min.	Lesson 3
Domino Effect individual Students write speeches explaining Johnson's domino theory to the American public.	paper, pencils	1 session 20 min.	Lesson 3
Policy Paper: Vietnamization individual Students write policy papers for the president about a plan for *Vietnamization*.	paper, pencils	1 session 25 min.	Lesson 3
Pen Pals individual Students write letters to Vietnamese boys or girls their own age as if they were pen pals.	paper, pencils	1 session 20 min.	Lesson 3
Reporter's Journal: Détente individual Students write as if they are journalists traveling with President Nixon on his landmark journey to China.	paper, pencils	1 session 25 min.	Lesson 3
Chapter 20 Citizenship Project page 190			
Honesty whole class Students create a list of questions for a survey on the importance of history.	paper, pencils, BLM p. 191	1 session 45 min.	Lesson 3

# Unit 7 Long-Term Project

Face the Press

What if you could call together some of the major players of the twentieth century and question them about their moments in history? Your students can—with this Long-Term Project.

Week 1 — Preview and Prepare

 whole class   30–45 minutes

Materials: clipboard, paper, pens

Advance Preparation: *Copy and hand out the blackline master on page 179.*

To begin, preview the unit with your class. Explain that it covers most of the twentieth century. Ask students what some of the major events are from the twentieth century and who was associated with each event. Have them record all the major figures that come out of this brainstorming session on the blackline master. People mentioned might include Queen Victoria, Kaiser Wilhelm II, Vladimir Lenin, Woodrow Wilson, Emperor Hirohito, Joseph Stalin, Winston Churchill, Franklin D. Roosevelt, Eleanor Roosevelt, Douglas MacArthur, Harry Truman, Anne Frank, Nikita Khrushchev, John F. Kennedy, Mao Ze-dong, Richard Nixon, and Lyndon Johnson. (Or have students name groups of people, such as World War I nurses, World War II fighter pilots, Korean refugees, or Vietnam War protesters.)

Week 2 — Research and Reflect

 group   30–45 minutes

Materials: index cards, pens or pencils, research materials (textbook, other books, the Internet)

Divide the class into groups. Explain that each group will research one figure or group from the twentieth century. Students read and take notes on index cards about the person or group. Encourage them to organize their notes by subject on the cards (they can write the subject at the top of the card). The group then assembles its cards.

Week 3 — Creating the Questions

group · 30–45 minutes

Materials: group note cards, pencils

Invite your class to consider how journalism has influenced the way in which we learn about the events of the world. Explain that each group will use its notes to role-play a scene. Each group chooses students to play the person or people the group has researched as well as the advisors' roles. Others will play journalists. Challenge each group to create a list of questions by reviewing its notes. Each group pools its questions and writes them on index cards for journalists to use.

Week 4 — Asking the Questions

group · 30–45 minutes

Materials: same as those for Week 3

Set up a table and chairs for the role-playing scenes. One at a time, groups go before the class and role-play their scenes. The person or people sit in the middle next to the advisors. The journalists pose their questions. The figures can consult with aides before answering, or invite aides to answer. Aides can also refer to their notes. Afterward, the group may choose to open up the forum to the public (rest of class), and invite questions from the public.

Unit 7 Drama Scenarios: A World in Opposition

From life in the trenches to life in the streets, the twentieth century is on the move. And everywhere, people have something to say. Stage some scenes from a world in opposition.

Life in the Trenches

Create "trenches" by making two parallel rows of desks. Arrange them so the audience can look down the row and watch the scene. Research life for the soldiers during World War I. What was a typical day in the trenches? What did soldiers eat? Did they get mail? How? What happened when the enemy attacked? What do you think they talked about? Where were the soldiers from? How long had they been in the trenches? What did they think their chances were of ever going home? What did they think that war was about? What was the news from home? Create a realistic scene and act it out.

March 1917: Revolution in Moscow

It's 1917 and the Russian army has suffered huge casualties on the eastern front. The economy has collapsed. Food and fuel are limited. On top of it all, the people are fed up with a government that denies them personal freedoms. The soldiers have joined the citizens to overthrow the czar! Communists, led by Lenin, are promising peace, bread, and land to all citizens. Stage a scene as the people march and revolt. Have a journalist conduct on-the-street interviews with different people such as a peasant, a soldier, a shopkeeper, an aristocrat, and a student. Does everyone feel the same? Why are the masses revolting? What do they want?

Secret Meeting in the North Atlantic

In August 1941, U.S. President Franklin Roosevelt met secretly with British Prime Minister Winston Churchill aboard a ship in the North Atlantic. The meeting was crucial for many reasons. Roosevelt knew his country would have to join the war and was already laying the groundwork for U.S. involvement, but the American public was not yet convinced. Churchill desperately needed U.S. support. What did the two talk about? How did they get along? Did they like each other? What were their feelings about Stalin? Could they trust him? Would the U.S. public support the president and enter the war? Ask students to research the Atlantic Charter and stage a meeting between the two great leaders.

Sent to Work in the Fields: The Chinese Cultural Revolution

Ask students to suppose they live in the Chinese capital of Beijing and go to school. They are very good students and hope one day to go to the university. But the Cultural Revolution has come. To change the country, the leaders say, people have to learn to work with their hands. Students are taken away from their families and sent to work in the fields. The work is long and the living conditions are very primitive. Ask students: You want to support your country, but are you worried about your family? What is happening to them back in the city? Are you beginning to have doubts about this Cultural Revolution? Whom can you talk to? What can you do? Stage scenes in the life of a young person in China during the Cultural Revolution.

The Home Front

Unit 7 Drama Play

Students gain insights about the impact of World War II on family life by acting out some scenes.

The Parts: (5 players)
- Mother
- Billy, little brother
- Radio Announcer
- Alice, older sister
- Frannie, little sister

 Director's Notes: Make a stand-up picture of an old-fashioned radio with knobs. Place it on a kitchen table. Seat the radio announcer at a second table with a "microphone" made from tin foil. Find a recording of 1940s dance music such as Count Basie or Benny Goodman, for example.

Invite someone to write an essay about freedom to use as Frannie's speech/essay at the end of the play.

(Mother is cooking dinner. Billy and Frannie sit at the kitchen table doing their homework. Alice comes in from outside.)

Alice: Hey, how about some music around here? *(Turns on the radio. Some 1940s dance music is heard.)* Hey, Billy, let's dance.

Mother: Let Billy alone, he's got to finish his homework.

Alice: How about you, Sis?

Frannie: I've got to finish my essay.

Alice: Nobody wants to dance with me. *(Picks up the broom.)* How about you, sir? Would you like to dance? *(Dances with the broom.)*

Billy: Hey, Alice, how many battleships did you girls build today at work?

Alice: *(turning off the radio and siting at the table)* You don't build a whole battleship in a day, silly. We build one destroyer escort and two landing craft every week.

170 Unit 7 Drama Play Social Studies Plus!

Billy: How do you build them?

Alice: I go down forty feet into the bottom of the ship because I'm a tacker. I hold the welding rod with one hand and the torch fire in the other, like this. *(Demonstrates.)* You put the rod where two metal plates meet and melt the steel till you seam it. Then you brush it off with a steel brush. It's just like crocheting.

Frannie: I wish I were old enough to work in the shipyard like you, Alice. I want to do something for the war effort too.

Mother: You all do lots of things for the war effort, Frannie.

Frannie: Like what?

Billy: I collect tin and rubber and old toothpaste tubes.

Frannie: What good will they do?

Alice: The government needs as much tin and rubber and aluminum as we can get, Frannie. To build new planes and tanks.

Mother: And what about our Victory Garden, Frannie?

Frannie: Well, if you can win a war by growing fruit and vegetables, I guess we'll win. We had a bumper crop of zucchini in the summer, and the apple tree has never had so many apples as this fall. I thought we'd never get them all canned.

Alice: What's for dinner, anyway? All this talk of food is making me hungry.

Mother: I saved up a few coupons from our ration book and bought us a fine piece of meat today at the butcher. He saved it for me. So we'll have a pot roast tonight with broiled potatoes. And then we got our two-week ration coupons today for butter and sugar, so guess what? With some of Frannie's delicious canned apples, I made an apple pie—for dessert!

Alice: Meat for dinner and apple pie for dessert! Mother, what are we celebrating? Did you get a letter from Wally?

Mother: Yes, I did.

Alice, Billy, and Frannie: What does he say? What does he say?

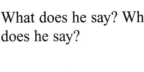

The Home Front *continued*

Mother: *(taking the letter out of her apron pocket and reading)* Dear Mother, Alice, Frannie, and Billy, I'm writing to you from my berth (that's what sailors call a bed) on the ship. We've been (censored) weeks at sea now.

Billy: *(interrupting)* How many weeks?

Frannie: That's the part they've censored. You know, the sailors' letters get censored to make sure they don't reveal any information if the letter falls into enemy hands.

Alice: Hush, let Mother read the letter.

Mother: *(reading)* We saw some action yesterday. A *(censored)* ship suffered a direct hit. We picked up a bunch of the crew out of the water and returned them to their fleet. I had to get them some dry clothes, and then the captain sent me over to deliver them. To thank us for saving his men, their captain gave us some ice cream from their stores and we exchanged some movies. Boy, we were getting tired of watching the same movies over and over, so tonight we're all looking forward to some ice cream and a new movie. Rita Hayworth, I hope.

Gee, speaking of food, I sure miss your cooking, Mother. Our ship's cook does the best he can, but it sure doesn't measure up to one of your pot roasts with potatoes, and a hot apple pie for dessert!

(Entire family stops eating and looks at one another.)

Mother: *(reading)* I sure wish I were sitting at the kitchen table with you all right now, having dinner together.

Frannie: We wish you were here right now, too, Wally!

Mother: *(reading)* Hey, Billy, how many pounds of tin and aluminum have you collected? I'm real proud of you. And, Alice, keep up the good work. You and the girls are building the ships that will bring us home. Frannie, how's that Victory Garden of yours? Mother, don't worry about me. I'm fine and healthy, and watching out for myself. That's all I got time for now. I'm on the next watch. Love to you all, Wally.

Billy: Gee, ice cream and movies. It must be fun to be a sailor.

Alice: It's a lot of hard work, Billy. Wally only tells us about the good parts, so we won't worry so much.

Mother: It's time for the news. Turn on the radio. *(Billy turns it on. All lean close and listen.)*

Radio Announcer: And now it's time for the news. In Europe: Allied forces are beginning to turn back the German army in Belgium. The fighting is fierce in what soldiers are calling the Battle of the Bulge. But Allied forces are determined. Germany's army is being battered on the ground, and its cities pounded from the air.

In the Pacific: American marines have landed at Iwo Jima. Reports from the area say there is fierce fighting and heavy losses on both sides. General MacArthur is reported to be ready to return to the Philippines.

Meanwhile, President Roosevelt has flown to Yalta, in the Crimea, to meet with British Prime Minister Winston Churchill, and Russian ruler Joseph Stalin. They are said to be planning strategies for the final phases of the war. The Big Three have also called for a meeting of all the world's nations in San Francisco in April to form a world peacekeeping organization called the United Nations.

And now for a word from our sponsors . . .

Mother: *(turning off radio)* Perhaps it *will* be over soon.

Frannie: The United Nations! Now I know how I'll end my essay.

Alice: What are you working on, Frannie?

Mother: Her teacher invited her to submit an essay to an essay contest.

Mother: What's the subject?

Frannie: *(writing)* Freedom. *(Finishes writing.)* Do you want to hear what I wrote?

All: Yes!

Frannie: *(starting to read)* What Freedom Means to Me . . .

Chapter 18: Short-Term Projects

The Great War (World War I) was a bloody, brutal conflict that affected millions of lives all around the world. These short-term projects bring students to terms with facts and themes from this time.

On the Eve of the Great War

individual   30–45 minutes

Materials: research materials; paper; markers, colored pencils or tempera paint and paintbrushes

Challenge your students to make world maps showing the colonial possessions of the European powers on the eve of World War I. Ask them to color-code the maps and include keys. Invite them to present their work to the class and point out the size and extent of each European country's empire. Ask students: How did competition for colonial holdings play a role in the outbreak of war?

European Royals

individual   30–45 minutes

Materials: research materials, paper, colored pencils or markers

Invite your students to make books about the European royal families on the eve of World War I. Have them draw portraits of royal family members and label pictures with the person's name and country. They can include the family's crest or coat of arms and may also want to show the costumes of the times. Can students tell how these families were interrelated?

Parallel Time Lines

individual   30–45 minutes

Materials: research materials; paper; colored pens, pencils, or markers

Challenge your students to make parallel time lines for Europe and the United States during World War I. Battles were raging in Europe. What was going on in the United States? Invite them to include domestic developments in politics, science, the arts, and technology. Students may want to illustrate their time lines. Hang the parallel time lines up next to one another in the classroom.

World War I Aircraft

 individual   30–45 minutes

Materials: research materials; paper; colored pens, pencils, or markers

One of the technological innovations of World War I was aircraft. For the first time, airplanes were used in combat for reconnaissance, spying, and fighting. Some very famous battles took place in the air. Ask students to research and make a book about different kinds of aircraft used in World War I. Invite students to label their drawings with the names and use for each aircraft.

Poster Art: Comrades Unite!

 individual   30–45 minutes

Materials: research materials, copier, paper, scissors, glue, markers or colored pencils

During the Russian Revolution, artists were looking for new ways to present the events and ideas of a new age. The constructivist style was born, featuring the use of bold block letters, photomontage (collage using newspaper photos and headlines), and skewed perspectives. Challenge your students to research early Soviet-style poster art and invite each student to make a poster about the Russian Revolution in the constructivist style.

Remember! Keep working on that Long-Term Project.

League of Nations

 individual   30–45 minutes

Materials: paper, colored pencils or markers

President Woodrow Wilson called for a League of Nations to be created after World War I to help prevent future wars. The League of Nations did, in fact, come into being, but the U. S. never joined. Challenge your students to create emblems for the League of Nations. What symbols would they choose to represent this organization? What words or motto could they add?

Chapter 18: Writing Projects

They called it the Great War. Its costs in lives and destruction were huge. What were the underlying causes and the far-reaching effects? Students write from many of points of view about World War I.

Target Skill: Cause and Effect

The Archduke Ferdinand of Austria-Hungary and his wife have just been assassinated in Sarajevo! Who is responsible? Why did they do it? What will be the consequences? Invite your students to write news analyses of the causes and effects of this unexpected event that sparked the beginning of World War I.

Journal Entry: Soldier in the Trenches

The hours are long for a soldier in the trenches. There's plenty of time to write in a journal. Challenge your students to write entries in the journal of a World War I soldier. Encourage them to picture daily life in the trenches. How do the soldiers pass the time? Where are they located? What part of the war are they in? Have they seen any action? Have there been losses? Where are their homes? How long have they been in the war? How long do they think it will go on?

Letter Home

Invite your students to think of themselves as volunteer nurses in World War I. Challenge them to decide which theater of war they have been sent to. Invite them to write letters home describing daily life. What kinds of casualties are they treating? Do they have enough supplies? Are they glad they volunteered?

Newspaper Editorial: On the Sinking of the Lusitania

The Germans have sunk the British ship, the *Lusitania*. Nearly 1,200 died, including 128 Americans. Now that Americans have lost their lives, public opinion in the U.S. is leaning toward war. Up until now, the American public has favored staying out of Europe's conflict. Invite your students to write a newspaper editorial either supporting or opposing the entry of the United States into World War I. Challenge students to give reasons for their position.

Letter to the Editor

The Great War is over! The armistice has been signed. Now U.S. President Woodrow Wilson is traveling to France to present the Fourteen Points, his plan for a just and lasting peace in Europe. His position is that no one country should be singled out and punished for the war, or this will cause a lasting bitterness that may give way to future conflicts. French leader Georges Clemenceau and the French people do not agree. They want to punish Germany and weaken it, so it will never again threaten France. Challenge your students to write letters to the editor of a newspaper expressing their opinions on Wilson's proposal.

Biography: Wilfred Owen, Poet

Wilfred Owen was one of the generation of young men who fought in World War I. After being wounded, he was sent to the Craiglockhart War Hospital. There he began writing poetry about his experiences at the front. He edited a hospital literary journal called *The Hydra*. Sent back to the front, he died shortly before the armistice was declared. Invite your students to research and write a short biography of this man who wrote some of the most moving poetry to come out of World War I. Encourage them to read some of his poems.

Chapter 18 Citizenship

Fairness

At the Paris Conference in 1919, Geneva was chosen as the headquarters for the newly formed League of Nations. Why was the city of Geneva chosen?

Geneva has long been known as a city of fairness. A very old city (mentioned in the writings of Julius Caesar), it was situated at the crossroads of important trade routes and soon gained a reputation as a place of fair trade. During the Reformation, reformer John Calvin made it his home. It then became a place of refuge for Huguenots and other victims of religious persecution. During the eighteenth century, two of the greatest humanist philosophers, Rousseau and Voltaire, made Geneva their home and wrote many of their works there.

In 1863, a Geneva citizen named Jean-Henri Dunant founded the International Committee for Relief to the Wounded in Time of War, which later became the International Red Cross. (Clara Barton, the American Civil War nurse, founded the American Red Cross soon after.)

The first Geneva Convention, signed in 1864, established the concept of fairness in war, with protocols for the protection of wounded and captured soldiers and civilians. Several other Geneva conventions have been signed since then, and these protocols continue to uphold the international rights of people during war.

Challenge your class to find out about the city of Geneva and its long history of promoting fairness.

Name _____ Date _____

Major Events of Twentieth Century

List major events of the twentieth century below. Next to each event, write the names of major figures who were associated with the event.

_____

_____

_____

_____

_____

_____

_____

_____

_____

_____

_____

_____

_____

_____

Chapter 19: Short-Term Projects

Less than twenty years after the end of World War I, the world was at war again. Challenge your students to find out why with these short-term projects.

Map Skills: Axis Invasion

 individual 🕐 30–40 minutes

Materials: research materials; paper; colored pens, pencils, or markers

The Axis powers (Germany and Italy) invaded many lands in their effort to expand their territory and create a new empire. Challenge each student to draw a map of Europe showing the lands conquered by the Axis powers. Encourage students to label and color-code their maps and include keys.

Poster Art: Propaganda

 group 🕐 30–40 minutes

Materials: research materials, poster paper, colored pens or markers

The use of propaganda reached new heights during World War II. The Nazi regime used propaganda to spread prejudice and lies. Propaganda can also be used to shape opinion in a positive way. Challenge your students to create posters that use the techniques of propaganda to get across a positive message. They may want to research the photomontage counterpropaganda art of John Heartfield, the German artist who made many posters exposing the lies of the Nazi regime.

Recruiting Poster

 individual 🕐 45 minutes

Materials: poster paper, colored markers or pencils

Invite your students to make recruitment posters encouraging women to work in factories or join the United States war effort. Invite them to research World War II posters showing Rosie the Riveter, the character who represented women who worked in factories while the men were off at war.

"Life" Magazine Cover

individual — 30–40 minutes

Materials: paper, colored pencils

Life magazine, started in 1936 by publisher Henry Luce, quickly became one of America's most popular weekly news journals. Its covers were usually photographs by leading photographers of the day that captured important moments in time. Invite your students to design and create magazine covers for a person or event of World War II. Challenge them to draw pictures in realistic photographic style.

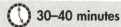

Remember! Keep working on that Long-Term Project.

World War II Memorial

individual — 30–40 minutes

Materials: paper, colored pencils or markers

What is the purpose of a memorial? Usually we want to remember and honor people who died. But the *way* different artists choose to remember can cause controversy. Invite your students to design memorials for people who died in World War II. These could be for people who died in combat (soldiers) or civilians. They could be designs for realistic statues or monuments or abstract designs to represent peace.

Universal Declaration of Rights

individual — 30 minutes

Materials: blackline master (page 185), paper, pens

As the U.S. delegate to the newly created United Nations, Eleanor Roosevelt took part in writing a Universal Declaration of Human Rights. Since then, the UN has sponsored declarations on basic economic, social, and cultural rights, and on the rights of children. Challenge your students to document what they think are the basic human rights of all people. Encourage them to name their documents and ask them to create emblems for the top. Use the copied blackline master.

Chapter 19 Writing Projects

From the Depression to another war, difficult times loom. Analysis is needed to understand mistakes of the past. Can we avoid them in the future? Writers wrestle with important ideas.

News Article: Stock Market Crash

What happened on October 29, 1929? As investors lost confidence in the stock market, the orders to sell stocks flooded in that morning. Within the first few hours, prices fell so far as to wipe out all the gains that had been made in the previous year. This was the beginning of the crash and the Depression that lasted many years. Challenge your students to write eyewitness accounts from the floor of the stock market or the streets of New York on the day that became known as Black Tuesday.

To Appease or Not to Appease?

British Prime Minister Neville Chamberlain has just returned with a freshly signed agreement from a meeting in Munich with Adolf Hitler. It says that Great Britain and her allies will let Germany take over Czechoslovakia. In return, Hitler promises not to take any more territory in Europe. Chamberlain is greeted by many as a hero. His policy, called appeasement, will avoid war in Europe, or so he believes. Invite students to write letters to Chamberlain either supporting or criticizing appeasement. Do they believe this policy will work? Why or why not?

Diplomatic Pouch

Ask students to suppose they are U.S. diplomats to Japan in the 1930s who carefully watch the political moves of Emperor Hirohito. They see the Japanese government encouraging the rise of nationalism and the worship of the emperor. Challenge your students to write dispatches to the home office reporting on their observations. What predictions can they make about Japan's plans for the future?

Journal Entry: The London Blitz

Invite your students to suppose they are living in London during the Battle of Britain. The Germans are bombing London night and day. But the Londoners are plucky. How do they keep up their courage? Where do they go for protection? Encourage students to use descriptive language to convey the sights, sounds, and feelings of this period in a journal entry.

World War II: Effects and Causes

The world paid a terrible toll for the conflicts that were settled by World War II. What were some of the effects of that terrible struggle? Ask students to write brief essays about the effects and what caused them. Challenge your students to look at short-term and long-term effects. Are we still feeling some of the effects of World War II today? In what ways? Ask students to give specific examples.

Letter to Anne Frank

Most people know the story of Anne Frank, a Jewish girl who went into hiding with her family in Holland during World War II. After living in an attic for two years, the Franks were discovered and sent to concentration camps, where most of the family died. Anne's father survived and, after the war, returned to the attic where they had hidden. He found a diary that Anne had kept during their period in hiding. The book was published and read by people all over the world. Invite your students to write letters to Anne Frank telling her how they feel about prospects for peace in the world today. Challenge them to write about the contributions they think children can make to peace. Invite them to talk about the effect the diary has had on people all over the world.

Chapter 19 Citizenship

Courage

More than fifty years ago, a Japanese girl named Sadako began folding paper cranes. She wanted to fold a thousand. According to legend, whoever folds a thousand cranes will have good health.

Sadako Sasaki was only two years old when the atomic bomb was dropped on Hiroshima. Although she suffered no immediate injury, the effects of the exposure caught up with her eventually. At the age of twelve, she was battling leukemia from exposure to radiation. In the course of her courageous battle, she folded 644 origami cranes. They hung around her hospital bed. She died before she could fold 1,000. Her classmates folded the rest.

Sadako's courage and faith inspired her friends and students all over the world to raise money for a memorial to the children who were the innocent victims of the atomic bomb. This movement led to the building of Peace Park in Hiroshima.

Every year, children and adults join together to fold paper cranes for the Children's Monument in Peace Park. Following this practice, paper cranes are now sent to a number of other peace parks and memorials around the world.

Read about the story of Sadako together with your class. Have your students research and discuss the symbolism of the crane. Challenge them to learn to fold paper cranes. Find links to schools participating in the paper crane project. You may want to join in an official paper crane project and send paper cranes to a peace site. Or you may simply make an exhibition in your classroom of paper cranes. Invite your students to write about Sadako's courage and what her story means to them.

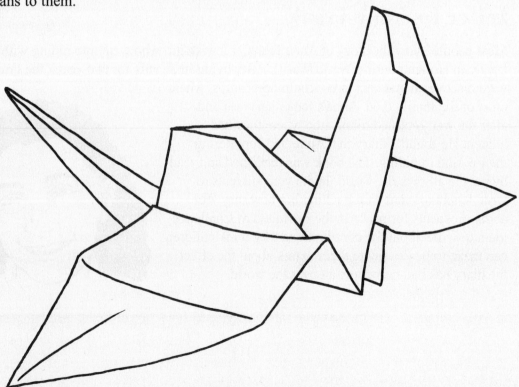

Name _____ Date _____

Basic Human Rights

_____

_____

_____

_____

_____

_____

_____

_____

_____

Chapter 20: Short-Term Projects

From events in China to environmental concerns, students learn more about historical events through these lively projects.

Cultural Revolution Comic Book 👤 individual 🕒 30–45 minutes

Materials: paper, markers or pens

Invite your students to create comic books about the Cultural Revolution in China. Who was responsible for it? What was it supposed to accomplish? Who supported it? Who did not? What happened to people who did not support it? What made it come to an end? Challenge them to tell the story in pictures with captions.

Person of the Year 👤 individual 🕒 30–40 minutes

Materials: paper; colored pens, pencils, or markers

Time magazine started publication in April 1923. Its format, short articles summarizing important events and issues, proved successful. Once a year, the magazine chooses a man or woman as the person of the year. A picture of the person is featured on the cover of that week's issue. Invite each student to choose a man or woman of the year for the cold war period and then create the magazine cover.

Two Sides of a Conflict: Vietnam 👤 individual 🕒 30–45 minutes

Materials: collage materials, paper, colored pencils or markers

Challenge your students to make two-paneled posters that show the two sides of the Vietnam War debate. They may want to look for images, headlines, or maps from that time to copy and use in a collage. Or they may draw pictures to illustrate their posters. Exhibit the sets of posters side by side.

Diorama: "Viking 1"

👤 individual   🕐 30–40 minutes

Materials: shoe boxes, modeling clay, pipe cleaners, tempera paints, paintbrushes

The moment has arrived: The *Viking 1* spacecraft probe is landing softly on Mars's craggy surface. NASA mission controllers switch on the probe's television cameras. The first images are transmitted back to Earth. They show a red landscape strewn with rocks under a pink sky. Challenge your students to make dioramas of the Mars landing of *Viking 1*. Invite them to research the spacecraft and the images that were sent back.

Energy Crisis Collage

👤 individual   🕐 30–45 minutes

Materials: pictures from magazines, paper, glue, scissors, markers

The energy crisis of 1973 made Americans aware of the nation's dependence on foreign oil. Arab oil-producing countries cut off shipments to the United States because of U.S. support for Israel. All over the country, long lines of cars appeared at gas stations. Prices for fuel and gas nearly doubled. Many gas stations and factories were forced to shut down before the embargo ended in March 1974. Invite your students to make a collage about the energy crisis, and possible solutions.

> Remember! Keep working on that Long-Term Project.

Health Craze Collage

👤 individual   🕐 30–45 minutes

Materials: magazine pictures, scissors, glue, poster paper, markers

During the 1970s, as people grew concerned about the environment, they also began to think about their own health. They demanded healthier foods without chemical additives. Whole wheat bread started appearing on supermarket shelves beside bleached white breads. Health food stores began to open, offering everything from algae to tofu products. At the same time, new forms of exercise became popular, such as jogging, yoga, and aerobics. Invite your students to make collages about Americans' new concern for their health.

Social Studies Plus!   Unit 7   Short-Term Projects   **187**

Chapter 20: Writing Projects

The cold war is on. Tensions are rising, as is the arms build-up. Is there a way out? Student writers search for solutions to these problems.

Eyewitness Report: The Cultural Revolution

Challenge your students to file a journalist's report from the midst of the Cultural Revolution in China. What is going on in the streets? Why are many people being transported to work in the country? Why are university professors under suspicion? Why are so many young people involved? Does everybody support this mass movement? What is its purpose? Is it being achieved?

Domino Effect

President Lyndon Johnson wants to rally the country to support his policy of continued involvement in Vietnam. Johnson inherited this conflict from his predecessors, Presidents Kennedy and Eisenhower, and is determined to continue. Challenge your students to suppose that they are speechwriters for Johnson. Invite them to write speeches explaining Johnson's domino theory to the American public. What is the domino theory? Challenge them to write persuasively about this policy.

Policy Paper: Vietnamization

Richard Nixon has just been elected president. He is looking for a way to change U.S. strategy in Vietnam. He wants to gradually ease U.S. troops out of this conflict, where so many have already been lost. Invite your students to suppose that they are aides to President Nixon. Challenge them to write policy papers for the president about a plan for *Vietnamization*. Explain how this policy would work. What is its goal? What are its chances for success?

Pen Pals

Ask your students to write a letter to Vietnamese boys or girls their own age as if they were pen pals. Suggest some questions they could ask. How did the war affect their country? How has life changed since the end of the war? What effects did the war have on the United States? Are any of these effects still with us today?

Reporter's Journal: Détente

Invite your students to write as if they are journalists traveling with President Nixon on his landmark journey to China. With U.S. involvement in the Vietnam War winding down, the president is hoping to start a period of détente, or relaxation of tensions, with the Soviet Union and China. Ask students to write press releases that describe the meeting between Nixon and the aging Mao Ze-dong. What do they say about cold war tensions, Vietnam, the United States' relationship with Taiwan, and the lingering effects of the Korean War? What role does Henry Kissinger play? What will be the effects of this historic meeting?

Cold War Biography

During the cold war, artists and athletes from Communist countries were sent as cultural ambassadors to the West. Some of these people decided to defect, or not return to their country. Invite your students to research and write a short biography of a prominent person who defected from a Communist country. Some examples are Mikhail Baryshnikov (dancer), Galina Vishnevskaya (opera singer), and Martina Navratilova (tennis player).

Chapter 20

Citizenship

Honesty

Robert McNamara, President Johnson's Secretary of Defense, once said about the Vietnam War: "We ... acted according to what we thought were the principles ... of this nation. We were wrong. We were terribly wrong."

Discuss with your students how the study of history is an exercise in hindsight. Being honest about what happened is a step toward understanding the mistakes of the past. Discuss the importance of studying and understanding—and being honest about—history.

Why is it important to study history? Are there really lessons to be learned from the past? Can being honest about the past help us in the present and the future? How, or in what ways? Ask students: What era in history is important to you, and why? What can we learn from it?

Have the students use the blackline master on page 191 to create a list of questions for a survey on the importance of history. Brainstorm a list of people to whom they could send the survey. Among recipients could be a local television or radio station, business bureau, local mayor's office, or state or federal representative. Invite students to write cover letters to accompany the survey, explaining that they are concluding a year's history project with this questionnaire.

Name _____   Date _____

Survey

Lessons Learned from the Past

1. _____

2. _____

3. _____

4. _____

5. _____

6. _____

7. _____

8. _____

9. _____

10. _____

Teacher Planner

Long-Term Project pages 194–195	Materials	⏱	Lesson Link
United Nations Students set up a classroom United Nations, discussing important global issues.			Lessons 1–3
Week 1 group Students decide which country they wish to represent in the classroom United Nations.	no materials needed	1 session 30–40 min.	
Week 2 group Students begin researching the major issues of their countries and regions.	research materials, index cards, pens	1 session 45 min.	
Week 3 group Students compile a list of regional problems.	notes, index cards, pens	1 session 45 min.	
Week 4 whole class Students present their region's problems and put questions on the agenda.	notes, index cards, pens	1 session 1 hr.	

Unit Drama pages 196–201

	Materials	⏱	Lesson Link
Scenarios: The Old Ways Change group Students role-play skits about some dramatic moments in recent global history.	props (optional)	5 sessions 30 min. each	Lessons 1–3
Play: Sooner or Later, Every Wall Must Fall group Students perform a play about the issues surrounding the Berlin Wall.	props, costumes (optional)	1 session 2 hrs.	Lesson 3

Chapter 21 Short-Term Projects pages 202–203

	Materials	⏱	Lesson Link
Design a Flag individual Students design flags for a new nation that has thrown off its old colonial status.	paper, colored pencils, markers or paints	1 session 30–40 min.	Lesson 1
Nonviolent Comic Book individual Students create comic books about using nonviolence to achieve justice.	paper, colored pens, pencils or markers	1 session 30–40 min.	Lessons 1–3
Israeli-Palestinian Peace Mural individual/group Students create murals promoting peace in the Mideast.	butcher paper, pencils, paints and brushes	1 session 30–45 min.	Lesson 2
Design a Peace Medal individual Students design their own peace medals, using the Nobel Peace Prize as an inspiration.	paper, colored pencils or markers	1 session 30 min.	Lesson 2
Berlin Wall Painting individual Students make paintings of the Berlin Wall.	butcher paper and paints, or paper and colored pencils	1 session 30–40 min.	Lesson 3

Chapter 21 Writing Projects pages 204–205

	Materials	⏱	Lesson Link
Award to Nelson Mandela individual Students write speeches for an award ceremony honoring a freedom award to Nelson Mandela for fighting apartheid.	paper, pens	1 session 20 min.	Lesson 1

© Scott Foresman 6

Chapter 21 Writing Projects pages 204–205	Materials	🕐	Lesson Link
Great Britain Returns Hong Kong to China individual Students write about their thoughts and feelings regarding Great Britain's return of Hong Kong to China.	paper, pens	1 session 20 min.	Lesson 1
Civil Disobedience individual Students write about what civil disobedience means to them.	paper, pens	1 session 20 min.	Lesson 1
Israeli-Palestinian Pen Pals individual Students write letters to a pen pal on the opposite side of the conflict in the Mideast.	paper, pens	1 session 30 min.	Lesson 2
East-West Cousins individual Students write letters to a cousin on the other side of the Berlin Wall.	paper, pens	1 session 20 min.	Lesson 3
Gorbachev Remembers: A Conclusion individual Students write articles about Gorbachev's memories of the times during Communism.	paper, pens	1 session 20 min.	Lesson 3

Chapter 21 Citizenship Project page 206			
Courage whole class Students create conflict scenarios and role-play solving the conflicts using mediation steps they have established.	BLM p. 207, paper, pens	1 session 45 min.	Lesson 1

Chapter 22 Short-Term Projects pages 208–209			
New Money individual/group Students design their own form of currency.	paper, colored pens, pencils or markers	1 session 30 min.	Lesson 1
Board Game: Common Market individual Students make a board game about a common market.	cardboard or paper, pens or markers	1 session 45 min.	Lesson 1
The Human Family: A Collage individual Students make posters celebrating our diversity and unity.	paper or poster board, paints, magazine pictures, scissors, glue	1 session 30–40 min.	Lesson 2
People Who Work for Peace individual Students make portraits of a woman or man who currently works for human rights and peace.	poster paper, paints and brushes	1 session 30–40 min.	Lesson 2
Heroes in Action individual Students make posters honoring those heroes who responded to the terrorist attacks on the World Trade Center.	poster board, paints and brushes, collage materials	1 session 30–40 min.	Lesson 3
Cartogram: World Hunger individual Students make cartograms representing their findings on world hunger.	research materials, paper, colored markers	1 session 30–45 min.	Lesson 3

Chapter 22 Writing Projects pages 210–211			
NAFTA: Yes or No? individual Students write newspaper editorials either supporting or opposing NAFTA.	paper, colored pens, pencils or markers	1 session 30 min.	Lesson 1

Unit 8 Teacher Planner

Chapter 22 Writing Projects continued	Materials	⏱	Lesson Link
Seattle and the WTO individual Students write reports as roving journalists about the World Trade Organization.	paper, pens	1 session 25 min.	Lesson 1
For a Multiethnic Culture individual Students give specific examples of the problems and strengths of a multiethnic culture.	paper, pens	1 session 30 min.	Lesson 2
Journal Entry: Refugee individual Students write entries in the journals they keep as refugees.	paper, pens	1 session 20 min.	Lesson 2
Reporter on the Scene: Tiananmen Square individual Students write reports from journalists on the scene, citing reasons for the students' protest.	paper, pens	1 session 25 min.	Lesson 2
Letter to a Firefighter individual Students write letters to a firefighter expressing their feelings about the events of September 11.	paper, pens	1 session 20 min.	Lesson 3

Chapter 22 Citizenship Project page 212

	Materials	⏱	Lesson Link
Respect whole class Students consider what we gain by living in a multiethnic culture.	paper, pens	1 session 45 min.	Lessons 1–3

Chapter 23 Short-Term Projects pages 214–215

	Materials	⏱	Lesson Link
Urban Planning: Megacity individual Students make plans for a megacity.	paper, colored pencils or markers	1 session 30–40 min.	Lesson 1
Immigrants and Cultural Change individual Students make poster collages representing the multiethnic culture of the United States.	poster board, markers, magazine pictures, library resources	1 session 30–40 min.	Lesson 1
Map Skills individual/group Students make distribution maps.	research materials, markers, paper	1 session 40 min.	Lesson 1
Make Your Own 3-D Goggles! individual Students make 3-D goggles from oaktag and cellophane.	oaktag, red and blue cellophane, scissors, glue, Internet	1 session 20 min.	Lessons 1–3
Bioethics: A Comic Book individual/partners Students make comic books about issues in the field of bioethics.	paper, pens or markers	1 session 30–45 min.	Lesson 2
Recycling Collage individual/group Students make collages about recycling.	recycled objects from the classroom, glue, oaktag	1 session 30–45 min.	Lesson 2

Chapter 23 Writing Projects pages 216–217

	Materials	⏱	Lesson Link
Target Skill: Draw Conclusions individual Students write speeches about population trends in developing nations.	paper, pens	1 session 20 min.	Lesson 1

Chapter 23 **Writing Projects** *continued*	Materials	🕐	Lesson Link
Celebrating Diversity individual Students write about an immigrant group and its contributions.	paper, pens	1 session 25 min.	Lesson 1
Biography: Rachel Carson individual Students write biographies of early environmentalist Rachel Carson.	paper, pens	1 session 30 min.	Lesson 2
A Place You Love individual Students write descriptions of a natural setting that they have visited.	paper, pens	1 session 20 min.	Lesson 2
Alternative Energy Sources individual Students write summaries of their findings on alternative energy sources.	paper, pens	1 session 20 min.	Lesson 2
Science Fiction individual Students write stories about a world of the future.	paper, pens	1 session 25 min.	Lesson 3
Chapter 23 **Citizenship Project** page 218			
Responsibility whole class Students discuss the principles of sustainable development, and the responsibility of today's planners to consider the needs of tomorrow's citizens.	paper, pens	1 session 45 min.	Lesson 1

Social Studies Plus!   Unit 8 Teacher Planner   **193B**

Long-Term Project

United Nations

How can we be national citizens and global citizens at the same time? What happens if national, regional, and global concerns collide? Can they be resolved? Put these questions to the test in a classroom United Nations.

Introduce and Plan

Week 1   group   30–40 minutes

Materials: none

Explain to students that together they will create a United Nations in the classroom. The General Assembly will consider the question: How can we address our different national and regional concerns while at the same time fulfilling our role as global citizens? Ask students to decide which country they wish to represent. Invite them to meet in regional groups: Asia, Pacific island nations, North America (including Canada, United States, Mexico), South and Central America, Europe, Russian federation, and Africa.

Research and Report

Week 2   group   45 minutes

Materials: research materials (library, the Internet), index cards, pens

Challenge students to begin researching the major issues of their countries and regions. Encourage them to take notes on index cards ordered in the following way: political, economic, social, cultural, and environmental.

Week 3 — Regional Planning

 group 45 minutes

Materials: notes, index cards, pens

Have the regional groups meet so that individuals can compare notes on their findings. Each group compiles a list of regional problems. Give the groups time to discuss the issues they want to raise at the General Assembly. Ask students: What are the possible solutions to some of the problems? How can the United Nations support their regions in solving problems? Invite students who want to serve as General Assembly moderator to put their names up for a vote, or you may want to choose a student to be the moderator.

Week 4 — The General Assembly Meets

 whole class 1 hour

Materials: notes, index cards, pens

Have each student write a place card with the name of the nation he or she is representing. If possible, set up the tables in a large circle. Each regional group chooses a place to sit with all its members. The moderator takes his or her place in the circle and opens the session. Each group presents its problems and puts questions on the agenda. After all groups have presented their concerns, debate can begin. Have the moderator work with a clock to time discussion so that all or most of the questions on the agenda will receive attention. At the end of debate on each question, the moderator holds a vote. At the end of the session, the moderator reads a list of the resolutions that have been agreed on by vote.

Unit 8 Drama Scenarios: The Old Ways Change

As the modern era begins, old ideologies die out. New nations are born, and new ways of thinking. The human spirit tries to create a brave new world. Students absorb some dramatic moments in recent history.

African Leaders Discuss Independence

Kwame Nkrumah (Ghana), Jomo Kenyatta (Kenya), and Julius Nyerere (Tanzania) get together to discuss the new era in sub-Saharan Africa. Their countries are all newly independent. The colonial period is over. But what does the future hold? Ask students to do some research and some role-playing to find out how these African leaders think.

John Atanasoff and Clifford Berry Build a Computer

Professor John Atanasoff is working with Clifford Berry, a gifted electrical engineer. Atanasoff has an idea: to build a computing device that uses electricity and that works with binary numbers. Together they build the world's first computer! It is the size of a small room, weighs thirty tons, and contains a mile of wire. It can calculate about 1 operation every fifteen seconds. (Today a computer can calculate 150 billion operations in fifteen seconds!) Stage the scene as Atanasoff and Berry work on their project. What do they talk about? Do they realize the implications of their invention?

Taking the Initiative

A family hiking in the mountains wants to spend their holiday enjoying the natural beauty of the landscape. But what do they come upon all along the trail? Soda cans, discarded bags of chips, and other garbage of fellow hikers. The family decides to take action and pick up the garbage along the way. Stage the scene as the family hikes along the trail. What happens when they meet other hikers? Improvise some dialogue.

Aboard the Mir

Two Soviet cosmonauts are orbiting the earth aboard the Soviet space station *Mir*. As they circle the planet, incredible changes are going on in their homeland far below. Their country, the Soviet Union, is going out of existence. Eleven of the twelve former Soviet republics have proclaimed independence. A *putsch* is underway to overthrow Soviet President Mikhail Gorbachev! Meanwhile, the economic structure of the country is collapsing. The space program is experiencing cutbacks—its future is uncertain. Sergei Krikalev and Alexander Volkov learn all these facts as they communicate daily with ground control and continue to orbit above—wondering when, and how, they will ever come home and what they will find. Improvise some scenes as the men orbit and speculate.

Code Crackers: The Human Genome Project

Francis Collins is the director of the Human Genome Project (HGP), a government-financed research project. Since 1990, the HGP has been slowly working to identify and sequence the code for the human genome. Craig Venter is part of the team, but he is frustrated by the slow pace and decides to start his own team. He founds a private company, Celera, and uses robots and computers to break down genetic material. His team is pulling ahead. But Collins criticizes Venter's team for selling the research to pharmaceutical 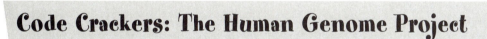 companies. Stage some scenes in the war of words between the two major players in the race to crack the code of the human genome.

Unit 8 Drama Play

Sooner or Later, Every Wall Must Fall

What happens when citizens go to sleep one night and wake up in the morning to find there is a wall dividing their city? In this play students find out about the Berlin Wall!

The Parts:
- Narrator
- Sister 1
- Sister 2
- Western Bloc Soldier
- Eastern Bloc Soldier
- West Berlin Citizen 1
- West Berlin Citizen 2
- East Berlin Citizen 1/West Berlin Citizen 3
- East Berlin Citizen 2/West Berlin Citizen 4

Director's Notes: *Truemmerfrauen* (TROOM er FROW in) were the "rubble women" who sifted through the rubble of the city after the war. The two sisters wear kerchiefs while they play truemmerfrauen.

Each soldier carries a sign saying You Are Now Entering the Eastern (or Western) Sector.

For the wall, place a row of desks close together, or paint a wall on butcher paper. Place the wall so the audience can see scenes on both sides.

The citizens who cross from East to West become West Berlin Citizens 3 and 4 in Part 2 of play.

Part 1

Narrator: At the end of World War II, the city of Berlin lay in ruins. Once one of the busiest cities of Europe, it now was nothing but a bombed-out pile of bricks. But the city did not go under. Immediately after the war, the women (who else was there?) set to work trimming old mortar from the bricks with hammers.

Sisters 1 & 2: *(as truemmerfrauen stooping over to pick up bricks)* We will build this city again, brick by brick by brick by brick . . . *(Exit.)*

Narrator: After a war, to the victor go the spoils. The city of Berlin was divided into four sectors, one for each of the Allied Powers. *(Two Soldiers appear.)* The eastern part went to the Russians. *(Eastern Bloc Soldier salutes and takes up a position in the "East.")* The other Allied Powers—France, Great Britain, and the United States—divided the Western part of the city among themselves. *(Western Bloc Soldier takes up position in the "West." Citizens and Sisters pass between Soldiers from West to East and East to West.)*

Sister 1: At first, there was no problem. The city was open, and we were free to come and go as we pleased.

Sister 2: We lived in a house that was now in the Western sector. Every day I visited my sister. She lived with her family in a house down the street—but in the Eastern sector now. *(Citizens and Sisters exit.)*

Narrator: But many people did not want to live under the Russian regime. They left the Eastern side of the city. So one night, in the early hours of August 13, 1961, they erected the wall. *(Eastern Bloc Soldier lines up desks or sets up painted wall.)*

Sister 2: Imagine our surprise in the morning when we woke up . . .

Sister 1: And found a wall dividing our little street in two!

Sister 2: No longer could I visit my sister and her family.

Sister 1: No longer could I visit my parents who lived with my sister!

Sister 2: We couldn't believe this had happened! *(Exits.)*

Sister 1: We never thought it would last. *(Exits.)*

Narrator: Life became very different on the two sides of the wall.

W/B Citizen 1: West Berlin was rebuilt with money from the Allies. Goods and services flowed in.

W/B Citizen 2: The shops were full and people could buy whatever they wanted or needed. *(Gives out an apple or banana to the other West Berlin citizen who begins eating.)*

W/B Citizen 1: But the news we got from the other side was disturbing.

E/B Citizen 1: The Russian system could not keep up with production.

E/B Citizen 2: The shelves in the stores were often empty, and we had to learn to do without.

E/B Citizen 1: What was worse, the East German government set up a system of spies to hear if anybody was grumbling. *(E.B. Citizen 1 listens carefully to E.B. Citizen 2.)*

E/B Citizen 2: You never knew who might be a spy, and you had to be careful about what you said. *(E.B. Citizen 1 whispers to E.B. Citizen 2.)*

Social Studies Plus!

Sooner or Later, Every Wall Must Fall *continued*

Part 2

Narrator: Many people tried to escape. They tried to escape in different ways. Some people tunneled under the wall.

(E.B. Citizen 1 looks around carefully. Near the upstage end of the wall, he or she mimes climbing over. Glancing around all the time, he or she motions to E.B. Citizen 2 who also climbs in pantomime or goes around the wall. W.B. Citizens 1 and 2 greet E.B. Citizens 1 and 2 as they arrive.)

Narrator: Once a family built a hot air balloon on the roof of their house. In the night they filled it up, got in, and flew across the wall. *(Soldiers and Citizens point and look up as if watching a balloon sail across.)*

Narrator: Some people tried to climb over the wall. Many died in the attempt . . . . It went on this way for twenty-eight years. People thought it would never change. When one day . . .

W/B Citizen 1: *(reading newspaper)* The new Soviet leader Gorbachev has declared a new policy.

W/B Citizen 2: *(reading newspaper)* Perestroika. Openness. What does it mean?

W/B Citizen 3: *(reading newspaper)* It says here the Soviet satellite country of Hungary is opening its border to the West!

W/B Citizen 4: *(reading newspaper)* People are flocking to Hungary! The border is open! People are free to go out!

W/B Citizen 3: *(throwing down the newspaper)* If the border is open in Hungary, it should be open here!

W/B Citizen 4: Down with the wall! Down with the wall! *(The chant is picked up by Sisters on both sides of the wall.)*

Sister 2: At first I couldn't believe it! Could it be true? After so many years?

Sister 1: We heard it on the radio that night. The border would be open—effective immediately.

Sister 2: There was only one thing to do. We went to the wall.

Sister 1: Like everybody else, I went to the wall. The poor soldier there had not gotten any orders. (*Eastern Bloc Soldier looks at Sister 1 who wants to pass through. Shrugs his shoulders. Sister 1 passes through. Soldier shrugs again and follows. They are greeted on the other side by hugs and cheers. They mime taking down the wall. All celebrate. Players form a line facing the audience, holding hands.*)

Player 1: How we danced that night!

Player 2: We danced on top of the wall!

Player 3: We danced all over the city!

Player 4: And all over the world, people celebrated with us!

Player 5: We celebrated that night and for many days to follow.

Player 1: Families were reunited.

Player 2: We all became citizens of one country again!

Player 3: Germany was reunited, and the cold war was over, once and for all.

Player 4: But in real life, there are no easy endings.

Player 5: Many challenges lay ahead, for citizens of the East and West.

Player 1: So many years had gone by, and the wall had changed us.

Player 2: Can we still learn to live together?

Player 3: Can we break down the walls in our minds?

All: We can do it! Sooner or later—every wall must fall!

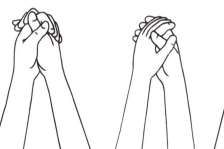

Chapter 21 Short-Term Projects

Colonies gain independence! Nonviolence works! In some places, peace does not hold. But some walls do fall! The end of the twentieth century heralds change. Invite students to join in the spirit.

Design a Flag

 individual   30–40 minutes

Materials: paper; colored pencils, markers, or paints

In the early 1960s, many nations in sub-Saharan Africa cast off their colonial ties with European countries and won their independence. These new nations celebrated their independence by writing their own constitutions, electing their own leaders—and by creating their own flags! Invite students to design flags for a new nation that has thrown off its old colonial status. What symbols and colors would they use? What do these symbols and colors represent?

Berlin Wall Painting

 individual   30–40 minutes

Materials: butcher paper and tempera paints, or paper and colored pencils

When the East German government built a wall in Berlin, they separated the East side of the city from the West. Families, neighbors, and neighborhoods were now divided. For nearly thirty years, that wall stood. On the East side, residents could not even approach the wall. Armed guards patrolled it and prevented people from approaching. Many people died trying to get under or over it. On the West side, however, the wall bordered on a sidewalk. Anyone could walk along it. Artists used it as a canvas for their thoughts and feelings. Soon it was painted from one end to the other with artistic calls for peace and unity. Invite your students to make Berlin Wall paintings. Challenge them to find photos of the original Berlin Wall paintings.

Remember! Keep working on that Long-Term Project.

Israeli-Palestinian Peace Mural   individual/group   30–45 minutes

Materials: large piece of butcher paper, pencils, tempera paints, paintbrushes

Peace for all the world is something that we all hope for. Yet some conflicts have been going on for a long time, such as that between Israel and the Palestinians. How can students show their hopes for peace? Invite them to create a mural promoting peace in the Mideast. Individuals can make sketches, or small groups can work together to create a full-sized work. Challenge students to use a map of the region as the background for their murals. Invite them to feature children in their drawings.

Design a Peace Medal   individual   30 minutes

Materials: paper, colored pencils or markers

The Nobel Prize for Peace is awarded to someone every year for his or her efforts in promoting peace in the world. In the year 2001, it was awarded to the United Nations and its leader, Kofi Annan. In his acceptance speech, Annan said, "In this new century, we must start from the understanding that peace belongs not only to states or peoples, but to each and every member of those communities." Challenge your students to design peace medals of their own.

Nonviolent Comic Book   individual   30–40 minutes

Materials: paper; colored pens, pencils, or markers

What happens in a comic book when there's a problem? There's always a superhero around to step in and help out in the cause of justice! But what if the superhero is dedicated to the principle of nonviolence—like Mohandas Gandhi or Martin Luther King Jr.? Challenge students to create comic books about using nonviolence to achieve justice. The books can feature real or fictional people and events.

Chapter 21: Writing Projects

Modern times: writers needed to explain complicated issues, publicize important achievements, maintain contacts with counterparts in other lands, and promote peace and understanding!

Award to Nelson Mandela

Invite your students to suppose they have been chosen to present a freedom award to Nelson Mandela for fighting apartheid and restoring democracy to his country, South Africa. Challenge them to write speeches for the award ceremony. Encourage them to explain why Mandela has earned this award. They may also say what Mandela's struggle means to them personally. What does it mean to his nation, to Africa, and to people everywhere?

Great Britain Returns Hong Kong to China

Challenge your students to suppose they have lived with their families in Hong Kong as British subjects for many years. Now, under a new agreement, Great Britain is returning the island colony to China. What will this change mean? Why is it happening? What will your family do? Invite them to write about their thoughts and feelings on the eve of this historic change.

Civil Disobedience

What is *civil disobedience?* Challenge students to define it and write about what it means to them. Ask them to give examples of how it *could be* used to address problems in the world. Ask them to give examples of how it *has been* used to gain freedom and civil rights for people in different parts of the world.

Israeli-Palestinian Pen Pals

Invite your students to suppose they are either Israeli or Palestinian students living in the troubled Mideast. Ask them to write letters to a pen pal on the opposite side of the conflict. Ask students: What questions would you ask, and what do you think your pen pal would want to know about you? Have students describe their hopes for peace in the Mideast. Ask students: What obstacles to peace do you foresee, and how can they be overcome?

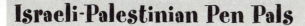

East-West Cousins

Ask your students to suppose they live in the divided city of Berlin. When the wall was built, it split their families. Half now live in East Berlin, and half in West Berlin. That means that they live in different countries with different governments. Invite students to write letters to a cousin on the other side of the wall. How are your lives the same? How are they different? What kinds of opportunities exist on both sides? How do you see the future? Do you think the wall will ever come down?

Gorbachev Remembers: A Conclusion

Soviet leader Mikhail Gorbachev called for economic and social changes in the rigid Communist empire. Due in large part to his policies, the Communist empire fell, giving way to a new era. Challenge your students to suppose they are Gorbachev in retirement and that a magazine publisher has asked him to write an article about his memories of that time. Why did Gorbachev think change was necessary? Ask students to explain perestroika and glasnost and draw conclusions about the effects of these policies.

Citizenship

Courage

Gandhi led his country, India, to independence from Great Britain through a long campaign of nonviolent resistance. Forty years later, Martin Luther King Jr. adopted the same techniques and philosophy in the campaign for civil rights.

Advance Preparation: *Copy and pass out the blackline master on page 207.*

What does nonviolence mean? Ask students if they think it really can be a way to resolve conflict. Study and discuss the principles of nonviolence together with your class. How does nonviolence work? Does a nonviolent approach to conflict take courage?

Invite the class to research organizations that explain and promote nonviolence. Have students contact these groups for information about programs for students. Students can also look for interactive sites.

Organizations that promote peer mediation also take a nonviolent approach to conflict resolution. Challenge the class to create rules for their own peer mediation initiative. Then invite students to create some conflict scenarios. Encourage them to role-play solving the conflicts using the mediation steps they created.

Afterwards discuss the effectiveness of peer mediation and the principle of nonviolent problem solving. Ask students to write about how they think nonviolence can make a difference in the world.

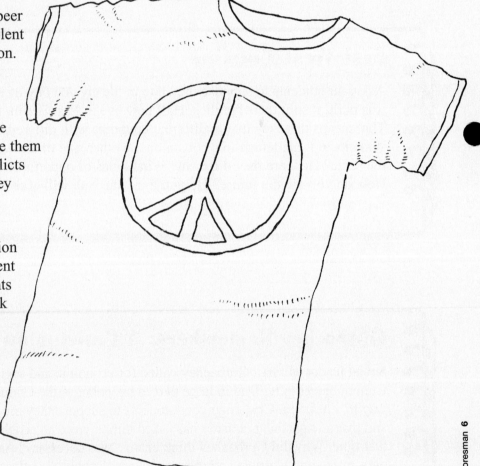

Name _____ Date _____

Rules for Peer Mediation

Social Studies Plus!   Unit 8   Blackline Master   207

Chapter 22: Short-Term Projects

All the world's becoming a common market! We are all part of the human family! Students show their colors on these short-term projects that are all about today.

New Money

 individual/group   30 minutes

Materials: paper, colored pens, pencils or markers

The euro is the new currency issued by the European Union (EU) to replace the different currencies of its member nations with one uniform money system. This will simplify trade and commerce. The EU had one problem when it was planning for the euro: What pictures would they put on the new bills? What images would symbolize the new Europe? Challenge students to design and name a new currency. Invite them to draw up pictures for the $1, $5, $10, $50, and $100 bills.

Board Game: Common Market

 individual   45 minutes

Materials: cardboard or paper, pens or markers

Advance Preparation: *Copy and pass out the blackline master on page 213.*

Challenge your students to make up a board game about a common market. They may work as individuals or in small groups to create the game. They could show a part of the world or a fictional land, and they should make game pieces for players, play money, or tokens of exchange. Ask students: Which nations have entered into a common market agreement? How does that affect trade? Invite students to write down the instructions and play the game!

The Human Family: A Collage

 individual   30–40 minutes

Materials: paper or poster board, tempera paints, pictures from magazines, scissors, glue

Nobel Peace Prize winner Mairead Corrigan Maguire is a peace activist who works to end the fighting in Northern Ireland. In her opinion, "It is fine to celebrate our diversity and our roots, but somehow we must . . . understand the most important identity that we have . . . [is] the human family." Invite your students to make posters celebrating our diversity *and* unity.

People Who Work for Peace

 individual 30–40 minutes

Materials: poster paper, tempera paints and paintbrushes

Invite your students to make a portrait of a woman or man who currently works for human rights and peace. Some examples are Mary Robinson (UN High Commissioner for Human Rights), Aung San Suu Kyi (Burma rights activist), and Rigoberta Menchù (Guatemala peace activist). Students may want to conduct research, or they may want to honor someone they know—perhaps a teacher or family member.

Heroes in Action

 individual 30–40 minutes

Materials: poster board, tempera paints, paintbrushes, collage materials

The men and women who responded to the terrorist attacks on the World Trade Center in New York City showed great courage. Their acts of valor saved the lives of many and inspired people all around the world.

Sadly, however, many firefighters died as they tried to help people escape. Invite your students to make posters honoring those (firefighters, police officers, and others) who responded to this tragedy with courage. Students may use collage techniques (pictures, headlines, etc. cut from newspapers or magazines) or may paint or draw to make their posters.

> Remember! Keep working on that Long-Term Project.

Cartogram: World Hunger

 individual 30–45 minutes

Materials: research materials, paper, colored markers

A cartogram is a special kind of graph based on a map. It stretches and bends map outlines to represent data or information. Invite students to research hunger in the world today. Encourage them to use resource materials such as an almanac, encyclopedia, or the Internet. Then challenge them to make cartograms to represent their findings. Remind them to label their cartograms and to provide a key.

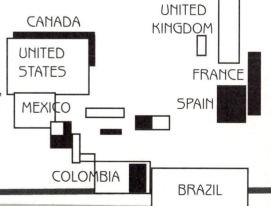

Chapter 22 Writing Projects

Report on free trade. Assess the strengths of multiethnic nations. Wear the shoes of refugees looking for safe havens. Write to firefighters. Students have a job to do.

NAFTA: Yes or No?

The North American Free Trade Agreement (NAFTA) created a free trade zone between the United States, Canada, and Mexico in 1994. But it sparked a lot of debate. Many people questioned the effect it would have on jobs, unions, pay scales, and standards of living for citizens in each country. Ask students to write newspaper editorials either supporting or opposing NAFTA, using specific details.

Seattle and The WTO

When the World Trade Organization (WTO) convened in Seattle in 1999, it met with a lot of unexpected, but highly organized, protest on the streets. A coalition of many different groups opposed many WTO policies and came out to say so. Invite students to do research on that meeting and then write reports as roving journalists. What's the controversy all about, and what policies do protesters oppose? Remind students to include responses of officials from the WTO.

For a Multiethnic Culture

Many of today's conflicts come out of ethnic differences. Yet according to UN Secretary-General Kofi Annan, "People of different religions and cultures live side by side in almost every part of the world, and most of us have overlapping identities which unite us with very different groups." Challenge students to give specific examples of the problems and strengths of a multiethnic culture. Ask them what conclusions they can draw about multiethnic cultures.

Journal Entry: Refugee

Ask students to suppose they have been forced to leave their homeland because of a conflict there. Have them consider where they would go, how they would live, and who would help them. Challenge students to write entries in the journals they keep as refugees. Ask them: Do you think you will ever be able to return to your homeland, and where does your future lie?

Reporter on the Scene: Tiananmen Square

Chinese students planned a peaceful demonstration in Tiananmen Square. They wanted more freedoms such as freedom of speech. The Chinese government responded with force and crushed the protest. Invite students to write reports as journalists on the scene, citing reasons for the protest. Ask students: Why does the government respond so brutally?

Letter to a Firefighter

When tragedy struck on September 11, 2001, the first people on the scene were the firefighters. They raced into and up the stairs of the World Trade Towers to try to help people get out. They were successful in helping many people escape. If not for their efforts, many more might have been injured or killed. Hundreds of firefighters, however, lost their lives as the buildings came down. Invite your students to write letters to a firefighter expressing their feelings about the events of September 11, and their gratitude for the role firefighters play in our communities.

Social Studies Plus!

Chapter 22 Citizenship

Respect

Many conflicts in today's world are between different ethnic or religious groups. Learning to live together in a multiethnic world seems to be the challenge that lies ahead, if we want to live in peace.

How can people learn to **respect** each other and each other's differences in culture and religion?

Challenge your students to discuss this difficult issue. Take notes on ideas that come out of the discussion. Specifically ask them about the main obstacles to understanding and respecting different customs. Ask students: What happens when you meet someone from a culture unfamiliar to you? Ask students to notice whether people dress differently, speak a different language, eat different food, or celebrate different holidays. Ask them to say what happens when they encounter something unfamiliar. Point out that often people are either shy or curious, and describe some appropriate responses to these feelings (being friendly, asking questions, sharing a custom of their own, etc.).

You may want to list the different cultures represented by the students in your classroom.

Challenge your students to consider what we gain by living in a multiethnic culture. Does it make a society strong? Does it make a democracy strong?

212 Unit 8 **Short-Term Projects**

Social Studies Plus!

Name _____ Date _____

Common Market Board Game

Objective:

_____

_____

_____

Number of Players:

_____

How to Play the Game:

_____

_____

_____

_____

_____

_____

_____

_____

_____

_____

_____

Chapter 23: Short-Term Projects

Living in this century, students face challenges. Invite them to zero in on molecular structures with 3-D glasses or zoom out to a world distribution map. Either way, perceptions will change!

Urban Planning: Megacity

👤 individual   🕐 30–40 minutes

Materials: paper, colored pencils or markers

Invite your students to draw up plans for a megacity (city of over ten million people). What kind of housing would they provide? Ask them to specify the houses: massive housing blocks, smaller-scale developments, or both. Where would schools, hospitals, entertainment, and shopping be placed? Should cars be encouraged or limited within the city? Should there be mass transit? Where would businesses be located? Remind students to label their plans for a megacity.

Immigrants and Cultural Change

👤 individual   🕐 30–40 minutes

Materials: poster board, markers, pictures from magazines, dictionary that shows word origins, blackline master (page 219)

Invite your students to make poster collages representing the multiethnic culture of the United States. Encourage them to show the variety of food, clothing, customs, and holidays of different ethnic groups. Challenge them to use the blackline master and a dictionary to research words that originated in other cultures and have become part of the English language (*shampoo*, Hindi; *barbecue*, Taino; *solo*, Italian; *kindergarten*, German).

Map Skills

👤 individual/group 👥   🕐 40 minutes

Materials: research materials (almanac, the Internet), markers, paper (or copy of map)

Invite your students to make distribution maps. They may work as individuals or in small groups. Encourage them to choose a feature or element to research (such as wildlife, deserts, forests or rain forests, or oil deposits). They may want to work with a world map, or they could make a distribution map of your state or region. Remind them to color code the maps, create keys, and, of course, create titles.

Make Your Own 3-D Goggles!

👤 individual 🕐 20 minutes

Materials: oaktag, red and blue cellophane, scissors, glue or tape, Internet access

3-D glasses are cool! They're easy to make and fun to use. Invite students to cut out pairs of eyeglasses from oak tag paper. Tell them to cut out holes for the "lenses" and tape in red cellophane on the left side and blue cellophane on the right side. Encourage them to go to scientific Web sites that feature 3-D pictures. Check out 3-D photographs of microchip technology inside a computer or 3-D molecular photographs of DNA structures. Invite them to use their 3-D glasses to view these sites.

Bioethics: A Comic Book

👤 individual/partners 👥 🕐 30–45 minutes

Materials: paper, pens or markers

Bioethics is a relatively new field. It deals with ethical issues that come out of new advances in biology. Things that were once unthinkable, such as cloning, are now fast becoming technically possible. Challenge your students to make comic books about an issue in the field of bioethics. Invite them to make stories that show the problems and challenges of this issue. They may want to create science fiction stories to illustrate the possibilities or dangers of certain biotechnological advancements.

Remember! Keep working on that Long-Term Project.

Recycling Collage

👤 individual/group 👥 🕐 30–45 minutes

Materials: recycled objects from the classroom (plastic cups, straws, juice bottles, tin foil, etc.), glue, oaktag

Invite your students to make collages about recycling. Challenge them to use recyclable materials from the classroom and show how these materials could be recycled or reused. Or ask them to show why recycling is important. Ask them: What would happen if we just threw everything away without recycling? Challenge them to consider how they can convince more people to recycle.

© Scott Foresman 6

Social Studies Plus! Unit 8 Short-Term Projects **215**

Chapter 23: Writing Projects

Demographics, immigration, alternative energy, science fiction: here are some topics for writers to sink their teeth—and their pens—into.

Target Skill: Draw Conclusions

Challenge your students to think of themselves as demographers (scientists who study population trends). Ask them to suppose that they will be attending an upcoming conference on population growth. Invite them to write speeches about population trends in developing nations. Ask students: What problems do developing nations face because of high population growth? How can we address these problems? What conclusions can you draw about the status of women in a society in relation to population growth?

Celebrating Diversity

Immigrants have made huge contributions to the United States from its earliest days. And today is no different, as new immigrants come, following in the footsteps of others, in search of better opportunities for themselves and their families. Invite your students to select and write about an immigrant group and the contributions (cultural, scientific, or political) it has made to American society. Or, your students may want to write about individual immigrants who made important contributions (a historical figure or someone they know, such as a family member).

Biography: Rachel Carson

How did Rachel Carson come to take such an interest in nature? What made her begin to question the use of pesticides? Was she surprised at the effect her book *Silent Spring* had on the public? Invite students to research and write short biographies of early environmentalist Rachel Carson. Challenge them to write conclusions about the future of environmental protection.

216 Unit 8 Writing Projects

Social Studies Plus!

A Place You Love

Ask students: Is there a place of natural beauty that you love? Invite them to write descriptions of such a natural setting that they have visited. Challenge them to use descriptive words to show how these places look, smell, feel, and sound. Ask them to explain how these settings make them feel and why.

Alternative Energy Sources

As the world demand for energy and power increases, scientists are looking for new sources of energy. This search for low-cost alternative energy is leading to some new ways of thinking about how to power the future. Challenge students to do some research on new ideas for energy sources, such as geothermal energy, or dual-powered (gas-*and*-electric-powered) cars. Invite them to write up summaries of their findings. Ask them to draw conclusions from the research about possible energy sources of the future.

Science Fiction

When Jules Verne wrote a novel about a boat that could travel under water, it seemed a fantastic notion. That was at the end of the nineteenth century, before submarines had been invented! But today many of his ideas are reality! Challenge your students to write stories about a world of the future. Ask students: How will technology be used to communicate and to travel? What inventions will change the way people live? What will be the problems of the future? Will technology create new problems—or help to solve them?

Social Studies Plus!

Chapter 23 Citizenship

Responsibility

What is a *sustainable community*? This new term is beginning to carry a lot of weight with planners who make decisions about community development. These people understand that the decisions they make will affect not only the present population, but also future generations. This is a great responsibility.

"Sustainable communities are defined as towns and cities that have taken steps to remain healthy over the long term. Sustainable communities have a strong sense of place . . . These communities value healthy ecosystems, use resources efficiently, and actively seek to retain and enhance a locally based economy" as defined by the Institute for Sustainable Communities. Another way of defining the term is "development that meets the needs of the present without compromising the ability of future generations to meet their own needs." (the Brundtland Commission)

Invite your students to research and discuss the ideas and principles of sustainable development. Challenge them to discuss the responsibilities of today's planners to think about the needs of tomorrow's citizens. Invite them to find out how community planners make decisions about community development.

Find out about plans for development in your local region. Do your students think the plans meet the standards of sustainable development? Why or why not? Do these plans take into consideration economic, ecological, and human quality-of-life factors? Will these plans create problems for future generations?

Name _____   Date _____

Words from Other Cultures

Word	Comes from
_____	_____
_____	_____
_____	_____
_____	_____
_____	_____
_____	_____
_____	_____
_____	_____
_____	_____
_____	_____
_____	_____
_____	_____
_____	_____
_____	_____

Additional Prop Suggestions for Unit Drama

Unit 5

Sundiata: The Hungering Lion

Suggested Props: buffalo mask; 11 cut-out figures, for sons of Sassonma; 2 mop handles to serve as rod and stick; 1 cardboard spear; chair; cloth or towel

If suggested props are too complex, have players mime the actions.

Unit 7

The Home Front

Suggested Props: broom or mop, some 1940s music, cardboard cutout of 1940s radio, aluminum foil microphone

Unit 8

Sooner or Later All Walls Must Fall

Suggested Props: 2 kerchiefs, 2 apples or bananas, wall painted on butcher paper if possible, 3 newspapers

History and Holidays
12 Month Calendar

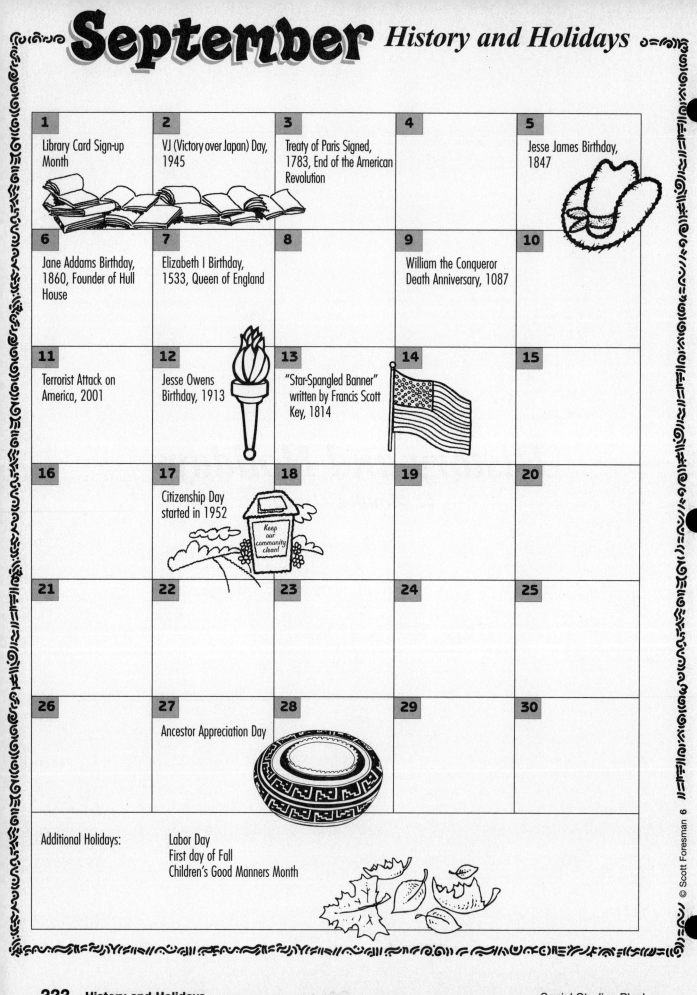

October History and Holidays

1	**2** Mohandas "Mahatma" Gandhi Birthday, 1869	**3**	**4**	**5** Tecumseh Death Anniversary, 1813, Shawnee chief
6	**7**	**8**	**9**	**10**
11	**12** Columbus Day	**13** White House cornerstone laid, 1792	**14**	**15**
16 Dictionary Day, Noah Webster Birthday, 1758; World Food Day	**17**	**18**	**19**	**20**
21	**22**	**23**	**24** United Nations Day	**25** Pablo Picasso Birthday, 1881, Cubist painter
26	**27** Theodore Roosevelt Birthday, 1858, 26th president	**28** Statue of Liberty Dedication at New York Harbor, 1886	**29** Stock Market Crash, 1929	**30**
31 Halloween				

Social Studies Plus!

History and Holidays

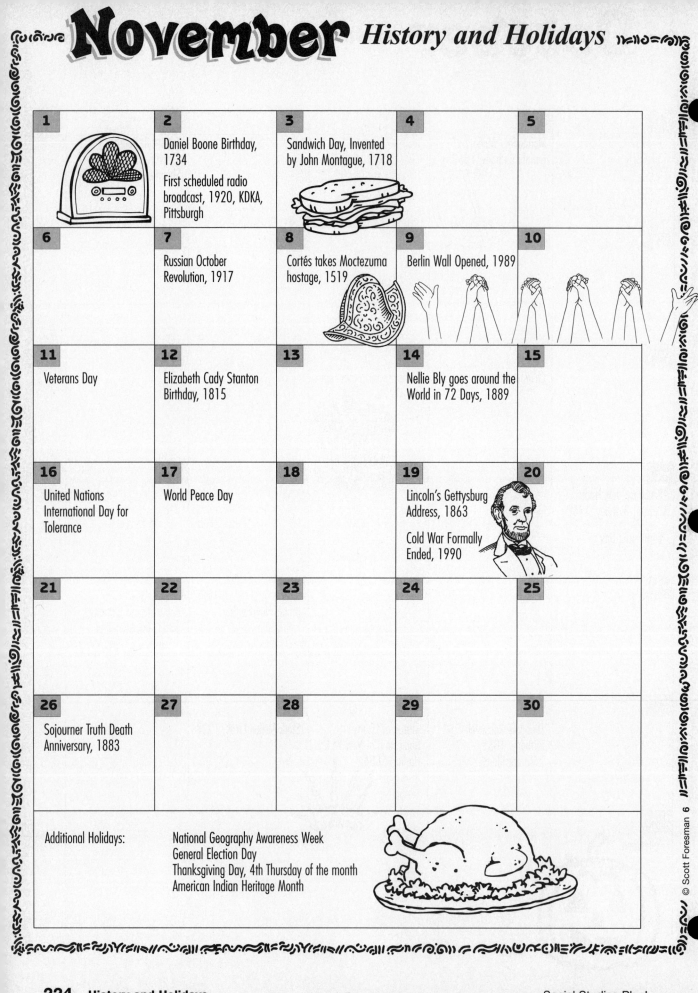

December History and Holidays

1 Rosa Parks Day, Anniversary of arrest, 1955	**2**	**3**	**4**	**5** Phillis Wheatley Death Anniversary, 1784
6	**7** National Pearl Harbor Remembrance Day, 1941	**8**	**9**	**10** Human Rights Day / Nobel Prize first given, 1901
11	**12** Jamhuri Day, 1963, Kenya wins independence from Britain	**13**	**14**	**15** Bill of Rights Day
16 Boston Tea Party, 1773 / Battle of the Bulge, 1944	**17** Aztec Calendar Stone Discovered, 1790 / Wright Brothers' first powered flight, 1903	**18**	**19**	**20**
21 Pilgrim landing at Plymouth Rock, 1620	**22**	**23**	**24**	**25**
26 Mao Tse-Tung Birthday, 1893	**27**	**28** Pledge of Allegiance Recognized, 1945	**29**	**30**
31	Additional Holidays: First day of Winter			

Social Studies Plus!

History and Holidays **225**

January *History and Holidays*

1 Paul Revere Birthday, 1735; Betsy Ross Birthday, 1752; Ellis Island Opens, 1892; Euro becomes official currency of the E.U., 2002	**2**	**3**	**4**	**5** George Washington Carver Death Anniversary, 1943
6	**7**	**8** Marco Polo Death Anniversary, 1324	**9**	**10** League of Nations founded, 1920
11	**12**	**13**	**14**	**15** Martin Luther King, Jr. Birthday, 1929
16	**17** Benjamin Franklin Birthday, 1706	**18**	**19** Robert E. Lee Birthday, 1807	**20**
21	**22**	**23** School Nurse Day; National Compliment Day (compliment at least 5 people)	**24** California gold discovered at Sutter's Creek, 1848	**25**
26	**27** Vietnam Peace Agreement Signed, 1973	**28** Challenger Space Shuttle Explosion, 1986 (11:39 A.M.)	**29**	**30**
31 Jackie Robinson Birthday, 1919, First African American pro-baseball player				

March History and Holidays

1	2	3	4	5 Boston Massacre, 1770
6 Fall of the Alamo, 1836, in present-day San Antonio Michelangelo Birthday, 1475	7	8	9	10 Harriet Tubman Death Anniversary, 1913, Leader, Underground Railroad First telephone call, 1876, by Alexander Graham Bell
11	12	13	14	15 Ides of March (Julius Caesar assassinated, 44 B.C.)
16	17 Saint Patrick's Day South Africa ends minority rule, 1992	18	19	20
21	22 World Day for Water (UN)	23 Liberty Day	24	25 Triangle Shirtwaist Fire, 1911, NYC
26 Soviet Cosmonaut returns to new country, 1992	27	28	29	30 Anesthetic first used in surgery, 1842
31	Additional Holidays:	Women's History Month First day of Spring		

April History and Holidays

1 April Fools' Day	**2** International Children's Book Day / Ponce de León Discovers Florida, 1513	**3**	**4**	**5**
6 North Pole Discovered, 1909	**7**	**8**	**9** Lee surrenders to Grant at Appomattox, 1865, End of the Civil War	**10**
11 Civil Rights Act of 1968	**12** Polio Vaccine, 1955, Developed by Dr. Jonas E. Salk / First Space Shuttle flight, Columbia, 1981	**13** Thomas Jefferson Birthday, 1743	**14** Moment of Laughter Day	**15** Sinking of the Titanic, 1912
16	**17**	**18** Paul Revere's "Midnight Ride," 1775	**19**	**20**
21	**22** Earth Day, 1970	**23** William Shakespeare, Birth and Death, m1564/1616	**24**	**25** Take Our Daughters and Sons To Work Day
26 Arbor Day, National day for planting trees	**27** Ulysses Simpson Grant Birthday, 1822, 18th president	**28**	**29**	**30**

Social Studies Plus!

May History and Holidays

1	2	3	4	5
May Day, Work celebration Law Day Leonardo Da Vinci Death Anniversary, 1519	Robert's Rules Day			Cinco De Mayo, Mexico, Anniversary of Battle of Puebla, 1862
6	7	8	9	10
		V-E Day, 1945, Germany surrenders to Allies		
11	12	13	14	15
			Lewis and Clark Expedition, 1804 Jamestown, Virginia, founded, 1607	National Bike to Work Day UN International Day of Families
16	17	18	19	20
	World Telecommunication Day (U.N.)			Homestead Act, 1862, Signed by President Lincoln
21	22	23	24	25
American Red Cross founded, 1881			First telegraph message sent, 1844, by Samuel Morse	Constitutional Convention, Philadelphia, 1787
26	27	28	29	30
	Rachel Louise Carson Birthday, 1907		John Fitzgerald Kennedy Birthday, 1917, 35th president	
31				

Additional Holidays:
National Family Week, 1st week in May
Mother's Day, 2nd Sunday in May
Memorial Day, Last Monday in May
National Pet Week

June History and Holidays

1	**2**	**3**	**4** Tiananmen Square democracy demonstration, 1989	**5**
6 D-Day Anniversary, 1944	**7**	**8**	**9**	**10**
11	**12**	**13**	**14** Flag Day, Proclaimed 1916; Harriet Beecher Stowe Birthday, 1811, *Uncle Tom's Cabin* author	**15** Magna Carta, 1215
16	**17**	**18** Dr. Sally Ride, First American woman in space, 1983	**19** Juneteenth, 1868, News of the Emancipation Proclamation reached Texas	**20**
21	**22**	**23**	**24**	**25** Last Great Buffalo Hunt, 1882
26 Francesco Pizarro Death, 1541, Conquered Peru	**27** "Happy Birthday To You" composed, 1859	**28** Treaty of Versailles, 1919, End of WWI	**29**	**30** Britain returns Hong Kong to China, 1997

Additional Holidays:
Father's Day
First day of Summer

July History and Holidays

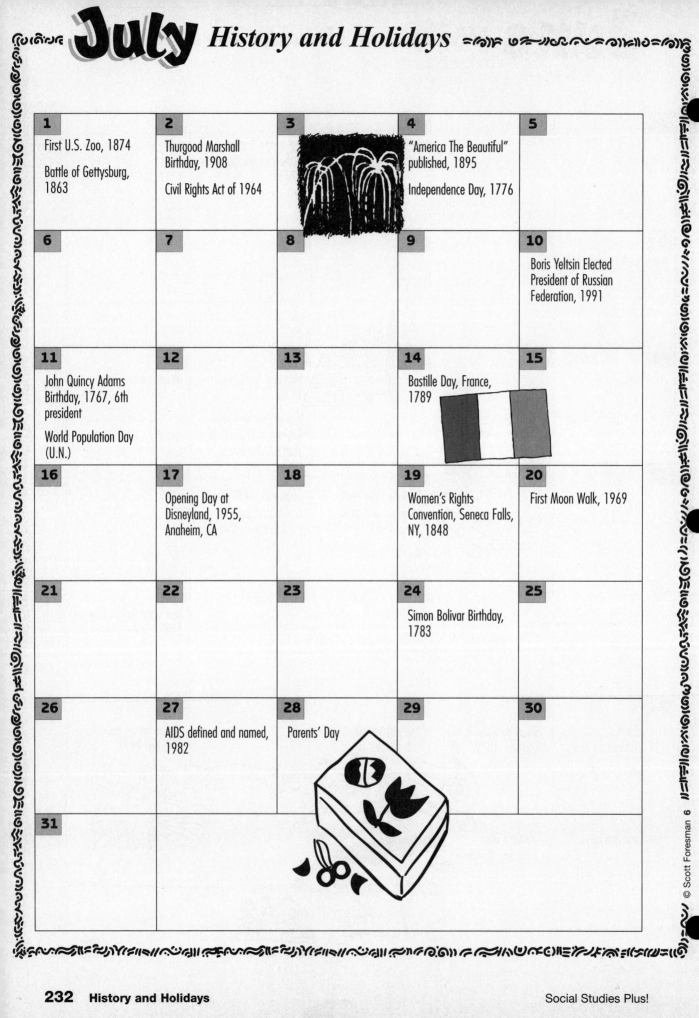

1 First U.S. Zoo, 1874; Battle of Gettysburg, 1863	**2** Thurgood Marshall Birthday, 1908; Civil Rights Act of 1964	**3**	**4** "America The Beautiful" published, 1895; Independence Day, 1776	**5**
6	**7**	**8**	**9**	**10** Boris Yeltsin Elected President of Russian Federation, 1991
11 John Quincy Adams Birthday, 1767, 6th president; World Population Day (U.N.)	**12**	**13**	**14** Bastille Day, France, 1789	**15**
16	**17** Opening Day at Disneyland, 1955, Anaheim, CA	**18**	**19** Women's Rights Convention, Seneca Falls, NY, 1848	**20** First Moon Walk, 1969
21	**22**	**23**	**24** Simon Bolivar Birthday, 1783	**25**
26	**27** AIDS defined and named, 1982	**28** Parents' Day	**29**	**30**
31				

232 History and Holidays

Social Studies Plus!

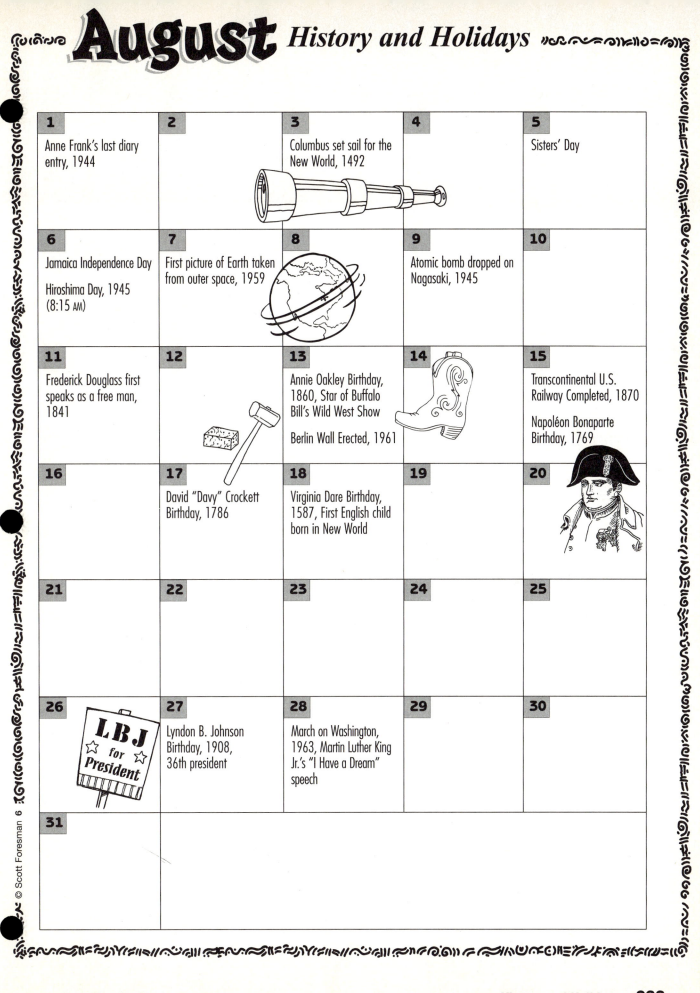

NOTES

NOTES

NOTES

NOTES

NOTES

NOTES

NOTES